WHY I BURNED MY BOOK

AND OTHER ESSAYS ON DISABILITY

In the series

American Subjects

edited by Robert Dawidoff

WHY I BURNED MY BOOK

AND OTHER ESSAYS

ON DISABILITY

Paul K. Longmore

 Temple University Press

PHILADELPHIA

To Carol and Larry

Mentors, Comrades, Friends

Temple University Press, Philadelphia 19122
Copyright © 2003 by Temple University
All rights reserved
Published 2003
Printed in the United States of America

♾ The paper used in this publication meets the requirements of
the American National Standard for Information Sciences—Permanence of
Paper for Printed Library Materials, ANSI Z39.48-1984

Library of Congress Cataloging-in-Publication Data

Longmore, Paul K.
    Why I burned my book and other essays on disability / Paul K. Longmore.
        p.   cm. — (American subjects)
    Includes bibliographical references and index.
    ISBN 1-59213-023-2 (cloth : alk. paper) — ISBN 1-59213-024-0 (pbk. : alk. paper)
        1. People with disabilities—United States—History. 2. People with disabilities—
Civil rights—United States—History. 3. Sociology of disability—United States.
4. People with disabilities in motion pictures. I. Title. II. Series.

HV1568 .L66 2003
305.9'0816'0973—dc21

                                                                            2002035272

2 4 6 8 9 7 5 3

Contents

Foreword

Why do so many of us see disability as a frightening subject? Perhaps because it seems to force upon us an awareness of the precariousness of the human condition. Race, gender, sexuality, class and other commonly addressed forms of human difference share a certain permanence, which may be why the transgendered, the bisexual, and the mixed race or ethnicity person still challenge our accustomed categories of understanding and action. The study of disability, however, challenges our uncomfortable, if usually repressed, awareness that anyone can become disabled and that the greater life expectancy some of us enjoy extends the risk and perhaps increases the odds that one will. We regard disability as a kind of *memento mori*, except that we take it as reminding us of a difficult and torturous life rather than the inevitability of death. Yet as Paul Longmore shows, the disabled different is not simply natural, but embedded in law and custom and belief. His essays explore the paradoxical effects of attempts to "help" people with disabilities at the same time society and culture maintain a false distinction between their "abnormal" bodies and minds and our putatively healthy normal ones.

I have worked with Paul Longmore since he was a graduate student in history at the Claremont Graduate University. His disability was a logistical element in our work together, one his essay "Why I Burned My Book" recounts. The challenges his disability presented to his graduate study included the perverse social-service system that had so little understanding of the individuals it was created to "serve," posing instead what seemed to us at the time obstacles to his real purpose, the study of history. The thought of his disability as a substantive issue, one that deserved his historical and analytic attention, began to form, as he recounts in his concluding essay, into a scholarly and active concern as the immediate demands of his graduate education receded, and he was doing the work he was meant to do. As a historian, he had begun to reflect on the issue of disability with his brilliant essay about Randolph Bourne (reprinted here). In the years since, he has developed into one of the nation's original and leading historians of disability.

Simultaneously, Longmore assumed an active role in the struggles of people with disabilities against discrimination, ill treatment, bad laws, and an interlocking set of notions masquerading as informed ideas. He also began to speak and write as an activist. He initially hesitated to assemble this volume because he was not sure that his writings as a scholar and as an activist could be understood together, that his activist writing might be confused with his scholarship. While it is not hard to understand this unease, since so much genuinely groundbreaking scholarship in areas that require contemporary as well as historical attention has been dismissed as "politics," it was this very quality that made this collection the very thing for this series. The point of doing the American Subjects series has been to present neglected subjects of our national story and to preserve the related narrative of how they come into being. It is hard to imagine a better account of a subject and how one comes to it as scholar, citizen, and reader than *Why I Burned My Book*. This collection rediscovers the historicity of disability and illuminates the subject position of disabled people as elements of our common history and humanity. The activism that has made Paul Longmore so important to the disability rights movement partners his scholarship. The arguments in such action-oriented essays as "The Resistance: The Disability Rights Movement and Assisted Suicide" take root in Longmore's scholarship. The truths he has discovered about disability as an American historical subject require forceful presentation to gain a hearing from an academic and reading public that resists the subject position of disabled people.

In the main, his essays inform us about people with disabilities as a group covered by laws, misrepresented by culture, and prey to a complex of social and political attitudes, and as individuals, whether Randolph Bourne or Elizabeth Bouvia, who experience those conditions. Especially important is his essay "The League of the Physically Handicapped and the Great Depression," which gives historians a model of "the new disability history"; along with "Uncovering the Hidden History of Disabled People," it demonstrates how the history of disability is done and why it should be studied. Longmore explains why historians must attend to the subject of disability and be prepared to find that the history of the marginalization and misunderstanding of disabled people is central to the history of the United States and suggests powerful reconsiderations of American society.

Among the many qualities Longmore brings to his writing is his witty and comprehensive approach to American popular culture. Attitudes toward people with disabilities take hold in popular and elite culture, making Longmore's placing of disabled people smack-dab in the middle of American culture of signal interest. He is careful to show how that culture operated within him and affected his own professional practice. He brings the varied work of scholars across the disciplines to bear, with the result that we can see the subject from more than the historian's perspective. History in the professional sense is importantly here in these essays. But history as the Founders understood it, the "experience" which they relied upon to guide their fateful decisions, as Douglass Adair memorably phrased it, is here too. We need them both.

I remember when Paul burned his book. I was shocked by this brilliantly conceived symbolic act until I tried to understand why he had done it. In that moment, I began to understand why disability studies *and* the activism of resistance are each and both the proper work of a historian like Paul Longmore. He is a rare example of the historian whose scholarly conscience pervades all his writing. He was, to use an old-fashioned term, *called* to his vocation as a historian. His subjects here are what a transdisciplinary subject and a human condition both require. When you read this book, you will understand not only why he burned that book but why he has written this one.

Robert Dawidoff

Introduction

The pieces gathered here include both works of scholarship and instances of political advocacy. Many meld the two. The last is largely autobiographical. At the same time, the entire collection represents something more than the understanding of an individual. It reflects a broader transformation in social consciousness and societal practices: the disability rights revolution. Written or delivered over a period of twenty years, these articles and speeches are themselves, on one level, documents of that revolution. Though prepared for a variety of audiences and for particular purposes, they are grounded in an overarching perspective about disability that constitutes the foundation of both disability rights activism and disability studies research. They attempt to explain contemporary advocacy and current academic studies as responses to a historical pattern of systemic prejudice and institutionalized discrimination against people with disabilities. In a sense, all of these pieces taken together describe the historical and contemporary background, the cultural and political context, that explains why I burned my book. Hence the title of the collection.

Underlying both activism and academic work is a basic reconceptualization of "disability." The new mode of analysis challenges the medical paradigm that has generally shaped modern social practices. The medical model assumes that pathological physiological conditions are the primary obstacle to disabled people's social integration. Defining disability as limitations in social and vocational functioning, it makes disability the exclusive and inevitable consequence of physiological impairments. It renders disability as a series of physiological, psychological, and functional pathologies originating within the bodies of individuals.

1

The new conceptualization of disability grew out of the efforts of activists to address the problems and obstacles faced by people with disabilities. Those advocates have recognized that for most people with most kinds of disabilities most of the time the greatest limitations are not somatic but social: prejudice and discrimination, inaccessibility and lack of accommodations. They explain the difficulties of people with disabilities in social and vocational functioning not as the exclusive and inevitable consequences of bodily impairments, but as products of the interaction between the social and built environment as presently arranged and individuals who look or function in nonstandard ways. In particular, they ascribe disabled people's typically disadvantaged status to deep-seated, pervasive cultural devaluation and systemic institutionalized discrimination. They regard people with disabilities as sharing a common social experience and therefore needing to engage in collective political action. Activists in the United States formulated the new approach as the minority group model of disability, while their counterparts in the United Kingdom fashioned what they call the social model. Both paradigms shift the focus from individuals and pathologies to institutions and ideologies.

This transformative analysis of the social sources and character of disability has generated new public policies and social practices. For example, it forged innovative concepts in American civil-rights theory, such as equal access and reasonable accommodations, community-based living and independent living, mainstreaming and education in the least restrictive environment. In the process, the activists, individually and collectively, have been redefining the social identities of people with disabilities. They have also been forming disability communities and subcultures. In all of this, they have been recasting what disability actually is. Many of the pieces collected here either exemplify or seek to explain those objectives.

Disability studies emerged in the 1980s as the academic counterpart to disability rights advocacy. It aims to do the work of research and critical analysis necessary to any effort at social reconstruction. It critically analyzes the ideas about disability that have shaped societal organization and public policies, cultural values and architectural design, individual behavior and interpersonal encounters, professional training and delivery of services. It also explores disability experiences and identities, communities and cultures, from the perspectives of people with disabilities themselves. In addition and just as important, this field raises profound questions about basic values and arrangements in every sphere of society.

The study of disability was, of course, already present throughout academic research and teaching. For instance, a quick survey at San Francisco State University, where I teach, found 257 courses that addressed disability-related topics. They instructed students in nine bachelor's degree programs, twenty-two master's programs, thirteen minors, ten certificate programs, and six credential programs. A search for comparable curricula at neighboring Stanford University counted courses in every school and many disciplines: business, education, engineering, ethics, feminist studies, human biology, law, linguistics, medicine, philosophy, policy studies, population studies, religious studies.

The frequency of disability as a subject of study will no doubt surprise most people. It takes only a moment's reflection to recognize that disability appears frequently in teaching and research because it is a common feature of human existence. It is a major category of modern social organization and policy formulation. In its socioeconomic, ethical, and policy significance, it is comparable to class, gender, and race or ethnicity. The problem, then, is not that the academy neglects disability, but rather the ways in which this subject is addressed. The danger is not that we will ignore disability, but that we will reach intellectual, sociocultural, ethical, political, and policy conclusions about disabled people without examining the ignorance, fear, and prejudice that deeply influence our thinking.

In 1995, the National Institute on Disability and Rehabilitation Research of the U.S. Department of Education noted the failure of research "to assess the comprehensive phenomenon of disability and its complex interaction with all aspects of society, particularly from the perspective of individuals with disabilities."[1] That deficiency characterizes academic research not only in the applied fields, but also in the social sciences and humanities. Beyond the academy, that defect impairs professional practice in a wide array of disability-related fields, including education, medicine, policy making, psychology, social work, and vocational rehabilitation.

The problem with academic consideration of disability stems from the paradigms that shape research and teaching. The medical model remains the typical perspective not only in medicine, rehabilitation, special education, and other applied fields, but in the social sciences and humanities as well. As a result, traditional academic study represents disability as a defect located in individuals that requires corrective treatments. This approach not only medicalizes disability, it thereby individualizes and privatizes what is in fundamental ways a social and political problem. Academic research and teaching still typically operate from old modes of analysis that do not adequately explain, let alone remedy, the social and economic disadvantages endured by people with disabilities. Current academic discourse fails to examine disability as a "comprehensive phenomenon" that interacts "with all aspects of society" in complex ways.

Disability studies seeks to remedy these deficiencies. It is a multidisciplinary project that analyzes the intricate interaction of social, cultural, political, and economic variables. The disability studies scholars Simi Linton and Lennard Davis sum up the approach. "Disability Studies," writes Linton, "challenges the idea that the social and economic status and assigned roles of people with disabilities are inevitable outcomes of their condition, an idea similar to the argument that women's roles and status are biologically determined."[2] Instead, explain Davis and Linton, "Disability studies centers the study of disability on its social construction, the processes that have accorded particular meaning to disability and that have determined the treatment and positioning of people with disabilities in society."[3]

As with disability rights legislation and activism, disability studies has arisen because of the deficiencies of traditional paradigms and the policies and practices derived from them in addressing the current changing circumstances and problems confronted by persons with disabilities. Because the reigning models frame disability as a defect in the individual that requires curative or rehabilitative treatment or other "special" remedial services, they usually overlook the impact of developments such as improved accessibility, disability rights activism and legislation, changing disability demographics, and the emergence of minority group identity across disability types. Nor have approaches based on medical models responded effectively to a range of controversial ethical and policy dilemmas. For example, the shriveling of public-sector resources has necessitated discussion about "entitlements" and "accommodations." How much can society afford? What do disabled people have a right to expect? Likewise, the crisis in the health care and health-financing systems has generated policy and ethical debates about who has a right to how much medical treatment. Innovations in medicine continue to prompt legal cases regarding both the right to treatment and the so-called right to die, not just for terminally ill persons, but for others who have disabilities. The medical model of disability cannot address these sorts of issues because they involve, not diagnoses of pathologies, but analyses of values. In contrast, disability studies takes as its domain the examination of cultural values regarding "disability" and their relationship to social arrangements, public policy, and professional practice.

It is necessary to distinguish in detail the differences between disability studies and other modes of studying disability in order to clear up a conflation and confusion that is currently befogging the field. Some researchers in rehabilitation and special education continue to use the medical model but have appropriated the term "disability studies" to legitimize their work and secure funding for it. But for more than twenty years, the basic theoretical texts in "disability studies" have laid out a mode of intellectual analysis based on a minority group or sociopolitical paradigm. This theoretical approach has been developed in part to critique disability research based on various versions of the medical pathology paradigm, including putatively progressive ones. To confound disability studies with these other ways of studying disability is erroneous and obfuscating. We must insist on accuracy and precision in academic labeling.

Disability studies, like disability rights, has encountered strong opposition. Some critics condemn it for pushing parochial ideologies and political agendas, for lacking intellectual credibility, and for contributing to the "balkanization" of learning. A senior fellow at the conservative Pacific Research Institute in San Francisco used that term and leveled all of those charges in commenting on a National Endowment for the Humanities Summer Institute for College Teachers I codirected in 2000 with the leading disability studies scholar Rosemarie Garland-Thomson. "Although he [the Pacific Research Institute critic] does not know much about the emerging field of disability studies," related a *San Francisco Chronicle* reporter, "he said he imagines it will be similar to the movement for ethnic or gay and lesbian studies. 'All these specialty studies end up being promotional studies for particular ideologies. . . . You don't really have a broad-based inquiry into the area; you tend to have an indoctrination into the area. It is not about open-minded philosophical inquiry. It is about people's special agendas.'"[4] One wonders how "open-minded" a "fellow" is who would dismiss an entire field he admits he doesn't know much about.

More important, reactions such as this indicate vast ignorance not merely about the historical and contemporary experience of people with disabilities, but also regarding the social significance of issues related to disability. By any measure, everything directly or indirectly connected with disability is being transformed. The vastness and complexity of the changes underway make necessary a thorough rethinking of public laws and policies, of social, professional, and institutional values and practices regarding persons with disabilities. The emergence of disability studies has profound implications for research, policy making, professional practice, and general academic inquiry.[5] The essays in this collection seek to demonstrate the importance of disability issues in virtually every sphere of society and the consequent necessity of serious scholarly inquiry into them. That is the "agenda" of disability studies.

Further, the charge that disability studies is narrow rather than "broad based" fails to recognize the implications of this emerging field for all areas of scholarship and thought, for values and practices in every sphere of society, for every dimension of human experience. It offers a new angle of vision regarding not only concepts of equality and community, minority status and justice, but also individualism and independence, fitness for citizenship and the "health" of the body politic, as well as gender, appearance, and sexuality. In short, the issues raised by disability studies reach into every discipline, into all spheres of intellectual inquiry.[6]

A growing number of academicians outside the applied fields traditionally assumed to be the proper academic home for the study of disability recognize the far-ranging social and intellectual significance of disability studies. For example, writing in the *Chronicle of Higher Education*, the literary scholar Michael Berubé urged his colleagues in the liberal arts to incorporate the study of disability into their work. "The cultural representation of people with disabilities," he said, not only "affects our understanding of what it means to be human; in more practical terms, it affects public policy, the allocation of social resources, and the meaning of 'civil rights.'"[7] In other words, disability studies has both philosophical and political implications, and academic inquiry ought to explore the linkage between the two.

Finally, the accusation that disability studies merely promotes a particular ideology, that it indoctrinates rather than engaging in "open-minded philosophical inquiry," is, to put it charitably, naive about the processes and products of academic scholarship and intellectual inquiry. All analyses, all arguments, are consciously or unconsciously shaped by moral values, philosophical presuppositions, sociocultural norms, and political premises. Some forms of knowledge are privileged and others marginalized. Every philosophical position has implicit political content. In every inquiry, specific interests are at stake; they are represented in every explanation. The intellectual and political debates in American society during the past four decades should have taught all of us by now that public discourse and intellectual analysis are enriched when we examine and critique the premises and interests underlying each particular position. In addition, the controversies of the last two generations should have alerted us to the value of critical perspectives developed from the margins of society.

That is why the pieces that follow give particular attention to issues of voice and authority. What sociocultural mechanisms and social actors have the power to define the social identities and roles permitted to or required of people with disabilities? Who is competent to decide what the real problems and needs of disabled people are? Who gets to frame disability-related agendas for public policies and professional programs or for social and political change? What have been the framers' motives and purposes?

These issues of authority and agency have become more complicated, more controversial, and more important because of the frequent discrepancy between disabled and nondisabled understandings of disability issues. People with disabilities and people without disabilities often perceive "disability" in very different ways. Indeed, many times their assumptions and perceptions radically conflict. As a result, their expectations and prescriptions of "what needs to be done" clash too. This disparity in understanding and disjuncture of agendas has intensified since the advent of mass disability rights movements, but it is not a recent historical development. It seems to have been a feature of the historical experience of disability throughout, at least, the modern era. The pieces gathered here recount those historical oppositions and call attention to their current prevalence.

In addition, much of the time, in the present as in the past, nondisabled perspectives have dominated, while disabled views have typically been regarded as illegitimate. Nondisabled voices have automatically assumed authority to declare what "disability" is and what disabled people need. Disabled people have often been considered unqualified to speak for themselves, to interpret their own experience. They have frequently been rendered voiceless.

The essays and speeches that follow depict these disparities of power. They examine the material interests at stake. They also report, and at times represent, the historical and current attempts of people with disabilities, singly as well as collectively, to claim our voices. The struggle of disabled people seems always to have been a struggle for both self-determination and self-definition.

This collection also reflects my own commitment and effort to labor simultaneously as an academic and an activist, a historian and an advocate. These pieces move back and forth between analysis and activism, sometimes within the same essay or speech. I make no pretense of a spurious objectivity, no false pose of a stance outside and therefore independent of the welter of human concerns and contentions. I trust that not only my commitments but also my controlling assumptions stand forth plainly in the pieces that follow.

Yet scholar-activists betray the causes we espouse if we seek merely to legitimate dissenting dogmas and validate alternative mythologies by festooning them with footnotes. It has seemed to me that I could most usefully contribute to advancing social justice for people with disabilities by producing and facilitating rigorous disability studies scholarship, by applying it to current disability issues, and by critiquing disability rights advocacy and ideology from within. I have hoped that constant connection with disabled people would keep my work grounded in their lived experience of disability, in their daily confrontation with prejudice and discrimination. At the same time, I have wanted disability studies research to deepen and strengthen the analytical component of disability rights advocacy.

Disability studies scholars in every discipline, disability rights activists in every campaign, confront the selfsame skepticism. All must combat deeply embedded cultural assumptions about disability and disabled people. Both scholarship and advocacy must struggle against the entrenched power of the medical model to shape thinking about "disability." That model has naturalized what are, to a large extent, social constructions. It has presented historical artifacts as facts of nature. It has made cultural representations and ideological formulations seem merely a description of the personal and social consequences of physiological realities. In the case of disability, biology becomes the exclusive determinant of destiny. This medical discourse effectively removes from social, political, or historical analysis most of what people actually experience as *disability*. By portraying people with disabilities in certain limited ways, as, for instance, patients or clients, it renders invisible the true character of their social experience and of the social status "disabled."

The power of the medicalized perspective also masks or distorts the presence of disabled people in contemporary society, as well as in the historical record. As a result, when disability issues are addressed, when disability experiences are described, they are framed from the perspective of nondisabled people. Accounts of disability are told as the story of what nondisabled people have done for or to people with various kinds of disabilities. It is a story of treatments or derelictions, benefactions or neglect. As a result, disabled people are hidden or depicted as passive and inert. The essays collected here report how people with disabilities, past as well as present, have actively sought to shape their individual lives and collective destinies.

The contemporary disability rights campaigns are, of course, embedded in historical processes. Present concerns always prompt questions about the past: how did we, as individuals and communities, come to be who and what we are? As one would expect, many disabled activists have been asking about experiences of disability in earlier times. How did societies in previous eras regard and treat people with disabilities? What values underlay cultural constructions of disabled people's identities? What factors shaped their social careers? How did people with various disabilities view themselves? In what ways did disabled people embrace or resist reigning definitions of their identities? How did they attempt to influence or alter sociocultural beliefs and societal practices in order to manage their social identities and social careers? Were there communities and cultures of disability in the past? What are the connections between those many pasts and our present?

Some historians talk about constructing "usable pasts." I take that to mean the fashioning of historical explanations that can aid us in understanding our own present so that we can build a future that will be different, which is to say, more just than it would otherwise probably become. The explicit effort to forge a usable past is commonly and unsurprisingly an agenda of scholars who write the histories of currently marginalized groups. They hope to mold historical tools outsiders can use to shape contemporary change.

Critics often accuse this sort of historical scholarship of the fallacy of present-mindedness: the imposition on the past of present-day concerns and values, the distortion of earlier historical experiences by interpreting them, not on their own terms, but simply as precursors of ours. That danger is real, but it is a pitfall of all historiographical enterprises, not just those that are politically engaged on behalf of outsider groups. Moreover, we often fail to notice or acknowledge two basic realities in the reconstruction of history. Like the fellow at the Pacific Research Institute, we not only ignore that all historical writing is influenced by philosophical and political values; we also often disregard that virtually all interpretations of the past are put to use for present-day purposes. Some historiography is employed to effect societal change; much is marshaled to uphold elements of the status quo. The mid-1990s controversy over the *National Standards for History* illustrates that vital interests are at stake in the interpretation, teaching, and uses of history.[8] Likewise, proponents of explicating the U.S. Constitution according to the framers' alleged "original intent" obviously mean to make historical accounts serve a contemporary political agenda. Most pertinent to the subject of this book, opponents and supporters of the Americans with Disabilities Act, arguing before the U.S. Supreme Court in *Garrett v. University of Alabama* (2001), disputed whether or not Congress had compiled evidence of a historic pattern of state government discrimination against disabled persons sufficient to justify imposing the ADA on the states. The lead attorney for the State of Alabama asserted that the ADA "exaggerated" the extent of that discrimination. The Court accepted his argument. In that aspect of their ruling, the justices were embracing a particular interpretation of history.

Chronicles of the past that sustain presently reigning arrangements often go unquestioned because they are seen, not as interpretations, but simply as the way things were. The great English historian J. H. Plumb observed: "The personal ownership of the past has always been a vital strand in the ideology of all ruling classes."[9] Dissenting historical viewpoints, like dissenting political activism, have to establish their credibility against a presumption of partisanship. Outsiders must verify their claims to ownership of the past, must prove their qualification to explain their own history.

Many of the essays collected here are part of a search for a "usable past" for the disability rights movement. Even the pieces that address contemporary issues usually seek to locate those concerns in a larger and longer-term historical context. That historical agenda parallels the broader agenda of disability studies to forge the analytical tools necessary to the task of building a society that guarantees equal access, which is to say equal opportunity, to people with disabilities. The reconstruction of a usable past can contribute to the building of an accessible future.

Rereading these articles and speeches calls my attention not only to the issues I have tried to address, but also to those I have neglected. Unfortunately, occasional and fugitive pieces such as these do not permit the expansive systematic analysis a subject as complex as disability demands. In addition, many of the essays were composed during the first phase of disability studies. They were designed to help introduce and establish new ways of thinking about disability. They thus evidence, not only my own limitations of analysis, but, I think, the theoretical limitations of that stage of the disability studies and disability rights movements. In the present moment, the social and minority group models, as much as the medical model, stand in need of critique. The pieces that follow do not offer the critical examination of disability definitions and paradigms, disability rights ideology and campaigns, disability studies theories and methods we now need.

At the same time, some themes that do appear here deserve much fuller examination. The deeper I delve into disability history, the more I am persuaded that issues of gender are central to the historical and contemporary experience of disability. Gender, it is clear, has been a key factor in social constructions, social prescriptions, policy definitions, cultural representations, and political advocacy regarding disability. In practical terms, in terms of lived lives, ideologies of gender combining with ideologies of disability have shaped the daily experiences of every woman and man with every sort of disability. They have lived at the intersection of gender and disability. Although some of my work has touched on issues of gender, that theme demands much more attention.

The articles that follow tend often to focus on people with physical disabilities because that is the experience I understand best and can explicate with most assurance. It is risky to extrapolate from one type of disability experience to all disability experiences. "Disability" is not a monolithic category. Disability experiences are not homogeneous. We need careful studies of disability-specific histories and contemporary experiences as the foundation for rigorous analysis of disability as a common category.

This collection only briefly refers to a disability-based critique of dominant culture. I have long believed that disability experiences can supply the tools for a profound analysis of modern cultures in general and American culture in particular. The very features of disability that have caused those cultures to devalue people with disabilities so fiercely can provide disabled people a degree of cultural—and moral—independence, the clarifying distance of outsidership. From the perceptual advantage of that position, disabled intellectuals could formulate a distinctive critical inspection of contemporary societies, disabled people could fashion a distinctive set of values rooted in disability experience that could serve as an alternative to dominant values. A few of the pieces gathered here touch on this potential for analysis. Although I have elsewhere attempted a somewhat lengthier cultural critique from a disability perspective, we need more thorough analyses.[10]

Some of the disability- and gender-related terminology used in these essays will seem archaic. That language, now outdated, reflects either the historical era I was examining, or the historical moment in which I myself was writing.

I hope that these preliminary efforts can help to stimulate more sophisticated work. Perhaps their explanations can serve as part of the provisional framework that should and will give way to more thorough empirical research and shrewder and deeper analysis. Much work remains for us to do, work that critiques and improves on itself.

During my two decades of reading and research, of talking and thinking and writing, countless numbers of people have deepened my understanding and encouraged my work. In an introductory endnote to each essay, I have expressed my thanks to the individuals who particularly contributed to the production of that piece. Cathy Kudlick, Carol Sue Richardson, Sue Schweik, Lauri Umansky, and two anonymous readers gave me helpful and generous feedback on the entire collection. Over the years, I have also learned and received encouragement from academic colleagues and community activists, in particular Rosemarie Garland-Thomson, Mary Johnson, Richard Scotch, Sandy Sufian, Anthony Tusler, Cheryl Marie Wade, and the late Barbara Waxman and Irv Zola. None of this work would have been possible without the logistical support of a battalion of transcriptionists, research assistants, and personal aides. I especially want to thank Diane Banks, Barbara Berglund, Judith Engle, Laura Meek, Diane Reichwein, Christine Stapp, Abby Stoner, Alan Waldman, and Brooke Wirtschafter. The article on the League of the Physically Handicapped would never have been written without the partnership of David Goldberger. Robert Dawidoff proposed that I do this book. I hope it justifies his encouragement and faith.

Returning to these essays has prompted me to think about the influences that have helped to shape my thinking about disability. Although many experiences and people have furthered and helped me to refine my views, several individuals have had a particularly profound influence.

Harlan Hahn and William Roth introduced me to the minority group model of disability analysis. In the early 1980s, their writings contributed to the intellectual foundation of disability rights and what would become disability studies. Their theoretical explorations combined social science scholarship with policy analysis and advocacy. Their expositions of a minority paradigm of disability supplied me with the groundwork on which to build my own ideas.[11]

If these and other academic colleagues handed me scholarly tools of analysis, a great many community activists offered me models of advocacy that generated its own populist political and cultural analysis. In particular, Doug Martin, for decades a leading national advocate of policy reform, taught me many of the most important things I know about disability policy and disability politics.

Over the years, time and time again, men and women in the disability community have instructed me. In their savviness and tenacity at surviving in a society that so often oppresses them, in their wise and complex understanding of the disability experience—an understanding often richer and more profound than that of academicians in either traditional rehabilitation research or transformative disability studies—in their dedication to securing freedom and dignity for their disabled brothers and sisters, they have taught me and (to use a word that often makes disabled people bristle, but that in this case is the only appropriate word) inspired me. The fact is that every movement for justice needs its heroes. Some heroes become famous for doing great deeds. Others never get their names in the history books. The latter form of heroism consists simply in this: in the face of society's contempt, they just live their lives. Two women, Mary Helen Fisk and Emma Saenz Eivers, represent for me the heroism of a great many disabled people. They instructed me in how to live my life as a disabled person as I watched how they lived theirs.

There is strength and pride and wisdom and clear-eyed good sense in the disability community at its best. Larry Voss epitomizes those qualities. He is for me a model of disabled manhood.

Carol Gill has influenced my thinking about disability more than any other individual. Her comprehensive, rigorous, subtle, honest, and profound grasp of the experience of disability in all its sociological and psychological, cultural and political, physical and medical elements has not only instructed me, but stimulated me to work harder at thinking about these issues.

In the end, as I reread my own work, one central theme, one main point, stands out. More than anything else, in various ways, yet over and over, I seem to have been saying: "Disability" is not what most of us commonly think it is. People with disabilities are not who or what we have been taught to assume they are. The experience of disability is not what we have been told. Much of the reigning social thought about disability is distorted. Most of the conventional wisdom about disabled people is wrong. The disabled poet Cheryl Marie Wade made the same point succinctly when she wrote: "I emphatically demonstrate / It ain't what it seems."[12]

The danger is that dominant ideologies of disability will pinion our perceptions, shackling efforts to think in new ways about disability and disabled people, and about "normality" too. Describing this sort of constricted mindset, e. e. cummings wrote: "he does not have to think because he knows / . . . because he knows, he cannot understand."[13] All of us, disabled and nondisabled alike, will never truly understand disability experiences and identities unless we examine what we think we know. We all have a lot of relearning to do.

Notes

1. Office of Special Education and Rehabilitative Services, National Institute on Disability and Rehabilitation Research, U.S. Department of Education, "Notice Inviting Applications under the Innovation Grants Program for Fiscal Year (FY) 1995," *Federal Register* 60(85) (May 3, 1995), 21940, Federal Register Online via GPO Access [wais.access.gpo.gov] [DOCID:fr03my95-115] http://frwebgate6.access.gpo.gov/cgi-bin/waisgate.cgi?WAISdocID=565092316578+9+0+0&WAISaction=retrieve

2. Simi Linton, "The Disability Studies Project: Broadening the Parameters of Diversity," in Elaine Makas and Lynn Schlesinger, eds., *End Results and Starting Points: Expanding the Field of Disability Studies* (Portland, Maine, 1996), 323–25.

3. Lennard J. Davis and Simi Linton, "Introduction: Disability Studies," *Radical Teacher* 48 (1985), 2–3.

4. Tanya Schevitz, "Scholars Take Fresh Look at Disability/Cultural Perspective Examined at S.F. State," *San Francisco Chronicle*, August 7, 2000.

5. See, for instance, Adrienne Asch and Michelle Fine, eds., *Women with Disabilities: Essays in Psychology, Culture, and Politics* (Philadelphia, 1988); Davis and Linton, "Introduction: Disability Studies"; Victor Finkelstein, *Attitudes and Disabled People: Issues for Discussion* (New York, 1980); Carol J. Gill, "A New Social Perspective on Disability and Its Implications for Rehabilitation," in *Occupational Therapy in Health Care* 7:1 (Spring 1987), and in F. S. Cromwell, ed., *Sociocultural Implications in Treatment Planning in Occupational Therapy* (New York, 1987); Harlan Hahn, "Disability Policy and the Problem of Discrimination," *American Behavioral Scientist* 8 (January–February 1985), 293–318; Harlan Hahn, "Paternalism and Public Policy," *Society*, March–April 1983, 36–46; Harlan Hahn, "Toward a Politics of Disability: Definitions, Disciplines, and Policies," *Social Science Journal* 22 (1985), 87–105; Simi Linton, "Reshaping Disability in Teacher Education and Beyond,"

Teaching Education 6:2 (1984), 9–20; Linton, "The Disability Studies Project"; Simi Linton, Susan Mello, and John O'Neill, "Disability Studies: Expanding the Parameters of Diversity," *Radical Teacher*, No. 47 (Fall 1995), 4–10; Martha Minow, *Making All the Difference: Exclusion, Inclusion, and American Law* (Ithaca, 1992); National Council on Disability, *Equality of Opportunity: The Making of the Americans with Disabilities Act* (Washington, D.C., 1997); National Council on Disability, *Back to School on Civil Rights: Advancing the Federal Commitment to Leave No Child Behind* (Washington, D.C., 2000); Richard K. Scotch, *From Good Will to Civil Rights: Transforming Federal Disability Policy* (Philadelphia, 1985); G. Tysse, ed., *The Legislative History of the Americans with Disabilities Act* (Horsham, Pa., 1991); Charles E. Vaughn, *The Struggle of Blind People for Self-Determination: The Dependency-Rehabilitation Conflict, Empowerment in the Blindness Community* (Springfield, Ill., 1993).

6. Linton, "The Disability Studies Project."

7. Michael Berubé, "The Cultural Representation of People with Disabilities Affects Us All," *Chronicle of Higher Education*, May 30, 1997, B4–5.

8. Gary B. Nash et al., *National Standards for History*, Basic Edition (Los Angeles, 1996); Gary B. Nash, Charlotte Crabtree, and Ross E. Dunn, *History on Trial: Culture Wars and the Teaching of the Past* (New York, 1997).

9. J. H. Plumb, *The Death of the Past* (Boston, 1970), 30n. 2.

10. Paul K. Longmore, "Conspicuous Contribution and American Cultural Dilemmas: Telethon Rituals of Cleansing and Renewal," in David Mitchell and Sharon Snyder, eds., *Discourses of Disability: The Body and Physical Difference in the Humanities* (Ann Arbor, 1997), 134–58.

11. Hahn, "Disability Policy," "Paternalism and Public Policy," and "Toward a Politics of Disability"; John Gliedman and William Roth, *The Unexpected Minority: Handicapped Children in America* (New York, 1978); William Roth, "Almsgiving in the 1980's: Social, Political, and Policy Aspects of Being Disabled in an Able-Bodied World," *Pediatric Social Work* 2:4 (1982), 105–10; William Roth, "Handicap as a Social Construct," *Society* 20:3 (March–April 1983), 56–61; William Roth and Richard Sugarman, "The Phenomenology of Disability: Implications for Vocational Rehabilitation," *Rehabilitation Literature* 45:11–12 (November–December 1984), 366–69.

12. Cheryl Marie Wade, "Cripple Lullaby (I'm Not a Reason to Die)," http://www.selfadvocacy.com/Panel%2010c%2025%20x%2034.pdf.

13. e. e. cummings, *Complete Poems, 1913–1962* (New York, 1972), 406.

ONE

ANALYSES AND RECONSTRUCTIONS

1

Disability Watch

In 1998, Disability Rights Advocates, a small but highly effective
public-interest law firm in Oakland, California, published the
first volume of *Disability Watch*, its periodic assessment of the
status of people with disabilities in the United States. DRA
asked me to write the introduction. As the new century begins,
the findings of that report still largely describe the situation of
Americans with disabilities. For that reason, my introduction to
Disability Watch can usefully serve to introduce this collection of
essays.

During the past generation, Americans with disabilities have pressed
for equal access to U.S. society, to school and work and public transportation and public places. Most observers regard passage of the Americans with Disabilities Act in 1990 as the high-water mark of that movement. Two-thirds of the disabled adults responding to one recent survey
reported that since ADA their "quality of life" has improved. The evidence presented in this *Disability Watch* does indicate important progress
in some areas.

Yet many people with disabilities continue to endure economic deprivation and social marginalization. Depending on age and definition of
disability, poverty rates among disabled people range anywhere from 50
percent to 300 percent higher than in the population at large, while a
large percentage live on the meager financial aid supplied by federal

Originally published in slightly different form as the "Introduction" to *Disability Watch: The
Status of People with Disabilities in the United States* (Oakland: Disability Rights Advocates, 1998),
1–10. Courtesy of Disability Rights Advocates. A shorter version appeared as "Disrepecting
Disabilities" in *California Lawyer* 18:1 (January 1998), 48–49, 84–87.

income-maintenance programs. People with disabilities are also less likely to complete high school or college and far less likely to get jobs. The unemployment rate among those who report any form of disability is five times the national average. If they do obtain jobs, it is more likely to be part-time, and on average they will be paid 20 percent less than nondisabled workers.

They tend to be socially isolated too. Despite some improvement in accessibility, people with disabilities are still far less likely than nondisabled Americans to go to restaurants, movies, concerts, sporting events, churches, or stores. They are twice as likely to live alone. Those who grow up with disabilities tend to marry later, if they marry at all. Disabled women in particular marry and form families significantly less often than nondisabled women or even disabled men.

Social isolation and economic deprivation are not new among Americans with disabilities. They have long experienced these stark disadvantages. But the disturbing finding of this *Disability Watch* is that since the mid-1980s these conditions have improved modestly or not at all, and in some areas such as earnings things have actually gotten worse. The question is: why?

Different observers typically offer one of two differing answers. They focus either on the individual or on the environment. They ascribe the socioeconomic disadvantages suffered by disabled persons to their "impairments," or attribute them to the synergy of public policies, institutionalized societal practices, and the built environment. These competing explanations respectively express two contending paradigms of disability: a medical model and a minority model.

The medical model locates the problem of disability in the bodies of "afflicted" persons. By defining disability as a pathological medical condition, it inevitably individualizes the causes of socioeconomic disadvantage: *impaired individuals* cannot function appropriately within society. Some of the studies drawn upon for *Disability Watch* adopt medical definitions of disability. That research defines disability as a limitation in performing "major activities," meaning the endeavors ordinarily "expected" of people in particular age groups. Thus, children are expected to attend school and to engage in play as their major activities. Working-age adults are expected to hold jobs outside the home or to keep house. Older adults are expected to manage their households and to care for themselves. By this yardstick, some 26.8 million Americans (10.3 percent of the total U.S. population) are defined as limited in their ability to perform the major activities expected of persons in their age group. Various studies also report that the most common form of "major activity limitation" is "work disability," a partial or total limitation in an individual's ability to perform a paid job. Such limitations reportedly restrict the employment capabilities of nineteen million working-age adults with disabilities. The trouble is that, as with all medical definitions of disability, these definitions of "work disability" and "major activity limitation" focus attention exclusively on individuals. The definitions implicitly assume that the limitation results from medical pathology and resides within individuals. These ways of measuring disability fail to consider the impact of external, societally created factors in limiting disabled persons' capacity to perform "expected" social roles.

In contrast, research based on a minority model of disability examines the architectural, socioeconomic, and policy environments within which people with disabilities must operate and that shape their experience of disability. Those sorts of studies, which provide the bulk of the data analyzed in *Disability Watch*, present markedly different explanations of the disadvantages suffered by many people with disabilities. The evidence gathered here offers a comprehensive picture of artificially created marginalization and deprivation.

One aim of this report is to assess the impact and effectiveness of the Americans with Disabilities Act. Itself based on a minority group model of disability, the ADA mandated conversion of the U.S. physical and social infrastructure to make it inclusive of people with disabilities. Seven years later, ramps and blue wheelchair-access symbols and Braille markers seem to have sprouted everywhere. Sign-language interpreters seem now always to interpret public events. Thus, the nondisabled public has the impression that society has been transformed and made accessible. Significant improvements have been made, but *Disability Watch* indicates that to a surprising extent U.S. society continues to restrict or exclude people with disabilities.

The problems begin with modes of transportation. Americans have long considered mobility a major issue, both a core value and, given the vast geography of the country, an inevitable public concern. They have come to regard freedom of movement as a basic right. Yet *Disability Watch* reports that Americans with many kinds of disabilities still often find their mobility rights restricted or denied.

Take for instance public transit. Although a majority of public buses now has wheelchair lifts, those lifts are often broken and bus drivers often receive little training in how to operate them. Because the ADA requires public-transit agencies to include wheelchair lifts only when they buy new equipment, few cars on light-rail, rapid-transit, intercity, and commuter-rail systems can accommodate wheelchair riders. And since the ADA orders full access only at newly built transit stations and at existing "key" stations, inaccessibility prevails in those places too. The U.S. Department of Transportation has designated a mere seven hundred stops nationwide as "key stations." It reports that nearly two-thirds of them are at least partially accessible to wheelchair and walker users, but that just a fifth are fully accessible to people with mobility or sensory impairments. But those figures overstate the effective accessibility of some transit systems. Both Atlanta's MARTA and the San Francisco Bay Area's BART profess to be fully wheelchair-accessible, yet disabled riders report that ticket-vending machines and booths and turnstiles are often inaccessible and that elevators regularly break down. In New York City's commuter-rail system, a mere 28 of 104 "key" stations meet legal access requirements, while the rest of the 490 stations remain unusable. Around the United States, all forms of public transit typically fail to provide the audible or visible information necessary for blind, deaf, or hard-of-hearing passengers to travel safely and effectively, even when such information is legally mandated. Thus, while many public-transit systems claim full accessibility, the vast majority of public-transit buses, cars, and stations still effectively exclude many passengers with disabilities.

When people with disabilities cannot use regular transit, ADA instructs local public-transit agencies to provide paratransit services. Three-fourths of those agencies reportedly offer such services in the form of "special" buses, vans, or taxis. But disability rights activists condemn paratransit as separate and unequal, and with good reason. Eligibility procedures often make new applicants wait months. Service is frequently costly and therefore limited, with lift-equipped vans often charging twenty dollars a ride and some subsidized taxi rides set at a maximum of one hundred dollars' worth of travel a month. Paratransit is also commonly inflexible and inconvenient. Agencies require advance reservations of anywhere from twenty-four hours to as long as two weeks—for each and every trip. As the authors of this report note, it is clear that some local agencies see paratransit, not as "an essential substitute for unusable public transit," but as a charity service for "special" trips such as doctor visits. Whatever the rationale, paratransit perpetuates the social marginalization of people with disabilities. Yet, because they have no other options, disabled passengers use paratransit heavily.

The inconveniences inherent in paratransit services and the pervasive inaccessibility of most public-transit systems have a profound impact on the lives of many Americans with disabilities. Those conditions contribute to their exclusion from community life and block them from gaining employment. In a 1994 survey, one out of four individuals with disabilities who were not working or working only part-time named the "lack of affordable, convenient, accessible public transit as an important reason they could not obtain a job."

If public transit is still largely inaccessible, commercial modes of long-distance travel present major access problems as well. Intercity bus lines, led by industry pacesetter Greyhound, vigorously resisted any ADA requirement that they provide wheelchair access. Thus, commercial intercity bus travel still completely excludes wheelchair riders.[1] Because of limited access to other modes of long-distance travel, people with disabilities that affect their mobility or vision use airlines heavily, yet no law guarantees them the right to fly. The ADA overlooks airline travel altogether, and the Air Carrier Access Act of 1986, the federal law that supposedly ensures disabled Americans' right to fly commercial airlines, in fact contains no guarantee of equal access. This weak law allows airlines to treat access and accommodations for passengers with disabilities "as an afterthought." *Disability Watch* recounts a litany of problems with boarding, seating, debarking, poorly trained personnel, and damage to wheelchairs and other equipment.[2]

The obstacles impeding air travelers with disabilities begin and end on the ground. Because federal law mandates retrofitting terminals for access only when they are renovated, many major airports—Kennedy in New York, Midway in Chicago, Miami, Philadelphia, and Fort Meyers —continue to have serious access problems. ADA does cover airport shuttle services, but under much more lenient requirements than those governing public transit. No surprise then that many airports have no accessible shuttle buses at all. This forces wheelchair riders to pay for costly lift-equipped vans. Some airports do offer accessible shuttles, but these may operate more like paratransit systems than integrated services. For instance at Dallas/Ft. Worth Airport, nondisabled travelers may simply board any waiting shuttle bus, but wheelchair users must reserve a ride on the system's single wheelchair-accessible van twenty-four hours in advance, or they can hire another lift-equipped van at four times the cost. At many airports, shuttle-bus drivers lack adequate training to operate wheelchair lifts and tie-downs, at times endangering their passengers.

Car rental agencies have restrictive policies and practices too. They may not have vehicles equipped with hand controls or may offer them only on bigger, more expensive cars. Rental outlets also often require lengthy advance notice. And some agencies refuse to rent vehicles to disabled individuals unless they can drive the car themselves. Departing from this pattern, Avis recently agreed with the U.S. Department of Justice to change its policy. In the future, the company will permit non-driving customers with disabilities to assume financial liability for rented cars driven by another person.

At least people with mobility disabilities now have lots of places to park, or so many people assume. But in fact, a 1993 national survey by the U.S. Government Accounting Office found even that assumption mistaken. People with disabilities reported that in many public parking lots the spaces designated wheelchair accessible are too narrow or on a slope that is too steep. They also said they often can find no place to park at all, because many public lots have fewer accessible spaces than the ADA requires. GAO investigators confirmed these complaints. While some 5 percent of Americans have "severe mobility limitations," ADA requires smaller lots (under 400 spaces) to make only 4 percent of their spaces accessible, midsized lots (400–1,000 spaces) to have 2 percent accessible, and large lots a mere 1 percent accessible. Yet, the GAO found that well over a third (38 percent) of parking lots they inspected had even fewer accessible spaces than the already inadequate number mandated by ADA. In addition, 57 percent of spaces and aisles were too narrow and 88 percent of the inspected lots lacked the required number of "van-accessible" spaces.

Then there are all those ramps the nondisabled public takes as evidence that public places have been made accessible, implicitly thinking of access as an issue only for people who ride wheelchairs. But once again, subjective public perceptions are mistaken. Many ramps are too steep or too narrow or lack a handrail or lead to a door that cannot be opened. And access obstacles in public buildings do not end at the tops of ramps. Some building entryways are linked to security systems that require voice communication or sight. Wheelchair riders frequently find store aisles too narrow or blocked or carpeted, service counters too high or too narrow, restaurant tables too low, and drinking fountains inoperable. When theaters and lecture halls and other public venues do provide wheelchair-accessible spaces, they often segregate them from the rest of the seats, forcing wheelchair riders to sit apart from friends and colleagues.

Restricted access to information and communication in public buildings is another major problem. Most buildings lack enough signs indicating the location of accessible features or identifying rooms in Braille or raised print. Programs such as museum brochures and transit schedules are often unavailable in large print, Braille, or audiocassette or through staffers trained in sign language. Elevators usually lack either audible signals or Braille signs. Public telephones are often inaccessible. They are too high for wheelchair riders, lack signage appropriate for people with visual impairments, and lack text telephones for deaf people or phones with amplification for hard-of-hearing people. Businesses often do not have TDD numbers.

Inaccessibility in hotels remains a common problem too. The vast majority of U.S. hotels still have not instituted legally required access features. They do not supply devices to alert deaf guests of fire alarms, ringing phones, or someone knocking at the door. They fail to provide raised-print maps of hotel locations for visually impaired guests. They have too few rooms with wheelchair-accessible bathrooms.

One in four Americans with disabilities cites one or more of these various access obstacles as limiting their use of facilities that serve the general public.

If public buildings continue to have significant access problems, private housing remains pervasively exclusionary. A tiny fraction of U.S. houses and apartments are accessible or even readily adaptable for prospective residents with disabilities. One study cited in *Disability Watch* found that a mere "2.9 percent of Americans lived in homes with any kind of accessibility features," yet 29.2 percent of U.S. families included "at least one member with a disability." The extraordinary shortage of accessible or adaptable housing makes the search for suitable housing a seemingly futile quest. It forces many families with newly disabled members, who are often elderly, "to exclude" the member with the disability, which often means putting that person in an institution. Yet, unlike businesses, private homeowners have no tax credit available to subsidize and encourage modifications to residential housing. In addition, while the Fair Housing Amendment Act of 1988 requires property owners to allow disabled tenants to make necessary alterations, it puts the burden of those changes exclusively on the tenants. The act does mandate certain limited accessible and adaptable features in newly built multiunit housing and prohibits disability-based discrimination in the rental or sale of most multiunit apartment buildings and some single-family houses. But newspaper reports indicate that local authorities usually fail to enforce any of these provisions. Thus, this law is having only a very limited impact on the extreme shortage of accessible housing.

Perhaps the greatest progress toward the integration of people with disabilities has appeared in U.S. public schools. Americans have long viewed education as the key to economic opportunity and to full participation in society, yet for decades many states by law barred youngsters with specified disabilities from attending public schools. As of 1975, most children with disabilities in the United States either received no public education at all or were denied equal educational services. By the late 1990s, the impact of federal laws and the efforts of disability rights advocates have produced significant changes. Most children with disabilities now attend public schools. A growing proportion is mainstreamed. And a majority of teenagers with disabilities completes high school. High-school graduation, of course, greatly improves their job prospects.

But "mainstreaming" also has its negative side. Public-school districts too often assume that "mainstreaming" or "full inclusion" is the most appropriate solution for all children with disabilities. In fact, that strategy is proving disastrous for deaf children. Placing them in mainstream classrooms denies them the opportunity to learn American Sign Language, inhibits their acquisition and development of skills in any language, and effectively isolates them among hearing children. The Deaf community has vigorously opposed these ill-considered practices, but its cogent dissent has gone largely unheeded.

In addition, despite considerable progress toward integration of disabled students for whom mainstreaming is appropriate, many public schools still contain "formidable" physical barriers. Although no one gathers data nationally on accessibility in U.S. schools—a major deficiency that demands correction—a 1989 opinion survey did report that one-fifth of parents with children in special education and one-fifth of public-school educators rated access in their schools' physical facilities as only "fair" or "poor." Confirming these perceptions, a 1995 GAO study found that a majority of school districts needed to improve access and that in some large districts, such as Chicago and New Orleans, most school buildings were inaccessible. In addition, a court ruling against the Oakland, California, public-school system found "multiple, pervasive architectural barriers" in every one of its one hundred schools. These conditions persist despite the flexibility of federal laws that require "overall access to programs and activities," rather than removal of all physical barriers in every building. The greatest problems occur in central-city school districts that have more limited financial resources, whereas wealthier suburban districts have made better progress toward accessibility. Much work remains to be done in order to reach the goal of access to public education for all of America's children and youth.

Taken together, the data presented in *Disability Watch* show that, seven years after passage of the ADA, U.S. society still often limits or excludes people with disabilities. The evidence here suggests four reasons for the slow pace of compliance with disability rights laws and the continuing marginalization of Americans with disabilities.

First, there is as yet a great deal of ignorance about what constitutes accessibility and reasonable accommodation and regarding the achievability of those objectives. Many business people and property owners are misinformed and therefore anxious and angry. In particular, they mistakenly believe access and accommodations are costly. In fact, incorporating accessibility in the design of new buildings increases construction costs by no more than 2 percent. Retrofitting for access can prove more expensive, but ADA requires such modifications only when buildings are being renovated or when they are "readily achievable" in existing buildings and would not cause "undue" financial hardship. Most of the time the price of barrier removal and installation of accessible features is relatively low. In 1993, small businesses spent an average of $3,327 on retrofitting for access, with individually owned businesses spending even less, $2,535. And the federal government rebated 50 percent of these costs under the Disabled Access Tax Credit. The remaining expense should be more than reimbursed by the addition of new customers who have disabilities. Common fears about the price of job accommodations for employees with disabilities also overstate those costs. Nearly 70 percent of job accommodations cost $500 or less, with almost a fifth incurring no expense at all because they entail merely the rearrangement of work spaces or work patterns. Further, many business people overlook that the expense of job accommodations is usually much less than the cost of training a replacement employee. So, concludes *Disability Watch*, complaints about the financial impact of accommodations and accessibility are greatly exaggerated and cannot be used as an excuse to evade compliance with the law. Besides, compliance now will avoid costly lawsuits later.

Most architects are also still uneducated about how to design for equal access. *Disability Watch* urges readers to note two innovative approaches: "adaptable design," a strategy that incorporates certain basic access features and allows for others to be added conveniently later as they are needed, and "universal design," a scheme that plans spaces and equipment so that everyone can use them.

Second, social integration of Americans with disabilities is slow because federal laws and policies contain serious defects. Some civil rights statutes have weak enforcement provisions. For example, not only does the Air Carrier Access Act fail to guarantee travelers with disabilities equal access to airlines, it offers no injunctive relief in court, only administrative relief. And the ADA's requirements to make public transit accessible allow agencies as long as twenty years to comply. No wonder that, as *Disability Watch* notes, "some transit districts have not even begun the ADA-mandated planning phase for improving accessibility, let alone made any actual improvements."

Other federal policies continue to promote dependency rather than productivity. The government spends forty times as much on social-service benefits as on vocational rehabilitation. Its regulations and practices also still deter many disabled people from seeking employment by penalizing them with the loss of essential assistance or health insurance if they go to work. In one survey, almost a third of working-age adults with disabilities said that threat stood in the way of their taking a job. National policies could facilitate productivity by removing these work "disincentives." Policies could also foster competitive job skills among disabled individuals by subsidizing their acquisition of computer technology. In the midst of a technological revolution so often vaunted as liberating for people with disabilities, it is amazing that while one-tenth of disabled working-age adults say they would need adapted equipment to hold a job, only 1.3 percent actually own such equipment.

Federal policies also promote institutionalization rather than community integration. Not only is there no homeowners tax credit to encourage accessibility in residential housing, but Medicaid funding favors nursing-home placement over enabling disabled people to live in their own homes. As a result, the number of institutionalized disabled

Americans, the vast majority of them elderly, stands at an all-time high of 2.1 million.

In combination, these flaws in federal policies and laws effectively perpetuate the social segregation and economic deprivation of people with disabilities. Some policies actively promote marginalization. Other statutes delay removal of physical and social barriers to integration.

Third, even when the legal requirements for access and accommodations have already gone into effect, compliance is dilatory because local authorities often fail to enforce them. For example, a current lawsuit by disability rights activists charges San Francisco city building inspectors with routinely exempting new construction from state accessibility codes. As a result, hundreds of recently constructed buildings exclude wheelchair riders. Similar problems occur when local public-works departments neglect to remove barriers in streets and on sidewalks. Enforcement and compliance varies widely from community to community depending on three factors: the priorities of local public officials, the resources available to them, and the degree of activism by local disability communities. The last element is proving especially important.

In response to lax implementation and widespread violation of disability rights laws, activists around the United States are increasingly filing civil suits to compel vigorous enforcement. *Disability Watch* reports lawsuits against or settlements with the Days Inn hotel chain, Lone Star restaurants, United Artists movie theaters, Safeway stores, Planet Hollywood nightclubs, Bay Area Rapid Transit, Metropolitan Atlanta Rapid Transit, the San Diego municipal courts, and the operator of a parking-lot chain in San Diego. In all of these cases, the companies and agencies simply ignored the law, sometimes defiantly.

That conduct points to the fourth factor delaying integration of people with disabilities into American society: the refusal to comply with these various laws stems, not just from ignorance, but also from prejudice. Around the United States, people with disabilities report encountering prejudicial and discriminatory treatment. In some cities, bus drivers simply refuse to pick up passengers with visible disabilities. Airline employees are often tardy, uncooperative, or unresponsive and at times physically rough or humiliatingly rude. Working-age people with disabilities recount various forms of discrimination: they have been refused jobs, denied promotions, given less responsibility than nondisabled coworkers, or paid less than nondisabled colleagues doing similar work. In one survey, 40 percent of disabled adults who were unemployed or working only part-time declared employer bias was a factor.

Yet despite the persistence of discrimination against disabled Americans and lax enforcement of the laws to protect their rights, U.S. society cannot avoid disability-related issues. One reason documented in *Disability Watch* is the steadily growing number of Americans with disabilities. Depending on definitions of disability, there are now at least forty-one million, perhaps as many as forty-nine million, people with significant disabilities in the United States. Disability occurs more frequently in lower income groups and among racial minorities, but most of the numerical increase has resulted from the mounting size of the elder population. Here again though, *Disability Watch* corrects some common misconceptions. Most people with disabilities are not old. In fact, a majority (57.6 percent) are working-age, while more than one in ten are under age eighteen. And the most rapid rate of growth in the incidence of disability is occurring in those younger age groups. Among children and teens, much of the increase stems from the rising prevalence or more effective detection of asthma, emotional disabilities, mental retardation, and learning disabilities, while a growing proportion of young adults experience orthopedic, mental, and emotional disabilities. In addition, "disability" involves widely diverse conditions, with many of the more common, such as heart disease, back problems, arthritis, learning disabilities, and emotional disabilities, relatively hidden. Not only are Americans with disabilities a large and diverse population, the experience of disability is typical rather than rare. Nearly one-third of U.S. families have a member with a disability, and most families experience disability at some time. "Disability," conclude the authors of this report, "is a normal part of life."

The prevalence of disability compels greater efforts to address the socioeconomic disadvantages confronted by Americans with disabilities. That thrust should proceed on three related fronts. (1) Public education, particularly of business, to counter the widespread misinformation about the actual requirements of the ADA and other disability rights laws and to combat prejudice against people with disabilities. (2) Legislative correction of the defects in current laws and policies: to strengthen enforcement mechanisms in disability civil rights laws; to eliminate work disincentives in social-service policies; and to promote community integration rather than segregation and institutionalization. (3) Vigorous enforcement of existing laws.

The number of people with disabilities continues to grow. Their presence in American society, their needs and interests, increasingly make themselves felt. And, more and more, disabled Americans are asserting their right to participate in U.S. society, in its schools and places of work and places of business and community affairs. More and more, they are turning to legal and political activism to enforce those rights. As they become active, they are rejecting a medical model of disability and espousing a minority group model. In the end, *Disability Watch* should bring readers to at least this one conclusion: disability issues will not go away, because people with disabilities are not going away.

Notes

Acknowledgments: I thank Stephen Kaye, the principal author of *Disability Watch*, and Larry Paradis, Sid Wolinsky, and Pat Kirkpatrick of Disability Rights Advocates for giving me the opportunity to write this introductory essay.

1. After several years of complaints, lobbying, and protests by disability rights activists, Greyhound signed a settlement with the U.S. Department of Justice in November 1999 agreeing to comply with the ADA.

2. Subsequent to the publication of *Disability Watch*, the National Council on Disability issued its comprehensive report on access to airlines, *Enforcing the Civil Rights of Air Travelers with Disabilities: Recommendations for the Department of Transportation and Congress* (Washington, D.C., 1999).

2

The Life of Randolph Bourne
and the Need for a History
of Disabled People

The *Disability Watch* assessment of the status of Americans with
disabilities at the turn of the century may prompt us to ask how
that contemporary situation arose. In other words, what was the
historical experience of people with disabilities? What is the history of "disability"? I first began to think about disability history
in the late 1960s. In that same moment, I also encountered Randolph Bourne. Like many college students of my generation who
protested the war in Vietnam, I met Bourne through his powerful
antiwar writings that opposed U.S. involvement in World War I.
But unlike most of them, I also read his earlier essay "The Handicapped, by One of Them." There I discovered a physically disabled young intellectual who labored to make sense of his lifelong
confrontation with prejudice as he struggled to find a way to do
his work as a writer and critic, wrestled to make a place for himself in the world, strained to win some measure of self-respect
and social dignity. At that point in my life and in the development
of both my thinking about disability and my identity as a disabled
person, Bourne appealed to me because he explained his experience of disability in sociological rather than merely psychological
terms. Impressive as that articulation was for the era in which
Bourne lived, he sought at the same time to do something I found
even more remarkable. He endeavored to make the disability ex-

Review of Bruce Clayton, *Forgotten Prophet: The Life of Randolph Bourne*, originally published
in slightly different form in *Reviews in American History* 13 (December 1985), 581–87. Courtesy of Johns Hopkins University Press.

perience the starting point of a broad social critique. A close reading of his writings disclosed that his experience and perspective as a disabled person informed his approach to every subject and issue he addressed, from war to women's rights, from immigration to education, from literary criticism to social reform. Bourne made me see that *disability* could become a way of understanding the world, a mode of critically analyzing the social order. Just as important, the failure of his biographers and other historians to recognize the centrality of disability to his thought prompted me to think about the history of disability and the place of disability in history. Years later, Stanley Kutler, the editor of *Reviews in American History*, offered me the opportunity to review a new biography of Bourne and thereby gave me my first chance to sketch out some of those thoughts.

As the title of Bruce Clayton's new biography suggests, Randolph Bourne is now almost "forgotten," but in the teens of this century, he became a leading spokesman for the restlessness and revolt of a new generation of American intellectuals and reformers, voicing their rejection of the genteel tradition in literature and formalism in philosophy, their disgust with the sweeping of sordid social realities under the carpet, their fears of the stifling of individual personality in the new urban order, their optimism about the liberating possibilities of reform. Clayton's study, first and foremost an intellectual biography, explores Bourne's thought within the context of contemporaneous intellectual, cultural, and political history and offers the most thorough and useful examination of his ideas to date. The problem with it, as with all Bourne biographies, is its fundamental misunderstanding of his experience and identity as a disabled man in a society that intensively stigmatized him.

Christopher Lasch, in *The New Radicalism in America*, has seen Bourne as the exponent of a distinctively twentieth-century youth culture, interpreting his early essays *(Youth and Life*, 1913) as stating the premise of much of his later work: the source of social ills is not class conflict but inter-generational conflict, the repression of youth by age. Clayton, who repeatedly takes issue with Lasch, accusing him of undervaluing Bourne's ideas, disagrees, finding in these first forays a fight to safeguard individuality in a mass society, an attempt to create a distinctive literary persona, and a struggle between youthful romanticism and a deeper radicalism. Clayton also sharply criticizes Lasch's interpretations of Bourne's feminism. Despite his socialism, asserts Lasch, Bourne saw the oppression of women as a problem of Victorian values, not of economic exploitation, and by the end of his life had become thoroughly disillusioned with feminism. On the contrary, rejoins Clayton, he became disillusioned only with a particular brand of feminism that, advocating sexual exclusiveness, blamed women's oppression on men per se rather than on male economic domination. Further, says Clayton, Lasch and others ignore his subsequent optimistic appraisal of the resurgence among feminist women of just such an economic perspective.

Clayton, who takes Bourne's espousal of socialism more seriously than have earlier biographers, argues that he again suppressed his fundamentally radical perspective in *The Gary Schools* (1913), an influential tract propagating Deweyite educational philosophy. This uncritical celebration of progressive education with its emphasis on efficiency and technique ignored that movement's reactionary potential and perhaps motive to impose control on the new immigrants and the new urban industrial proletariat. Clayton suggests that he may have submerged his radicalism to fit in with *New Republic*–style liberals out of his own deep yearning to belong.

But Bourne soon followed with "Trans-National America" (*Atlantic Monthly*, July 1916), a radical critique not of the failure of the melting pot to absorb the new immigrants, but of the very aim of assimilation itself as undemocratic and reactionary, robbing both the immigrants and America of wellsprings of cultural and spiritual vitality. He advocated a confederation of cultures in America, a transnationality, what we now call cultural and ethnic pluralism. Braving the wartime whirlwind of xenophobic hysteria, he was arguing by 1917 that only the cultural diversity of immigrant "hyphenates" had held the country back from militaristic and chauvinistic nationalism. As Clayton importantly observes, this physically disabled outsider was the one prominent Anglo-American intellectual "to embrace cultural pluralism" (p. 196).

Bourne at last found his authentic and radical voice through his increasingly vehement dissent against the Great War but thereby "ruined his career and washed himself right out of the mainstream of American life and thought" (p. 203). He attacked head-on the liberals' illusion that war could be controlled as an instrument of international social betterment, denounced their complicity in domestic repression, demolished the preoccupation of Deweyite pragmatism with process and technique rather than values and ends, and, anticipating historians like Robert

Wiebe, notes Clayton, condemned this uncritical support of bureaucratic efficiency and order for serving the reactionary goals of conservatives who saw the war effort as a means "to discipline American society" (p. 225). Most devastating, Bourne asserted the utter impotence of individuals or the people to resist the coercive war-making power of the modem industrial state and declared that the "health" of that state depended on war. Liberals failed to see this and betrayed their ideals, Clayton argues, because, needing to feel influential, they found "powerlessness . . . unacceptable," while "Bourne could accept powerlessness precisely because, for all his yearning to count, he had always been a powerless outsider" (pp. 213–14).

Rejecting the notion of some historians that Bourne sank into disillusionment and negativism, Clayton reminds us that he optimistically "issued numerous prescriptions for an independent, radical intelligentsia," which should prepare for the necessary postwar intellectual, moral, and political reconstruction (p. 214). He also refutes the legend that Bourne died a persecuted and "penniless martyr" but does make clear that although he earned "a modest living" right up to his death in December 1918 in the great influenza epidemic, his radical stance killed the *Seven Arts* and shut him out from *The New Republic, The Dial,* and everywhere else he might have done the important and "real work [he] yearned to do" (pp. 254, 249). Despite his increasing political isolation, Clayton points out, he continued to contribute "very valuable literary criticism," remaining "a caustic, relentless, highly important critic of the genteel tradition," who condemned it for serving "reactionary elitist political and social values, . . . repressive sexual codes and narrow ethnic assumptions," and who helped to set the stage for the assault on "Puritanism" in the 1920s (pp. 236, 245). Throughout his career, his criticism called for a cultural tradition appropriate to contemporary needs, a literature sociologically, psychologically, and sexually honest, and a culture emancipated from English domination and reflecting the pluralistic reality of the American experience.

The difficulty with Clayton's and all Bourne biographies is their explanation of his experience as a disabled person and its relationship to his radicalism. Randolph Bourne had a highly visible disability, a twisted mouth, face, and ear from a difficult birth, a severely curved spine and stunted growth from childhood spinal tuberculosis. His handicap apparently involved little functional impairment. Thus, people reacted primarily, and often with extreme aversion, to his appearance. Ellery Sedgwick, editor of the *Atlantic Monthly*, could not overcome his revulsion and invite the young man to stay for luncheon at New York's exclusive Century Club. In Paris, concierges, catching sight of him, repeatedly refused him lodgings, until after two days he finally found a vermin-ridden flat. At Columbia University, recalled a friend, some were "instinctively hostile to him, either because of his radical ideas, or because of his personal appearance." "His writing shows he is a cripple," said Amy Lowell. "Deformed body, deformed mind."[1] Other enemies of his agreed.

Bias also limited his educational and employment prospects. In 1903, his uncle, who financially aided the fatherless family and would soon support Randolph's sister in college, refused to help him attend Princeton. For the next two years, he futilely hunted a job in New York City. Invariably rejected because of his disability, he finally was forced to take work perforating piano rolls for meager wages. In 1909, he at last enrolled at Columbia on scholarship, but the searing previous six years left him permanently in terror of unemployment, feeling utterly powerless to combat such discrimination.

But the prejudice that wounded deepest was in his relationships with women. An almost instinctive feminist, who knew what it meant to be economically dependent, to have one's abilities discounted, to fight devaluing cultural beliefs as one struggled to fashion one's own independent personhood, he had many close women friends, but, recalled one, "he had only to venture an inch over a forbidden line to have them fly from him like shy birds."[2] That line was romantic interest on his part. Remembered another woman: "I always took it for granted he was cut off from the whole range of experience by his deformity" (p. 165).

Bourne lived in an era when prejudice and discrimination against disabled people seem to have been intensifying sharply. If in New York City he was rejected as a luncheon guest because of his "unsightliness," in Chicago he might have been arrested for showing up at all. A city ordinance warned: "No person who is diseased, maimed, mutilated, or in any way deformed so as to be an unsightly or disgusting object or improper person to be allowed in or on the public ways or other public places in this city, shall therein or thereon expose himself to public view." Unlike most handicapped children, Randolph had been allowed to get an education. Probably much more typical was the experience of a lad with cerebral palsy expelled from a Wisconsin public school in 1919 because, even though he had kept up with the rest of the class academically, the teachers and other children found him "depressing and nau-seating." Eugenicists and professionals who dealt with disabled people proposed segregation and sterilization of deaf people, blind people, people with developmental disabilities, even people like Bourne who had had tuberculosis. In 1912, the eugenic section of the American Breeders' Association, later renamed the American Genetics Association, drafted a model sterilization law to be applied to these "socially unfit" classes. By the beginning of World War I, sixteen states had adopted sterilization statutes. A few eugenicists even advocated the mercy killing of individuals with epilepsy or mental handicaps, especially those who were mildly mentally retarded. Eugenics, an international movement, reached its greatest extreme in Nazi Germany where between a quarter of a million and three hundred thousand people with a wide variety of disabilities were systematically exterminated.[3]

Clayton notes much of the biographical information about Bourne, but unawareness of the larger history of disabled people and prevailing cultural assumptions about disability cause him and other historians to explain Bourne's experience as primarily a personal tragedy to be over-come by emotional coping. They also assume social outsidership as virtually inherent in Bourne's physical condition. Clayton describes him as "star-crossed," "someone whom fate had rudely shoved to the side of life" (pp. 8, 28). He pledges to forego "psychological analysis" (p. 5), but much of his interpretation derives from the unexamined assumption that disability is mainly a problem of individual psychological adjustment. Lasch agrees: "It can be argued of course that all [his] disappointments and frustrations were the inevitable result of Bourne's deformity . . . and that they tell us nothing, therefore, about the society in which Bourne lived."[4] But social scientists studying the disability experience have increasingly turned to a minority group model, defining "disability" not as a fated and "inevitable" condition, but as a socially constructed identity and role triggered by a stigmatized biological trait.[5] Bourne's lifetime of discrimination and rejection was not inherent in his physical disability but part of that stigmatized social identity rooted in deep but unconscious cultural prejudice. The low self-esteem he battled was not a personal response to his handicap but the internalization of social bias.

Bourne's essay "The Handicapped," so often quoted and so little understood by his biographers, gropes toward that understanding of the disability experience in its strikingly sociological analysis of his "situation." When he describes his psychological struggle to achieve "self-respect," he clearly puts it within the context of a society that devalues him because of his disability. From the stigmatized social condition that had isolated him as an adolescent and had kept him unemployed as an adult, he knew of "no particular way of escape." He makes clear that his attempt to understand his experience as a disabled person caused him to question "inherited platitudes," and to seek "the reasons for the crass inequalities and injustices of the world." This led him to "the works of radical social philosophers, beginning with Henry George," and converted him to social and political radicalism. But later in the essay, he blames his failures on his "weak will" and declares hopefully that he will achieve happiness and success by individualistic overcoming. This very contradictoriness indicates the conflict in his mind between the social values he had internalized and his own struggling sense of the reality of his experience.[6]

Thoroughly misreading this essay, Clayton says that Bourne showed "no self-pity or recrimination, nor did he shake his fist at fate or plead with the 'normal' to change their attitudes." "Bourne never allows whining or blaming the oppressor" (pp. 54, 56). One cannot imagine a writer making such statements about a member of any other minority group. He does so because he views disabled people through the paradigm of personal misfortune. Distressingly, cultural biases about disabled people unconsciously but repeatedly lead Clayton, like all of Bourne's biographers, into stigmatizing language and perceptions. For example, on physically disabled people: "those with souls encased in marred, unsuitable bodies." On Bourne and his lover Esther Cornell: "Was this beauty coming to love the beast?" On Bourne's pacifism: "Like the sickly [William] James, Bourne was too masculine, as ironic as that sounds, too much of a man of his era to accept any idea that denied manliness" (pp. 54, 180, 217). Also, Clayton and his editors are obviously unaware that most physically handicapped people have long regarded such terms as "deformed," "misshapen," and especially "cripple" as prejudiced and highly offensive. Bourne seems never to have used the last two, and when he reprinted "The Handicapped," he consistently replaced the word "deformed" with "handicapped."

To avoid these sorts of misperceptions and misinterpretations, historians must apply a minority group analysis to the historical experience of disabled people. Past social practices and public policies affecting them require reexamination from this perspective, and the history of eugenics needs revising from the viewpoint of its primary victims, people with disabilities. We need to study literary and artistic images of disabled people and descriptions of individuals like Bourne in order to uncover cultural beliefs regarding such matters as body image, masculinity and femininity, personal autonomy and selfhood, and, of course, disability itself as they have impinged on disabled people. The history of these attitudes should also be investigated in relation to the parallel histories of attitudes toward other minorities and women. When devaluation and discrimination happen to one person, it is biography, but when, in all probability, similar experiences happened to millions, it is social history. We will continue to misunderstand individuals like Randolph Bourne as long as the history of disabled people as a distinct social minority remains largely unwritten and unknown.

Notes

1. Louis Filler, *Randolph Bourne* (Washington, D.C., 1943), 32, 96; John Adam Moreau, *Randolph Bourne: Legend and Reality* (Washington, D.C., 1966), 35.
2. Moreau, *Randolph Bourne: Legend and Reality*, 106.
3. Frank Bowe, *Handicapping America: Barriers to Disabled People* (New York, 1978), 186; Robert L. Burgdorf, Jr., ed., *The Legal Rights of Handicapped Persons: Cases, Materials, and Texts* (Baltimore, 1980), 59–63; Peter L. Tyor and Leland V. Bell, *Caring for the Retarded in America: A History* (Westport, 1984); Harlan Lane, *When the Mind Hears: A History of the Deaf* (New York, 1984); Wolf Wolfensberger, "The Extermination of Handicapped People in World War II Germany," *Mental Retardation* 19:1 (February 1981), 1–7.
4. Lasch, *The New Radicalism in America, 1889–1963: The Intellectual as a Social Type* (New York, 1965), 99–100. Lasch tries to connect Bourne's personal experience with "history" by arguing that he shared with many of his generation the conviction of "a moral duty" to resist rather than acquiesce in one's limitations, whatever those limitations might be (Lasch, 100–102, cf. 75–76).
5. Especially useful for a better understanding of Bourne's life and as an introduction to the minority group analysis of disability are Erving Goffman, *Stigma: Notes on the Management of Spoiled Identity* (Englewood Cliffs, 1963); John Gliedman and William Roth, *The Unexpected Minority: Handicapped Children in America* (New York, 1978) (Clayton relies on Erik Erikson's theories of identity formation, but Gliedman and Roth show both the probable inappropriateness of Eriksonian and other developmental psychologies in explaining the development of disabled youngsters and the importance of social prejudice in the shaping of their identities); Harlan Hahn, "Disability Policy and the Problem of Discrimination," *American Behavioral Scientist* 28:3 (January–February 1985), 293–318; Harlan Hahn, "Reconceptualizing

Disability: A Political Science Perspective," *Rehabilitation Literature* 47 (November–December 1984), 362–65, 374; Harlan Hahn, "Changing Perceptions of Disability and the Future of Rehabilitation," unpublished paper, Program in Disability and Society, University of Southern California, 1984.

    6. Randolph Bourne, "The Handicapped," in Olaf Hansen, ed., *The Radical Will: Randolph Bourne, Selected Writings, 1911–1918* (New York, 1977, reprinted Berkeley, 1992), 73–87, see especially pp. 78–80, 86–87.

Uncovering the Hidden
History of Disabled People

The preceding book review sought to alert scholars to the need
for a history of disability. Because Stanley Kutler, the editor of
Reviews in American History, recognized the importance of that
field, he authorized me to write the review essay that follows. In
it I tried to sketch out a preliminary general interpretation of
modern American disability history. I hoped to show that disability history is neither simple nor unitary, but instead complex and
multiple, comprising the experiences of various disability groups,
as well as the simultaneous histories of such things as public policy and cultural representations. At the same time, while those
several histories were distinct, they operated only semiauton-
omously. They also paralleled and interacted with one another.
In addition, given the culturally pervasive stereotype of people
with disabilities as dependent, and therefore helpless and passive,
I thought it important to call attention to their historical agency.
Although they often found themselves individually or collectively
dominated by nondisabled people, they also frequently acted individually or collectively to alter their social fates. Finally, I
wanted to propose a chronological framework for modern disability history. Periodization is not simply a way of segmenting
the past into convenient chunks. It is a mode of charting change

Originally published in slightly different form in *Reviews in American History* 15 (September
1987), 355–64, as a review of Hugh Gregory Gallagher, *FDR's Splendid Deception* (New York:
Dodd, Mead and Company, 1985); Harlan Lane, *When the Mind Hears: A History of the Deaf*
(New York: Random House, 1984); and Peter L. Tyor and Leland V. Bell, *Caring for the Re-
tarded in America: A History* (Westport: Greenwood Press, 1984). Courtesy of Johns Hopkins
University Press.

over time and identifying the causes of historical change. I wanted to periodize modern U.S. disability history, to try to demark its basic chronological and causational structure.

"Disability" encompasses a broad spectrum of medical conditions with diverse effects on appearance and functioning. The books under review examine the historical experience of people whose disabilities (physical, sensory, and developmental) significantly affect daily activities. These studies indicate that whatever the setting, whether in education, medicine, rehabilitation, social-service policy, or society at large, a common set of stigmatizing values and arrangements historically have operated against such persons. They also corroborate recent work in other disciplines that is redefining "disability" as primarily a socially constructed condition. Finally, written mostly by social scientists from those disciplines, they begin to open a field hitherto neglected by historians.

It seems likely that in Western societies, until the early modern era, disability was viewed as an immutable condition caused by supernatural agency. In the eighteenth century, a medical model emerged which redefined it as a biological insufficiency amenable to professional treatment that could, if not cure, at least correct most disabilities or their functional consequences enough for the individuals to perform socially or vocationally in an acceptable manner. These assumptions underlay the construction of enormous edifices in health care, social-service, special education, vocational rehabilitation, and private philanthropy. But in practice, professionals and the societies they represented expressed profound ambivalence toward those who were different, frequently defining them as incompetent to manage their own social careers, even as socially dangerous, and, therefore, proper objects of (often lifelong) supervision.

Harlan Lane's *When the Mind Hears: A History of the Deaf* recounts these developments with regard to Deaf people, tracing the warfare between sign language and oralist education from the advent of signed instruction around 1750 to the ultimate triumph of oralism by 1900.[1] Oralists condemned signing as disorderly, irrational gesticulation. Real thought and learning could only take place through oral or written language. Advocates of sign, hearing and Deaf, countered that it was capable of the greatest subtlety and abstraction. Teaching speech took enormous time, robbed that time from academic subjects, required virtual one-on-one tutoring, and succeeded only with postlingually deafened pupils. Sign is now acknowledged as an authentic language, but in the late eighteenth century even proponents of signed instruction did not fully recognize it as such. Abbé Charles-Michel de l'Epee, who launched signed education in Paris in the 1750s, reversing the previous educational neglect of deaf people, created "methodical sign" in conformance with French grammar because he thought his pupils' natural signing lacked a grammar of its own. Not until the early nineteenth century did hearing educators who used sign abandon such efforts, but they had grasped the necessary principle that academic instruction could only effectively take place through sign. By the 1870s, there were more than two hundred signing schools in Europe and the Americas, twenty-eight in the United States, including Gallaudet College. In France and America, signed education beat back repeated attempts to institute oralism. In Britain and Germany, oralism initially held sway, then succumbed in practice to sign because it failed to deliver on its promises.

The thousands of signing-school graduates entered a wide variety of occupations and formed a signing subculture with its own publications (the "silent press"), churches, and political organizations. Deaf people in France and America even discussed the possibility of separatist townships. A distinct Deaf subculture was precisely the great fear of oralists. "Deaf congregation," they warned, was leading to marriages and production of deaf offspring (the latter an erroneous assumption) and to the creation of an unmanageable social class. To prevent the development of such separate and disorderly classes, Samuel Gridley Howe, an ardent oralist and a pioneer of what became American special education, opposed marriage and even social intercourse among not only deaf, but also blind and mentally retarded people.

In the 1880s and 1890s in Europe and America, oralists and advocates of sign fought the final protracted battle. On one level, as Lane's account of the ferocious struggle between Alexander Graham Bell and Edward Gallaudet, the leaders of the two camps in America, implicitly makes clear, this was a clash among hearing professionals for control of deaf education. The conflict also reflected deepening prejudice against the Deaf minority in an era of intensifying bias against all minorities. Bell, an advocate of immigration restriction and eugenics, warned of the possible "Formation of a Deaf Variety of the Human Race" (1883) and advocated measures to disperse the Deaf community. Oralists avowedly aimed at "restoring the deaf to society," but this meant only those able to learn speech. The majority would be employed at manual labor in sheltered workshops or agriculture. Academic instruction gave way to lip reading and oral articulation. Schools purged deaf teachers. Students were punished for using sign. The international Deaf community protested vehemently but in vain. An astonished Italian oralist asked rhetorically: "Since when do we consult the patient on the nature of his treatment?" (p. 409). Lane ends his story with the oralist triumph of 1900 but notes the continued devastating effect of oralism on the educational achievement of deaf students through much of this century.[2]

Pathbreaking and prodigiously researched, Lane's work is nonetheless marred by present-mindedness. He has chosen to render much of his material as though it were a memoir written by Laurent Clerc, a leading nineteenth-century Deaf teacher who carried signed education from France to America. Lane wholly adopts, but Clerc only partly shared, the viewpoint of current Deaf activists that they belong to an oppressed linguistic minority. One is often uncertain which are Clerc's and which Lane's thoughts. Lane reports that many Deaf contemporaries of Clerc, including some defenders of sign, saw deafness as an affliction. Though he notes that hearing proponents of sign agreed with some oralist biases, he fails to explore fully the extent to which they shared the paternalistic assumptions of the medical model. For instance, Thomas and Edward Gallaudet, the major nineteenth-century American advocates of signed education, opposed deaf people marrying one another, and Edward, having no wish "to safeguard the signing community," also opposed Deaf organizations (pp. 366–67). The signing community was the creation of Deaf people and an inadvertent byproduct of signed education, but not the goal of their hearing benefactors. Clearly, there was no simple dichotomy between oralists and supporters of sign. We need a thorough historical analysis of the various ideologies of deafness and of the development of Deaf identity from that era to the present. Finally and distressingly, to counter prejudice against Deaf people, Lane stigmatizes people with other disabilities. A minority model fits Deaf people; the medical model applies to other handicapped people. In fact, a minority model that defines "disability" as primarily a socially constructed and stigmatized identity and that Lane so convincingly applies to the history of Deaf people also best explains the modern experience of blind people, physically handicapped people, and even most mentally retarded people.[3]

Mental retardation is very unlike deafness, but Peter L. Tyor and Leland V. Bell's *Caring for the Retarded in America: A History* presents striking parallels with Lane's account. Mentally retarded people, considered hopelessly damaged, had been confined in almshouses or insane asylums, farmed out on poor relief, or simply neglected. Then in the early nineteenth century, several French physicians, most notably Edouard Seguin, propounded a developmental model of retardation and an educational model of treatment, proposing specialized training to improve functional capabilities. After Seguin introduced his theories and methods to America at midcentury, a series of state schools were founded. Rejecting permanent custodial care, they admitted carefully screened pupils to ensure a high success ratio, implemented Seguin's program of "physiological instruction" and moral training to treat what are now called developmental deficits, trained students in basic trades and farming, required their discharge, usually by age sixteen, and sent them back to their communities, expecting them to be self-supporting. These educators, like the hearing benefactors of deaf people, aimed ultimately at assimilation. Perhaps unsurprisingly then, some involved themselves in both efforts. Early on, the American Asylum for the Deaf and Dumb in Hartford, Connecticut, the fountainhead of American sign language education, had begun to admit a few mentally retarded students, and the major figure in the field at midcentury was Samuel Gridley Howe.

By the 1880s and 1890s, more thorough census data were uncovering much higher numbers of mentally retarded persons than previously recognized, while a lower percentage of pupils than expected had achieved the degree of normalization promised. Increasingly, retardation was seen as one result of a loss of social stability and order and was incorporated into the pseudoscientific linkage between heredity and a whole array of social ills. Not only was "moral imbecility" falsely attributed to paupers, prostitutes, delinquents, and alcoholics, but, more important for our purposes here, mildly mentally retarded people, many of whom had been living and functioning undetected in the community, were blamed for poverty, vice, and crime. The solution: permanent sequestration. By 1900, retardation professionals had redefined their mission. Custodialism replaced education. Previously, parents or guardians could withdraw pupils at any time. Superintendents now demanded and won exclusive authority over discharges. "The menace of the feeble-minded," many authorities believed, also required sterilization to prevent them from reproducing. Martin Barr, a longtime leader in the profession, even advocated selective killing. Proposals for euthanasia apparently were never implemented in American law as they were in Nazi Germany, but by 1931 twenty-nine states had adopted sterilization statutes. Tyor and Bell unconvincingly assert that professional bias reached its peak around 1900. Yet between 1910 and 1923, at least sixteen states established new custodial facilities as the number of inmates increased 150 percent, and nearly half of the states that passed sterilization laws did so after 1917.[4]

Meanwhile, physically handicapped people encountered similar prejudice. In the early twentieth century, Hugh Gallagher reminds us in *FDR's Splendid Deception*, they "were kept at home, out of sight, in back bedrooms, by families who felt a mixture of embarrassment and shame about their presence." A New York State study found physically disabled children "neglected at home [and] rejected by the public schools" (p. 29). Medical rehabilitation was harsh, punitive, viewing disabled people as flawed physically and morally. Orthopedic treatment of post-polio patients involved "iron, cage-like equipment and frames—painful and ugly . . . to prevent increased deformity." One leading medical authority even advocated amputation of paralyzed limbs. "It is not inaccurate to state that . . . in the course of their treatments [hospitals] practiced maiming and torture" (pp. 31–32). This parallels Lane's appalling stories of medical experiments to make deaf students hear: bleeding, blistering, leeching, fracturing the skull just behind the ear with a hammer, piercing the eardrum, inserting a probe through the nose into the Eustachian tube and working it back and forth, all inflicting excruciating pain, all with no effect.

Why this social ostracism and these extreme measures? Partly because within the medical model, moral and social stigma persisted. The "deaf-mute," wrote a leading French oralist in 1889, "is by nature fickle and improvident, subject to idleness, drunkenness, and debauchery, easily duped and readily corrupted" (Lane, p. 407). Declared an influential orthopedic doctor in 1911: "A failure in the moral training of a cripple means the evolution of an individual detestable in character, a menace and burden to the community, who is only too apt to graduate into the mendicant and criminal classes" (Gallagher, p. 30). Retardation professionals made similar statements. Normalization and assimilation had proved apparently impossible. The only answer was segregation of all the "defective" classes, the "great neuropathic family," one expert called them, "the insane, epileptics, feeble-minded, the neurotic tramps, criminals, paupers, blind, deaf, and consumptive." Professionals made "few distinctions . . . among the different components," note Tyor and Bell, "but there was a sense of almost absolute separation between it and the remainder of humanity" (p. 104). We need studies of the ideologies of various disabilities, particularly among professionals, and of their place in the modern social history of the disability minorities.

Social attitudes apparently began to change with World War I. For instance, Congress passed the first federal vocational rehabilitation legislation for disabled veterans (1918) and civilians (1920). Still, prejudice remained pervasive. In this historical context, Franklin Delano Roosevelt became disabled and had thrust upon him a new social identity. His party's vice-presidential candidate in 1920, he contracted polio in 1921. "Now he is a cripple," said a friend of his mother, "will he ever be anything else?" (Gallagher, p. 28).

But his career became an ironic turning point in the history of handicapped people. In *F.D.R.'s Splendid Deception*, Gallagher explores his management of his disability, not simply physically and emotionally, but more important, interpersonally and politically. For nearly a quarter of a century, aided by family and staff, he conducted a careful strategy of public image making. Because society stigmatized those who used wheelchairs and leg braces, FDR must appear to depend on neither. He banned pictures of him in his wheelchair or of his aides lifting or helping him. Only two out of thirty-five thousand Hyde Park Library photos show him in his wheelchair. Every other picture shows him seated in a regular chair or standing with a cane, not crutches. To hide his leg braces, he wore black socks and had the metal braces painted black. To make it appear in public that he could "walk" up steps, two strong aides on either side would take hold of his elbows and lift him while he held his arms stiff. At a distance, he seemed to be climbing the steps himself, surrounded by a crowd of dignitaries. Knowing that a fall in public would be politically disastrous, he and his aides rehearsed how to catch and right him if he slipped and how to hide it all from view. More strenuous still, he had to manage his demeanor constantly. He must counter the expectation that a "cripple" would be dependent and depressed, must put at ease audiences and individuals unused to and anxious about a disabled man assuming so public a role. Studiously presenting himself as unselfconscious, buoyant, indomitable, in charge of every situation, he developed his considerable skills of self-presentation to an extraordinary degree. "[H]e once told Orson Welles, he considered the two of them . . . the finest actors in America" (p. 190). The demands of this ceaseless performance deepened the isolation of this emotionally solitary man, Gallagher shows, by preventing him from confronting his own feelings about his disability.

Despite the willing participation of the working press in FDR's "deception," literally millions of people witnessed his laborious public efforts to walk, knew of his handicap, though never of its full extent, and yet never "perceived [him] as being in any major sense disabled" (p. xiv).[5] Even those close to him shared that view. Said the wife of a former Roosevelt advisor, "We never, ever thought of the President as handicapped, we never thought of it at all" (p. 210). Surely she did not mean that they were oblivious to his physical condition. Rather, she and probably most Americans exempted FDR from the dependent social role and the devalued social identity typically imposed on people with disabilities. Responding to a question about the effect of her husband's "illness" on his "mentality," Eleanor Roosevelt once said, "Anyone who has gone through great suffering is bound to have a greater sympathy and understanding of the problems of mankind." Reportedly the "audience gave her a standing ovation" (p. 95). The deliberately fashioned image was not that of a "cured cripple," as Gallagher argues, but of a "charismatic cripple," a handicapped man who did not fit the stereotype and who triumphed daily over adversity. Who better to guide his people through the twin national adversities of the Great Depression and World War II?

That image became and has remained the preferred, even required, mode of self-presentation for people with physical and sensory (not mental) disabilities. It involved an implicit bargain in which the nonhandicapped majority extended provisional and partial tolerance of the public presence of handicapped individuals so long as they demonstrated continuous cheerful striving toward normalization. This arrangement defined disability as a private physical and emotional tragedy to be managed by psychological adjustment, rather than a stigmatized social condition, and it disallowed collective protest against prejudice and discrimination, permitting at most efforts to educate away "attitudinal barriers." Despite whispering campaigns of his disability-related incompetence, FDR succeeded in selling not just himself, but a new sort of disabled person. The efforts of the next three generations of disabled people to match that image achieved only limited social acceptance for the majority, while imposing an enormous burden of stigma management on them.[6] That image also coincided with the enormous expansion of vocational and medical rehabilitation, whose assumptions reinforced it.

Meanwhile the situation of mentally retarded people changed as well. In the 1920s, a shift began away from institutionalization. Demographic data now showed a retarded population far too large to be sequestered. Most had lived undetected in the community, working at menial jobs. The Depression and World War II forced cutbacks in institutional budgets. The "special" class in public schools (first established in the late 1890s) began to assume increasing importance as a cheaper and more effective way to train higher functioning retarded people. Postwar research demonstrated that retardation was not a fixed condition, but strongly influenced by environment. Horrendous conditions in large institutions provoked calls for their abolition. Parents' groups and professionals allied to upgrade institutional care or to replace it with community-based small-scale facilities. In the 1960s and 1970s, they lobbied for and won new federal policies, backed by federal money. Perhaps most remarkably, in a series of federal court cases and congressional legislation, they established that mentally retarded citizens have legal rights to habilitation if institutionalized, a free and appropriate education in the least restrictive environment, due process, and protection from involuntary sterilization, among other guarantees. Tyor and Bell probably overstate the extent of professional agreement with this new perspective and exaggerate its implementation in practice. They also ignore the persistence of public hostility toward retarded people. Proposals to establish group homes in various localities led to lawsuits, protests, threats, in a few cases even vandalism, beatings, and firebombings.[7]

From 1918 on, the federal funding and policy-making role in rehabilitation increased, and the definition of "handicapping conditions" broadened, but the underlying concept of disability remained constant: disability was a defect residing in the individual and therefore requiring individual medical rehabilitation, special education, and vocational training to improve employment prospects. In the 1960s and 1970s, a civil-rights movement of people with physical and sensory disabilities and some rehabilitation professionals began to espouse a major new conceptualization of disability: "handicaps" result from the interaction of individuals with the social and built environment; "disability" is primarily a socially constructed and stigmatized role. Out of this new perspective developed the concept of "access." It could have been restricted to physical modifications in the personal living environments of disabled individuals. Instead, a series of federal statutes established, at least in theory, a broad view of "access," which included participation as well as mobility throughout society and made it a legally protected civil right.[8]

The social definition of disability has been central to the interpretation of the fundamental civil-rights statute for handicapped citizens, the 1973 Rehabilitation Act's Section 504, which protects them from discrimination in federally funded programs. The regulations implementing 504 had to define discrimination and to prescribe corrective measures. Discrimination, as Richard Scotch notes in his study of 504, can sometimes be ended simply by ignoring the stigmatized attribute. At other times, "differential treatment has been sanctioned as a remedy to past discrimination . . . , [but] such remedies are typically justified as temporary adjustments to achieve parity among groups rather than as an intrinsic premise." In fact, the 504 regulations perpetuated differential treatment by rejecting, for reasons of political and financial expediency, a standard of total architectural accessibility, in favor of "program accessibility": all federally supported activities, but not all facilities, must be accessible. But 504 did creatively fuse "concepts from prior rehabilitation and civil rights laws" in an area Scotch neglects. Adaptive devices and services (e.g., wheelchairs and sign language interpreters) had been considered special benefits to those who were fundamentally dependent and incapacitated. Section 504 moved beyond these social-service notions by viewing such devices and services as simply different modes of functioning and departed from traditional civil-rights concepts by defining them as legitimate permanent differential treatment necessary to achieve and maintain equal access. This perspective was the heart of the emerging disability rights ideology.[9]

A four-year battle by disability rights activists, culminating in nationwide demonstrations in spring 1977, including a month-long sit-in at HEW's regional headquarters in San Francisco, pressured the newly installed Carter administration into publishing the 504 regulations. But civil-rights activism was not new to the disability minorities, as a glance at their considerable, neglected political history indicates. The Deaf communities in France and America were politically active throughout the nineteenth century defending their language rights. During the Great Depression, New York City's League of the Physically Handicapped, a group of disabled young adults, protested job discrimination, particularly in WPA projects. Beginning in the 1940s, the National Federation of the Blind adopted a strong civil-rights stance and lobbied for equal rights of all disabled persons. Tyor and Bell show the impact of politicized parents of mentally retarded people from the 1940s to the present. We need historical studies of the politics and ideologies of a great many organizations of disabled people, parents, and professionals and of the historical roots of the minority group consciousness currently developing among a younger generation of disabled people.[10]

We also need a systematic legal history of disability, not only social policy, but a vast corpus of laws and legislation affecting people with disabilities. Additionally, various states conducted censuses of their deaf, blind, or mentally handicapped inhabitants in the nineteenth century. Carefully used, these and later more thorough surveys could enable social historians to develop demographic historical profiles of these groups.

Several factors complicate the study of disabled people's history. Different disabilities make for different individual and group histories: the signing community developed out of the condition of deafness. And yet social attitudes, while recognizing some differences, have often lumped all disabled people in an undifferentiated mass, "the handicapped." That perception reflected a common set of social values and responses to "disability" which requires historical explanation. It also created a common base of experience that cut across disability categories. The National Association of the Deaf defending the signing subculture in the 1890s and New York City's League of the Physically Handicapped fighting job discrimination in the 1930s may have had similar notions about their social, economic, and political status. Further complicating historical analysis is the wide range of individuals' social careers. Mabel Hubbard, wife of Alexander Graham Bell, strictly practiced oralism and with deep antipathy shunned other deaf people, while Laurent Clerc spent his life as a teacher and leader within the signing community. Individual experiences encompassed a broad spectrum sociologically. Finally, because "passivity" is so often unconsciously ascribed to disabled persons, it is essential for scholars to keep in mind that they, like other minorities, have not been passive victims of oppression, but actors in their own history and their own lives, as the examples of FDR and the signing community make clear. The studies under review draw upon enormous deposits of unpublished and printed primary source materials. That nearly untouched terrain, the hidden history of disabled people, awaits excavation by historians.

Notes

1. The terms "deaf" and "Deaf" are used by scholars to distinguish between persons who merely have impaired hearing and those who are "culturally Deaf," that is, belong to the Deaf community and use a sign language as their primary language.

2. A 1973 Gallaudet College study of Scholastic Aptitude Test scores of some seventeen thousand deaf students found them reading at a fourth-grade level. Harlan Lane, *When the Mind Hears: A History of the Deaf* (New York, 1985), 399.

3. John Gliedman and William Roth, *The Unexpected Minority: Handicapped Children in America* (New York, 1978), 4–5.

4. Surprisingly, Tyor and Bell omit mention of *Buck v. Bell* (1927), in which the U.S. Supreme Court, with Mr. Justice Holmes writing for the majority, upheld state sterilization laws as "prevent[ing] those who are manifestly unfit from continuing their kind."

5. The press's acquiescence in the "deception" is perhaps less remarkable than Gallagher thinks. Journalists of that era accepted many more restrictions than do today's media outlets.

6. On stigma management, see Erving Goffman, *Stigma: Notes on the Management of Spoiled Identity* (Englewood Cliffs, 1963), 91–125. Goffman skillfully analyzes stigma management but does not recognize that it is a historically conditioned strategy.

7. Tyor and Bell omit the lengthy series of court battles from the late 1960s to the early 1980s which found that the wretched conditions at Willowbrook State Hospital in New York violated the civil rights of the mentally retarded inmates. On the latter litigation see David and Sheila Rothman, *The Willowbrook Wars* (New York, 1985).

8. See Frank Bowe, *Handicapping America* (New York, 1978); Frank Bowe, *Rehabilitating America* (New York, 1980).

9. Richard K. Scotch, *From Good Will to Civil Rights: Transforming Federal Disability Policy* (Philadelphia, 1985), 71, 152.

10. Development of this perspective among adults with disabilities aged eighteen to forty-four, in contrast to those over forty-five, is the most important finding of Louis Harris and Associates, *ICD Survey of Disabled Americans* (New York, 1986), see 109–11.

4

The League of the
Physically Handicapped
and the Great Depression

A Case Study in the New Disability History

In 1993 at a meeting of advocates working on disability policy
issues, I passed around a half-dozen photos of members of the
League of the Physically Handicapped. The pictures showed
league members walking a picket line, sitting on the stoop in
front of their New York City headquarters, camping out on the
Mall of the Washington Monument, relaxing at a picnic. The
advocates crowded around, full of questions about these activists
from the past, their political forebears. Every community, every
minority, every movement needs its heroes. Heroes instruct us
as to who we really are, who we can become, and what remarkable changes we can bring about if we act boldly and if we stick
together. The brief history of the league makes for an exciting
heroic story: in the depths of the Great Depression, a small group
of physically disabled young adults audaciously took on the United
States government and, in many ways, won. But the episode of
the league offers us much more than a tale of intrepid activists. It
serves as a window into the complex history of disability. An examination not only of the League of the Physically Handicapped,
but also of the larger historical context within which it emerged,

Coauthored with David Goldberger, a senior director at the Advisory Board Company, a health
care research firm in Washington, D.C. A slightly different version was originally published
in the *Journal of American History* 87:3 (December 2000), 888–922. Courtesy of *Journal of
American History*.

allowed my coauthor David Goldberger and me to explore the multiple interacting tracks of modern disability history and the many views and usages of "disability" in twentieth-century America.

On Wednesday, May 29, 1935, six young adults—three women and three men—entered New York City's Emergency Relief Bureau (ERB), demanding to see Director Oswald W. Knauth. Told he would be unavailable until the next week, they declared they would sit there till he met with them or, one vowed, "hell freezes over." The next day a large crowd backed the demonstrators and demanded jobs for themselves. Five and a half years into the Great Depression, such protests were common. But this one presented something different. The six protesters and some supporting picketers had physical disabilities. They claimed that they and other handicapped job seekers suffered disability-based discrimination at the hands of work-relief agencies and the federal government's Works Progress Administration (WPA). Their protest marked the beginning of the League of the Physically Handicapped. In the next few years, the militant league fought job discrimination and contested the ideology of disability that dominated early-twentieth-century public policies, professional practices, and societal arrangements.[1]

An examination of the league reveals not only how that ideology prescribed the social roles and identities of people with disabilities, but also how some such people politicized disability as they sought to redefine their identities and the nature of the obstacles they faced. That inquiry illuminates the interplay between social policy and cultural values by exploring the use of *disability* to mark its opposite, *normality*, and thereby to manage social—particularly class—relations in modern society. Finally, it deepens comparative historical analysis of U.S. social-reform movements by investigating one of many disability-based political crusades.[2]

Studying the league also directs attention to an emerging scholarship that shows disability's pervasive presence in history and its conspicuous absence from historiography. Since colonial times exclusion of aliens with disabilities has been a central, if uncontroversial, goal of American immigration law, yet immigration historians have failed to examine that practice, except to disparage attribution of disability as an excuse to bar certain ethnic groups. Likewise, though workers have frequently experienced disability, labor historians have typically ignored how cultural values regarding work, gender, and class have shaped working-class perceptions of disability and responses to it. Recent research confirms the historian Douglas Baynton's observation: "Disability is everywhere in history, once you begin looking for it."[3]

Why then have historians omitted disability from their accounts? They may have assumed a dearth of primary sources; in fact, new research demonstrates sources in abundance. Scholars may also have avoided the subject because, as psychological studies have substantiated, disability often elicits "existential anxiety." Most important, an ideology of disability as a product of nature has seemed to obviate the need or possibility of studying disability as an artifact or construct. The medical paradigm dominant in modern societies has framed disability as limitation in social or vocational functioning due to chronic medical problems. By casting it as a matter of pathology, the medicalized perspective has individualized and privatized disability, effectively restricting historical investigation or interpretation. A merely "personal" condition, it defies systematic study.[4]

While some medical historians have reconstructed the sociocultural experience of illness and the impact on public discourse and policy making of social values concerning disease and health care, they have largely focused on the functioning of health care institutions and responses to epidemics and the critical phase of diseases. Few people with disabilities spent much time in hospitals or institutions. The perception of them as socially impaired by medical pathology did impinge on them in other social settings in their contact with social workers, educators, vocational rehabilitation counselors, and other nonmedical professionals, but scholars have usually failed to look in those places. Historians of workers' health have examined workplaces, but the medical paradigm has focused their analyses on the evolving explanations of the causes and courses of occupational diseases and disabilities and on safety, treatment, and compensation measures. Though that scholarship frequently mentions job discrimination against workers regarded as disabled, it does not delve into that theme. Nonetheless, public health historiography bears importantly on disability history.[5]

In addition, the medical approach, by typically regarding disabled people as patients or dependent objects of charity, has thereby rendered them historically inert or invisible. Older histories of "the deaf" or "the blind" made them passive recipients of the benevolence of those regarded as the real historical agents: hearing or sighted professionals and philanthropists. Policy historians have similarly traced creation of the "disability category," but disabled people generally enter the story as historical actors only when, in the late twentieth century, a broad-based disability rights movement compels attention.[6] In many fields of historical inquiry where disability was significant, the medical pathology perspective has located the causes of alleged social incapacity within "afflicted" individuals, thereby excluding consideration of cultural, social, and political factors in the construction of disabled people's identities and roles and overlooking disabled persons as historical actors.

Recent scholarship has identified the early twentieth century as the moment when policy makers and health care, charity, social-service, and education professionals institutionalized the medical definition of disability that thereafter dominated public policy and professional practice. Generating more than individual diagnosis, this paradigm produced disability as a social problem that required policy makers' and professionals' attention while simultaneously depoliticizing it by placing it under the authority of medical and quasi-medical experts. On both the diagnostic and societal levels, the medical model also constructed the social identities and roles of millions of people with disabilities, not to mention hosts of professionals in various emerging fields. Moreover, that paradigm made disability a major category of social organization, policy formulation, and "cultural signification." Not just a label on groups with various conditions, "disability," argues Baynton, served as "the primary term in a fundamental binary opposition—'normal' versus 'disabled' . . . a signifier for relations of power." It has functioned as a ubiquitous, though unacknowledged, organizing concept and symbol in the modern world, operating synergistically as public problem, cultural metaphor, social identity, and mechanism for managing social relations. Disability, then, is at once a neglected set of historical experiences, an important theme overlooked in many fields, and a central component of history in general. As such, like gender, race, and class, it must become both a subject of comparative historical study and a standard, indispensable tool of historical analysis.[7]

Many people in the League of the Physically Handicapped limped or wore leg braces and used crutches or canes as a result of polio. A few had cerebral palsy, tuberculosis, or heart conditions. At least two had lost limbs in accidents. One had been gassed as a soldier in the Great War. None rode wheelchairs. None was deaf or blind.[8] League members did not identify with people whose disabilities differed substantially from their own, but neither did they dwell on the varying origins of members' physical conditions. Forming not as the League of Polio Survivors, but as the League of the Physically Handicapped, and rarely even mentioning impairment, they concentrated on discrimination rather than diagnosis. Their activism sought to alter public understanding of disability, shifting the focus from coping with impairment to managing identity, from experiencing polio to engaging in politics.

The league's approach highlights the basic features and dilemmas of disability as a historical phenomenon. The physical effects of illness or injury constitute merely one dimension of disability. At its crux is the sociocultural meaning attributed to physiological conditions. Despite the medical paradigm's pretensions to scientific certitude, from the beginning of that paradigm's reign the lived experience of disability generated knotty questions about just what disability is. All modern public policies regarding people with disabilities, whether benefits programs or civil-rights laws, have had to grapple with that issue, for the answer would determine who qualified for coverage and who did not. For example, benefits administrators relied on clinical medical examinations not merely to ascertain the presence of a physical or mental impairment, but to extrapolate from it "disability," limitation in socioeconomic functioning. Despite what David Rosner and Gerald Markowitz call "the allure of the medical expert," many policy makers, program administrators, medical and rehabilitation professionals, and lay people recognized not only that impairment and disability are two different things, but also that social contexts can largely create, mitigate, or eliminate disability. Although the experience of disability varies partly because individuals react differently to the same conditions, those responses stem from more than personal temperament. Ethnicity, class, generation, gender, and other factors always mediate individual responses. Physical and architectural environments, medical and technological developments, and public policies significantly shape how people experience disability. Further, cultural values and social ideas about impairment and disability have changed over time. A "cripple" on a public thoroughfare might have been seen as a divinely punished sinner in the 1830s, a potential rehabilitant in the 1950s, a political activist in the 1990s, and, in any era, a mendicant. The intricate interplay of those factors indicates that disability is never simply limitation in social or vocational functioning, never an objectively determinable, pathological clinical entity originating in the bodies of individuals. Rather, defying simple definition, it is an elastic social category shaped and reshaped by cultural values, societal arrangements, public policies, and professional practices. It is always an array of culturally constructed identities and highly mutable social roles.[9]

In the early twentieth century, the predominant social identity enjoined on people with *physical* disabilities was "the crippled." A persona with a long cultural history in the West, it began in the modern era to be aggregated with an array of other traditional classifications ("the blind," "the deaf," "the feebleminded," "the insane") into a generic category, "the disabled." Modern policy makers and administrators viewed those diverse groups as sharing enough to warrant lumping them under a single rubric. Still, outside of public policy, the crippled and the other ancient personas remained distinct.[10]

Public policies often devalued cripples and other disabled people. While some crippled adults were relegated to the long-established poor-relief system, some crippled children, including a few founders of the league, were segregated in the "special" classes and schools that had been expanding since their advent around the turn of the century. The vast majority of handicapped youngsters were completely excluded from public schools. Rehabilitation professionals favored educating them in more "appropriate" settings such as hospitals. Moreover, public resistance to educating them at all, whether in special or general classes, seems to have intensified during the 1930s. Those allowed entry were often stigmatized, although, as we shall see, special classes could also generate a sense of solidarity among handicapped youth. The courts and the laws frequently excluded handicapped people from other spheres of society. Court rulings upheld the right of railroads and public transit systems to refuse to carry disabled passengers. While some cities, such as New York, licensed cripples to beg, others, such as Chicago, adopted "unsightly beggar" ordinances to bar them from public places. Police officers often refused to enforce the latter laws, but whether local ordinances banned or allowed alms seeking, all regarded cripples as natural beggars.[11]

If school policies, court rulings, and local laws often segregated handicapped people within American communities, national immigration laws banned them from the country. Though officials labored throughout the nineteenth century to bar "the halt, the lame, and the blind," the "deformed, crippled, or maimed," immigration laws passed during the decades surrounding 1900 increasingly "lowered the threshold for exclusion and expanded the latitude" of examining officers to reject immigrants with disabilities. The Immigration Act of 1907 made the ban open-ended by barring anyone with a "mental or physical defect . . . which *may affect* the ability of such alien to earn a living." One officer remembered a young couple barred because the husband was thought "likely to become a public charge" due to his "game leg" and crutch. Such exclusion typified the treatment of handicapped immigrants. The disability-based bans turned away not only those considered potential public burdens, but also those perceived as threats to the national genetic stock. Though most league members were native-born, immigration policies declared people like them unworthy of citizenship.[12]

Restrictive immigration laws barred disabled people from the United States; eugenic laws aimed to prevent their existence. Model statutes sought sterilization, marriage restriction, and even incarceration to stop reproduction by the "unfit," among them the "Deformed (including the crippled)." None of the twenty-nine state statutes adopted by 1937 covered cripples, but eugenicists' calls for their sterilization indicated the thinking of many influential people about who was fit to be a citizen or even to live. Eugenics, as Martin S. Pernick has shown, was always closely associated with euthanasia. In 1915, public controversy erupted when a Chicago surgeon, Dr. Harry J. Haiselden, revealed that he had caused several disabled newborns to die. To promote euthanasia of "defective" infants, he produced *The Black Stork*, a motion picture about a doctor who foresees a life of rejection, misery, and murderous rage for a "deformed" boy and convinces the mother to let the baby die. Released in 1916, the year of a polio epidemic in which some future league leaders became disabled, the film portrayed its main character, Pernick tells us, "as a mentally normal hunchbacked boy who grows up to become an insane criminal" because of—according to an intertitle—"the constant humiliation and embarrassment caused by his deformity." Haiselden and his film were prominent in euthanasia advocacy during the 1910s, supported by some leading Progressives (Lillian Wald, Judge Ben Lindsey, Helen Keller) and opposed by others (Jane Addams). The euthanasia movement receded during the 1920s but regained momentum during the 1930s, allying with euthanasia advocates in Nazi Germany. Proponents used *The Black Stork* into the 1940s. Its intertitles labeled the handicapped character "The Monster." Reviews called him "The Defective" or "The Cripple." His appearance strongly resembles that of male league members in photos of them picketing.[13]

In other films, actors portrayed cripples as incapacitated for any valid social role. Lon Chaney reigned as a major star of the 1910s and 1920s often by playing a variety of cripples, the vast majority of them villains. In the 1920s, 1930s, and 1940s, movies presented characters with disabilities similar to those of league members as either uncontrollable villains or helpless victims. This continued a cultural motif in which disabled figures embodied the loss of control and the dependency Americans have found so troubling and have displaced onto outsider figures. Whether represented as menacing or pathetic, physically handicapped people were thereby defined as unfit for normal social roles.[14]

Professional charity fund-raisers also deployed the image of the cripple to generate donations for medical rehabilitation that allegedly would validate individuals discredited by disability. Instead, their techniques further branded physically handicapped people as the inversion of socially legitimate persons. In 1934, Paul King, the National Society for Crippled Children finance chair issued a stamp benefactors could purchase for a penny. That first Easter Seal showed a sad boy wearing leg braces and leaning forward on crutches in front of a white cross and the words "Help Crippled Children." The enthusiastic public response ensured the annual appearance of this fund-raising tool. Also in 1934, the National Foundation for Infantile Paralysis, founded by Franklin D. Roosevelt, sponsored some six thousand President's Birthday Balls using the slogan "Dance so that others may walk." In 1938, the foundation launched the even more successful March of Dimes. All of these solicitations established as a standard mode of disability-related fund-raising one version of the cripple image: a dependent child as an object of charity. The young adults in the league opposed such charity. One remarked acidly, "The old custom was to take the crippled children on a boat ride and have it reported that 'a good time was had by all.'" He condemned this practice as "the run-around," self-congratulatory philanthropy that avoided the real issues.[15]

If cultural image making symbolically segregated cripples and statutory law often formally excluded them, social practices might informally shut them out as well. In Dayton, Ohio, in the mid-1930s, Tom Hockenberry, a power company employee who had lost an arm in a power line accident, applied to join the Freemasons. That anti-Catholic, racially segregated fraternity overwhelmingly voted against him because of his disability. Families with disabled members also often imbibed society's prejudices. "In those days if you were handicapped, you were hidden," recalled one league member. "And the parents cooperated in that. Many of them were ashamed of having handicapped children." Another remembered painfully: "My father brought me up with the idea that he was punished for someone's sins and that's why he had a handicapped child. . . . [He] would walk out every time I walked into the room." Internalizing society's prejudices, handicapped individuals sometimes avoided public contact with other disabled people. One man recalled: "There was only one other handicapped boy in high school and when he saw me he used to go the other way. And when I saw him I would go the other way . . . because I didn't want to embarrass him and I didn't want to embarrass myself."[16]

In its several forms, the cripple image limned a set of interlocking traits. Cripples appeared variously as victims and villains in popular culture, dependent sentimentalized children in charity fund-raising, mendicants who should be allowed to beg, "unsightly or disgusting objects" who should be banned from public places, potentially dependent or dangerous denizens of society, worthy subjects of poor relief but unworthy citizens of the nation. Whatever the guise, they were represented as incapacitated for real participation in the community and the economy, incapable of usefully directing their lives, disruptive and disorderly, antithetical to those defined as *healthy* and *normal.* They were socially invalid. Given all that "cripple" signified, no wonder Tennessee Williams's semifictional Amanda Wingfield instructs her crippled daughter Laura never to use that word, and no wonder the real-life young adults who formed the League of the Physically Handicapped spurned it. A friend of Sara Roosevelt, pondering Franklin Roosevelt's new disability in 1921 and thinking less about his physical condition than about his social identity, touched on layers of social and cultural meaning when she asked: "Now he is a cripple, will he ever be anything else?"[17]

Both Franklin Roosevelt and the young adults active in the League of the Physically Handicapped resisted relegation to that negative status, but they adopted different modes of altering their social fates. FDR made himself and allowed himself to be made into the avatar of an emerging system of rehabilitation. Rehabilitation ideology refined and systematized already existing ideas about disability. It attested that disability was a medically caused limitation in the individual's capacity to achieve economic self-sufficiency and to fulfill expected social roles, even as it prescribed a route to productive independence and a socially legitimate identity. Disabled individuals must engage in continuous cheerful striving to recapture some semblance of social normality, a quest at once physical, psychological, and moral. FDR devoted years of strenuous effort to physical therapy, kept his disability largely hidden, and disclosed it only in ways that would display him as an indomitable victor over personal adversity. In the process, he became the classic role model of what succeeding generations of rehabilitation professionals and physically disabled Americans referred to as "overcoming." He made his way back to a socially valid identity and role, but he succeeded by largely denying and hiding the disabled parts of himself while ignoring societal prejudice and shouldering an enormous burden of stigma management. He and rehabilitation professionals promoted this mode of social validation.[18]

Meanwhile, in New York City a group of physically disabled young adults who also sought a route to social validity blazed a different, ultimately a political, path. Rejecting both the crippled and overcomer identities, they redefined themselves as "handicapped." Yearning for the self-dependence and dignity prized by able-bodied workers, they prepared to go to work. But they found that the biases about cripples in every other sphere of society had spawned discrimination in the job market too.[19]

Some businesses required applicants to undergo physical examinations unrelated to a job's tasks. Florence Haskell walked with crutches. Upon graduating from high school, she applied for a secretarial position. "The man told me . . . 'I'm afraid you'll have to take a physical.' . . . I was really hit between the eyes. I never visualized that [my handicap] would be a reason for me not to get a job. . . . He *disqualified* me. . . . I was very hurt, upset, and mad." Sylvia Flexer Bassoff, who used crutches and wore a leg brace, explained to a reporter at the time, "I wanted to teach English, or be a librarian, until I found out I couldn't get a job if I were trained for it." The memory was still vivid decades later. "Well, I found I couldn't get a job. But not because there was a Depression. I found I couldn't get a job because I was handicapped." So she enrolled at the Drake Business School, where she excelled at stenography and typing and on the adding machine. "In my naïveté, I figured, 'I'll graduate from the Drake Business School and they're all going to grab me.' . . . Well, nobody grabbed me. . . . Some people who graduated got jobs who weren't, they didn't begin to be as good as I was." Denied work in private business, she and other handicapped people felt humiliated at having to take jobs in charity-run sheltered workshops. "And finally I got a job," she remembered indignantly, "at the *Brooklyn Bureau* of *Charities*, who *only hired* handicapped people." She was paid three dollars and fifty cents for every thousand envelopes she addressed. "It was a mail-order, and it was the Brooklyn Bureau of Charities. . . . What a terrible name to work for. . . . It was a great injustice. And I didn't know what to do. I didn't know what to do." [20]

If a handicapped individual did land a job in private business, it might be only part-time or temporary and at lower pay. Born with cerebral palsy, Lou Razler attended business college for a year after high school, then spent five years fruitlessly searching for permanent work. By the spring of 1935, he was thoroughly fed up with his situation. Some handicapped people who found work felt they suffered from wage discrimination. In 1927, Jack Isaacs, who had lost a leg in an industrial accident, worked as a linotypist. He told a journalist that he "turned out just as much work" as the men alongside him, but they got three times his fifteen-dollar-a-week wages. He claimed his lower pay was because of his disability. [21]

Blocked by such barriers, these and other handicapped people looked to New Deal work programs to give them jobs just like those given to unemployed nonhandicapped workers. Instead, they found the culturally dominant image of the crippled had been inscribed in the avowedly innovative federal policies. In January 1935, President Roosevelt proposed the Works Progress Administration to provide jobs for the unemployed, but roughly 1.5 million individuals categorized as "unemployable"—mothers with dependent children, old people, and handicapped people—would be shunted to local relief. New York City's Emergency Relief Bureau had routinely selected some disabled home relief recipients for city jobs. Now, in line with the new federal policy, it automatically rejected handicapped persons for municipal work relief. [22]

Until the 1930s, local relief remained limited in scope, with the federal government playing only a small role in social welfare. But as millions of unemployed people overwhelmed private charities and state and local governments, the unprecedented crisis forced many Americans to rethink the federal government's role in ensuring the general welfare. Many working-class citizens decided that the state must guarantee social equity and economic justice by providing both adequate welfare and work relief. [23]

Handicapped job seekers too came to expect government action on their behalf. The news that their government would aid unemployed "able-bodied" Americans while classifying out-of-work handicapped persons as unemployable violated this newfound sense of their rights. When a group of young adults who frequented a Manhattan recreation center for handicapped people learned that WPA policy defined them as unable to work, shutting them out of both federal and local work relief, they felt outraged. "What started it," remembered one, "was finding out that jobs were available, that the government was handing out jobs. . . . Everybody was getting jobs: newspaper people, actresses, actors, painters, and only handicapped people weren't worthy of jobs. . . . Those of us who . . . were militant just refused to accept the fact that we were the only people who were looked upon as not worthy, not capable of work."[24]

Common backgrounds and shared experiences had already generated solidarity among members of the recreation center group. Besides having similar disabilities, most were children of working-class southern and eastern European immigrants. Most were Jewish. Their parents had encouraged some of them toward education and employment. As high school graduates, in some cases with additional vocational or college study, they were better educated than most physically handicapped people. Some had become friends in New York City's public elementary special-education classes during the 1920s, thereafter attending mainstream high schools. After graduation, they extended their web of friendships by socializing at summer camps and recreation centers run by social-service agencies or at "basement clubs" organized by handicapped young people. Members who grew up in families with leftist and labor ties were also predisposed to radical political analyses of social problems. Their common background spurred the group to action. Through activism they could combat both bias and the construction of disability as medical pathology, vocational incapacitation, and social invalidation by redefining them in political terms. As group members applied labor radicalism to their situation, they would push radical politics in new directions.[25]

One of the group was Florence Haskell, who had already found herself disqualified for a clerical job because of her disability. Another was a twenty-eight-year-old unemployed watch repairman, Hyman Abramowitz, who used leg braces and crutches due to childhood polio. His wife too had a disability, and the couple had a child to support. Abramowitz had been arrested for sitting in at a Brooklyn relief center. By late May 1935, he had emerged as a leader of the group.[26]

Abramowitz evidently argued that a delegation should go to the ERB and demand an end to disability-based discrimination in work relief. On Wednesday, May 29, 1935, Florence Haskell, age 19, Pauline Portugalo, 21, Sara Lasoff, 22, Harry Friedman, 24, and Morris Dolinsky, 26, went with Abramowitz to ERB headquarters. Director Knauth's aides said he could see them the following week, but the six rejected the delay as unacceptable. Angry and frustrated and, it seems, without any real plan, they did what Abramowitz had warned them they might have to do: they "refused to budge" until Knauth met with them.[27]

For the next twenty-four hours, they sat there without attracting public attention. On Thursday afternoon, Abramowitz's wife tried to enter the building. When the watchman, following orders, refused to let her in, she departed for a Communist-sponsored United Youth Day parade in nearby Madison Square and returned "with a score of husky young men." Soon hundreds of protesters, then thousands of onlookers, thronged before the ERB. Members of the Writers Union, the Young Communists of America, and the City Committee of the Unemployment Council picketed to support the sit-in and to demand jobs for themselves. Some demonstrators "besieged" the building for an hour, tried to rush the doors, and ended their "riot" with a snake dance in the street. As quickly as it had gathered, the crowd evaporated. By late afternoon, only Mrs. Abramowitz and "a crippled friend" remained. But the turmoil in the street alerted the press to the disabled protesters upstairs. Hyman Abramowitz charged the ERB with discriminating against handicapped people in assigning relief jobs. He told reporters, "We are not able to go out seeking manual labor . . . , but we still feel that the city should provide us with jobs." The day before they had sought merely to see Knauth. Now Abramowitz announced, "We are going to stay here until fifty of our organization get jobs." In fact, there was no organization as yet. They were playing the protest by ear, developing their strategy and demands as they went along. They had accidentally captured media attention.[28]

Trying various stratagems to force the protesters to give up, ERB officials at first refused to allow any food to be brought in. The tactic backfired. By Friday, three of the protesters had quit the sit-in, but Abramowitz, Dolinsky, and Portugalo hung on. While leftist supporters engaged in "mass and 'marathon' picketing," "the strikers" conducted "a series of interviews." In response, ERB officials switched their strategy, apparently to put themselves in a more sympathetic light. They would now feed the protesters but at no greater cost to the city than home relief. They would not forcibly evict them, ostensibly for fear of injuring them, but would no longer permit visitors. Perhaps "isolation of the cripples" would end the sit-in by cutting them off from public attention. The new tactics failed too.[29]

By Saturday, the number of nonhandicapped protesters on the sidewalk had dwindled, but nine handicapped picketers, five men and four women, conspicuously walked the line. They called themselves the Committee of Action for the Support of the Handicapped Unemployed. Lou Razler, the frustrated ex–business college student with cerebral palsy, learned of the protest in the *Daily News*. "As soon as I read about it, I went down," he recalled. Sara Lasoff spotted him "standing on the other side of the street. And I went over to him and said to him, 'Why don't you join the picket line?' . . . And he joined, and he became very active." Said Razler: "I joined the line. I figured, 'I got nothing to lose.'" All that Saturday, the neighborhood echoed with their chant to ERB director Knauth: "Knauth, come out, wherever you are!" That evening, continuing to emulate labor radicals, the protesters strategized for "mass support and mass demonstrations."[30]

On Monday, June 3, the sixth day, Knauth finally met with the three strikers. Again hiking their demands, they rejected both charity and segregated workshops. Abramowitz warned that unless its demands were met "the league of 100 cripples would expand to 1,000, and that jobs would have to be found for all of them." He demanded fifty jobs immediately and ten more each week, at wages of at least twenty-seven dollars a week for married workers, twenty-one dollars for single workers. Those hired must also be integrated with nonhandicapped workers, not shunted into separate projects. Knauth rejected the demands but promised to "investigate." "That's not a good enough answer," Abramowitz shot back. "We are not just as any other group. We are all handicapped and are being discriminated against." Probably with the WPA policy regarding "unemployables" in mind, he charged President Roosevelt with "trying to fix things so that no physically handicapped person can get a job, so that all of us will have to go on home relief." At least one handicapped person and probably others already felt disillusioned with FDR, the champion of American workers. "We don't want charity," demanded Abramowitz, "we want jobs." But Knauth hewed to the new policy. The city owed nothing beyond home relief, he said. "This is not an organization to give work to those who are permanently un-employable." Then, contradicting himself, he advised them to seek work from private businesses. Abramowitz blasted those who offered handi-capped people charity instead of work. "We'll have to be carried out," he declared.[31]

For three days more, the strikers stayed put. And each day the pick-eters, most of them handicapped, marched below. By Thursday, June 6, the ninth day, the noise of the "shouting and singing on the sidewalk" had become intolerable to workers in the building. Knauth directed the superintendent to call the police, who arrested eleven protesters, eight of them handicapped. Among the arrestees was Jack Isaacs, the one-legged ex-linotypist. Upstairs, the three strikers ended their sit-in. But that afternoon "about twenty-five crippled protesters and 300 sympa-thizers" rallied at Fifty-fourth Street and Eighth Avenue. Dispersed by police, they regrouped at the WMCA radio station, where Oswald Knauth was to deliver a speech celebrating the ERB's first anniversary. The group "stormed the lobby" and tried "to seize an elevator, but po-lice drove them out of the building."[32]

On Friday evening, June 7, the handicapped activists again met with Knauth. He said he could not promise jobs immediately but hoped federal funds would include some aid for that purpose. Downstairs, handicapped picketers passed out handbills announcing a Saturday dem-onstration at city hall. The next morning, ten to twelve disabled demon-strators and as many as fifty nonhandicapped supporters circled in City Hall Plaza. After unsuccessfully demanding an interview with Mayor Fiorello LaGuardia, they moved to Foley Square for some speech mak-ing, then dispersed. That marked the end of the first actions of these novice activists. For eleven days, they had captured the city's attention and forced relief officials to bargain with them.[33]

The eleven picketers arrested on June 6 were soon brought to trial. Judge Overton Harris seemed bewildered about how to handle the mil-itant young handicapped defendants who shouted slogans in his court-room. For ten days, the often tumultuous trial of "the Communist crip-ples" gave New Yorkers comic relief from the Depression. On the trial's first day, disabled protesters picketed at the ERB. On the second day, five were arrested. One was Lou Razler. "My family almost went nuts," he remembered. "I said, 'I don't give a damn. This is too much already.'" The five were paroled without bail. Two of them, along with four other

handicapped protesters, got themselves arrested at the ERB the following day. On June 28, Judge Harris convicted the original protesters of
disorderly conduct. Perhaps revealing his confusion over the incongru-
ous notion of "crippled pickets," he suspended the eight handicapped
defendants' sentences but gave their nonhandicapped supporters five
days in jail. That evening, police arrested fifteen handicapped demonstrators who "stormed" the ERB protesting those punishments.[34]

Judge Harris was not the only one struggling to resolve the seeming
oxymoron of disabled protesters. Municipal and media reaction reiter-
ated common but conflicting stereotypes about cripples. ERB officials
tried to discredit the demonstrators by charging that Communists had
staged the sit-in and were using the "cripples . . . for dramatic effect."
Shifting tactics, they then accused the strikers of "taking advantage of
their physical disabilities, knowing they will not be forced from the
building." The cripples were thus portrayed first as dupes and then as
manipulators. The police too claimed that "the [June 6] riot . . . was
Communist-inspired and planned." Not simply a standard way to discredit protesters, this narrative reinforced the notion that cripples were
incapable of carrying out such an action on their own. The press largely
presented the "crippled protesters" as shrill, irrational, and out of control, while it painted the police and bureaucrats as patient and carefully
compassionate. The *New York Herald Tribune* reported that "the crippled
picketers screamed hysterically and fought with forty patrolmen who
did everything they could to avoid violence." The *New York Post*, covering the June 8 city hall demonstration, displayed an even more barbed
antipathy toward league actions: "Ten vociferous cripples and a handful
of onlookers comprised a mass meeting . . . to protest treatment of invalids on relief rolls." Thus, antagonistic newspapers and public officials sought to discredit the disabled protesters by reinforcing culturally
dominant stereotypes about the crippled.[35]

The handicapped protesters' ostensible supporters on the Left also
used the crippled persona to promote their own political agenda. The
Daily Worker repeatedly depicted them in horrific stigmatizing language,
describing them as "dragging their own lame bodies back and forth,"
bodies "twisted by infantile paralysis." It also inaccurately reported that
the ERB strikers had been "crippled at birth or in bosses' factories." In
one instance, it fabricated police "brutality" against the picketers. A pho-
tograph of the June 6 demonstration that ran in both the mainstream
and radical press showed Florence Haskell sprawled on the sidewalk.

Some witnesses said the cops had kicked her crutches from under her. Others claimed she had thrown them away. Years later Sylvia Bassoff recalled that several picketers had deliberately fallen. But the *Daily Worker* claimed: "Brave LaGuardia Police Beat, Club, Jail Crippled Jobless." Just as public officials and the mainstream press used the cripple stereotypes of incompetency and manipulativeness to denigrate militant handicapped activism, the Communist paper exploited the stereotype of pathetic vulnerability to discredit the capitalist system. The radicals who supplied a model for the handicapped protesters and supported their demand for jobs also reinforced prejudice against them.[36]

The Left apparently understood no better than the establishment that the activists wanted not just jobs but valid social identities. The mainstream media labeled them "cripples," "paralytics," or "invalids." The *Daily Worker* sometimes referred to them as "paralysis victims" or "helpless crippled people." League leaders consistently identified themselves as "handicapped." The differences in language reflected opposing conceptions of disability identity and competing prescriptions for "what is to be done." The league's activist approach also tacitly addressed how the majority viewed physically handicapped people. Slogans such as "We Don't Want Tin Cups. We Want Jobs" and "We Are Lame But We Can Work" called for more than employment. They demanded respect, social dignity. League picketers who deliberately fell in order to discredit the police and to elicit public support did reinforce the very stereotypes of feebleness and manipulativeness they claimed to oppose. Despite such occasional inconsistency, however, the handicapped activists declared their rejection of society's devaluing verdict. That in itself was culturally radical.[37]

Their audacity is surprising given that era's attitudes toward cripples. To resist society's prejudice, they had to engage in public acts of defiance at a time when the president of the United States found it necessary to keep his disability largely hidden. "It was a very traumatic experience to even decide to get on a picket line, because we all shuffled along with braces and crutches," recalled Sylvia Bassoff. Public protests challenged not only the nonhandicapped majority's perceptions but league members' views of themselves. Explained Florence Haskell: "You have to understand that among our people, they were self-conscious about their physical disabilities. . . . They didn't like being stared at. They didn't want to be looked at. . . . I think it not only gave us jobs, but it gave us dignity, and a sense of, 'We are people too.'" In combining the issue politics of protesting job discrimination with an implicit identity politics of redefining disability, the league exemplified the character of disability-based political movements.[38]

The month-long series of actions in June 1935 generated a tremendous amount of public attention that spurred the protesters to formal organization and further agitation. They quickly settled on the name League of the Physically Handicapped. Hosting fund-raising parties and speaking at labor union meetings, they collected enough money to rent an office. They had already begun to recruit members among their handicapped acquaintances. "Pauline Portugalo came to me at the Brooklyn Bureau of Charities," recalled Sylvia Bassoff. "She says . . . 'There is a group of handicapped people organized for jobs. Suppose you come to the meeting tonight.' And I said, 'Jobs? Anything to get out of here.'" Electing officers, the group met weekly to talk strategy.[39]

The ERB protest in June 1935 was a spur-of-the-moment action springing from pent-up grievances and shaped more by militant enthusiasm than careful planning. Half a year later, league leaders were more skilled. Aware that the ERB had transferred some 100,000 work relief employees to the newly created New York City WPA, a group of picketers led by Jack Isaacs began marching in front of WPA headquarters on November 9. Seeking recognition as one contingent of the unemployed, the marchers wore sandwich-board signs that any unemployed workers might have borne. One proclaimed: "WE DON'T WANT THE RUN-AROUND—WE WANT JOBS." Another placard played off the common image of the jobless workers as "the Forgotten Man" by protesting: "WE HAVE NOT BEEN FORGOTTEN—WE'VE BEEN IGNORED." But, using their personal stories to explain the issues, the activists also insisted on acknowledgment of the bias handicapped job seekers faced. "The Physically Handicapped," declared their flyers,

> cannot get regular jobs as teachers or librarians in New York State. . . . Even a typist must pass a physical examination. . . . In private business the Physically Handicapped invariably are discriminated against. They work harder for less wages. [Given this disability-based employment bias,] our League *demands* that handicapped people receive a just share of the millions of jobs being given out by the government. . . . The Handicapped still are discriminated against by Private Industry. It is because of this discrimination that we *demand* the government recognize its obligation to make adequate provisions for handicapped people in the Works Relief Program.

Operating more shrewdly than it had the previous June, the league now not only identified with unemployed workers in general by adopting the rhetoric and tactics of labor radicalism; it also extended radical ideology to draw attention to disability-based discrimination and to politicize disability.[40]

Three weeks of picketing prodded local WPA director Victor Ridder to promise to hire approximately forty league members. Six months after their first demonstration, virtually all of the original protesters would get jobs. But Ridder had not conceded their claim of a government obligation to hire handicapped workers discriminated against by private industry. He just wanted to set up a "sort of demonstrating project . . . to show employers what the handicapped can do." League leaders saw an ulterior motive. The officials "figured if they hired the most active of [us] . . . it might kill the thing," claimed Lou Razler. "But instead of killing it, more handicapped came to the line." The momentum of success now propelled the activists not just to get jobs for themselves but to change local and federal policies toward all physically handicapped job seekers. By January 1936, they were again picketing the New York WPA.[41]

At last on April 5, Ridder granted that obstacles in the job market entitled handicapped people to government attention. He also admitted that handicapped people made up some 5 percent of New York's adult population but less than 1 percent of local WPA employees. So a new Bureau for the Physically Handicapped would be "the first step in a comprehensive plan to give closer attention to the employment problems of these people," while a special ERB "handicapped interviewing unit" would refer handicapped home relief recipients to the WPA. The *New York Times* announced "5,000 Physically Handicapped to Get W.P.A. Jobs," but league leaders called this "pure newspaper talk." The WPA did not guarantee jobs, only that handicapped workers would be considered for them. Five thousand was the number of handicapped home relief recipients the ERB classified as employable. Still, during the next year the WPA did give jobs to some fifteen hundred handicapped New Yorkers.[42]

Advised by Ridder's assistant that only Washington could address their concerns, league leaders sought a meeting with WPA chief Harry Hopkins and President Roosevelt. Getting no response, they boldly announced to Hopkins's staff on Friday, May 8, 1936, that they would arrive the next morning, "as per appointment through President Roosevelt." That evening, thirty-five delegates (fourteen women and twenty-one men), some of them risking their hard-won relief jobs, rode all night on a borrowed flatbed truck to the nation's capital. At WPA headquarters, labor relations director Nels Andersen explained that the WPA concerned itself only with work relief for "employables." Their problem, he said, was one for New York's municipal relief agencies. The delegates erupted. Twenty-one-year-old Sylvia Flexer Bassoff, now the league's president, took a vote and announced to reporters: "Unable to get any satisfaction in New York, we resolved to come here and ask the aid of Mr. Hopkins in providing WPA employment. They class us as unemployables, despite the fact that our members include . . . teachers, chemists, . . . and others who are professionally skilled. We are going to stay here until Mr. Hopkins does see us. Until then nothing can make us leave." League members, she said the next day, were "sick of the humiliation of poor jobs at best [and] often no work at all." They were tired too of "getting the same old stock phrases that the handicapped have been getting for years." They wanted, she said, "not sympathy—but a concrete plan to end discrimination . . . on W.P.A. projects." League press representative Harry Friedman demanded that the WPA set nationwide quotas for hiring handicapped workers. That night the protesters slept on office furniture. WPA officials ignored them all day Sunday. On Sunday evening, as they began settling in, deputy administrator Aubrey Williams promised to do "everything reasonable" but issued an ultimatum: Leave immediately for hotel accommodations at WPA expense or face the consequences of refusing to vacate a federal building. As they debated what to do, Hopkins telephoned. He agreed to meet five of them the next day.[43]

The meeting with Hopkins did not go as they had hoped. They demanded five thousand WPA jobs for handicapped New Yorkers, "a permanent relief program for the physically handicapped and a Nationwide census of the physically handicapped" conducted by the league but funded by the WPA. Hopkins rejected the charge that his agency was discriminating against handicapped people. He doubted that five thousand employable handicapped New Yorkers existed. He suggested that the league survey the New York situation, on its own. If they came back with proof, "a thesis . . . show[ing] such discrimination," he would "correct those conditions at once." As Friedman's questioning of Hopkins "grew sharper," "Hopkins' replies grew more impatient." At last the WPA chief abruptly picked up his famous hat and walked out. An assistant told the delegates that their hotel bill would be paid only until 6:00 P.M. League leaders unsuccessfully sought a conference with the president, though presidential secretary Marvin McIntyre did assure them that "in view of the President's long and sincere interest in the problem of physically handicapped persons . . . any constructive suggestions you may have will be given his personal consideration and study." With little money and nowhere else to go, they took the train home but promised to return to Washington with the "thesis" suggested by McIntyre as well as Hopkins.[44]

In early August 1936, the league sent its "Thesis on Conditions of Physically Handicapped" to Roosevelt and Hopkins and distributed it to the press. Drawing on members' own experiences, that ten-page memorandum analyzed handicapped persons' "struggle for social and economic security." It attributed their economic disadvantages, not to their disabilities, but to job discrimination, unjust policies, and haphazard, unfair rehabilitation and relief programs. Moving toward a comprehensive critique of policies and programs affecting handicapped Americans and implicitly rejecting the premises of modern policy making, it presented a handicapped perspective distinct from that of non-handicapped policy makers and professionals.[45]

While their disabilities "automatically closed . . . many fields of manual labor" to handicapped job seekers, the "Thesis" argued that "unjust restrictions" and "unfounded prejudices" shut them out of private-sector jobs in which "physical qualifications were irrelevant." "The Municipal, State and Federal Governments" also required "the most illogical and unnecessary physical qualifications . . . for positions, which the physically handicapped person, if given a chance, could fill most competently." In fact, noted the "Thesis," federal hiring did extend preference to disabled veterans. Since the only difference between them and disabled civilian job seekers was the cause of their disabilities, the league asked how "deterring and hindering" the latter could "be reconciled with [the] special consideration" of the former. Indeed, "the preference" to disabled veterans provided "ample precedent for giving [the civilians] some added consideration" in civil-service hiring. Associations of the Deaf made similar arguments about civil-service restrictions on hiring Deaf people. Both the "Thesis" and the Deaf groups also criticized government work relief policies and projects for bias in indiscriminately classifying handicapped and Deaf individuals as "unemployable."[46]

The "Thesis" next complained that state-sponsored vocational rehabilitation was "not only inadequate but also detrimental," as it created "the illusion that something constructive is being accomplished." Due to underfunding, New York State's Rehabilitation Bureau "had to turn thousands away," could offer only "very limited training" to "those few it did reach," and during the training "failed" to supply them with sufficient aid for "daily necessities." Meanwhile, the state employment agency typically placed handicapped workers in temporary jobs that paid "miserably low wages" and even went "so far as to send [them] out . . . as strike-breakers."[47]

Reflecting league members' suspicion of social-service professionals, the "Thesis" was especially critical of sheltered workshops. It censured three in particular: the Brooklyn Bureau of Charities, where Sylvia Flexer Bassoff had labored in frustration; the Altro Workshop, "an institution created for the rehabilitation of tuberculers," which probably was the "workshop for the TB" in which one league member had felt "very much exploited"; and the Institute for Crippled and Disabled, established by the Red Cross in 1917 as a model of vocational rehabilitation. Those workshops paid a meager three to five dollars a week. "Under the guise of social service," the league charged, they "actually engage in shameful exploitation." Sheltered workshops then and later won exemptions from minimum-wage requirements. Leading charity and rehabilitation professionals supported such exemptions, but the league condemned them, as did the "organized blind" movement and the Deaf associations. Disputes between professionals and advocates over workshops' subminimum wages have continued to the present. Such clashes caused the league to regard professionals as self-serving. Sylvia Bassoff recollected that the day after she attended her first league meeting, her boss at the sheltered workshop threatened to fire her if she went to any more. "I don't think they were too happy at handicapped people becoming independent. Because if handicapped people became independent economically and were able to get jobs, what do you need the Brooklyn Bureau of Charities for?" The "Thesis" proposed no reforms of vocational rehabilitation but did repeat its recommendations to Hopkins about work relief: the WPA should create jobs for the "thousands of unemployed handicapped" people and should conduct a survey to "gather the necessary information upon which to outline a permanent program." Because the league distrusted social-service agencies and professionals, it recommended that handicapped persons conduct the survey. Suspicion of nonhandicapped policy makers and service providers and the demand for a voice in policy making and program administration appeared in other disability-based political movements, becoming increasingly emphatic over time and reaching a crescendo in the late-twentieth-century declaration, "Nothing about us without us."[48]

Turning to home relief, the "Thesis" again delivered a distinctive handicapped critique. Denied the chance "to take their proper place in society to support themselves," many handicapped people were thrown back on their families, private charities, or home relief. As much as the league wanted jobs, it also wanted home relief expanded. If the home-relief allowance was inadequate for able-bodied recipients, it was "doubly insufficient" for handicapped persons who needed added funds for "mechanical appliances and medical care." Worse, even "this mere pittance" was often denied because of stringent eligibility requirements. Hundreds rejected for home relief were forced into "municipal lodging houses, while vast numbers of others [were] reduced to vagrancy . . . and [sank] to the level of beggars." And yet beggar ordinances banned or regulated cripples' alms seeking. "Something must be done to eliminate the necessity of any handicapped individual being forced to resort to begging," declared the "Thesis."[49]

As for federal efforts, the "Thesis" condemned "the whole Emergency Program and all the social legislation of the New Deal" as "consistently neglectful" of the problems of physically handicapped citizens. The league incorrectly claimed that the Social Security Act provided only for rural handicapped *children*. In fact, the act also had small components supporting state vocational rehabilitation programs and providing welfare for blind people. The administration had resisted including the latter, while blind activists would criticize it for its humiliating investigations and means test and for failing to promote employment. Those complaints paralleled the league's critique of home and work relief policies. Given the act's limited attention to disability issues, the league scornfully declared, "as far as the Administration was concerned, there were no such persons, there was no handicapped problem."[50]

In conclusion, the "Thesis" called its proposals "the very minimum necessary to alleviate the present grave situation of the handicapped," then added ironically, "Certainly the situation must be grave if [it has] finally made the handicapped articulate." The league had, in effect, articulated its rejection of the "disability category" in modern public policy.[51]

To create that category, modern policy makers combined old English Poor Law classifications of impairment to define disability rigorously as an absolute inability to engage in productive labor. Deborah Stone has elegantly explained this as an attempt in capitalist economies to demarcate a "need based" system and a "work based" system in order to limit access to the former and keep "able-bodied" workers in the labor market. Thus, relief policies dichotomized the "worthy" and "unworthy," the "deserving" and "undeserving," poor. While scholars have noted how those labels regulated poor and working-class people, some have seen the disability category as a "privileged" position that granted disabled people a "ticket" out of the labor force by "excusing" them from work. This ignores that those policies stigmatized and marginalized the "deserving" disabled poor. The category's formulators not only established allegedly objective clinical criteria to verify impairment and detect fraud but also sought to make relief the "least eligible" option by subjecting applicants to humiliating investigations. Assuming that only the truly needy would submit to such social degradation, legislators aimed to limit access to welfare funds.[52] State authorities dichotomized people with disabilities from "able-bodied and self-dependent" workers in order to regulate poor and laboring people, but they did so by presenting "the disabled" as "worthy" of poor relief but socially defiled. More than a medical and vocational classification, the designation imposed a socially delegitimating identity and role. The disability category thereby institutionalized the opposition of normal versus disabled that modern states have deployed to signify and manage relations of power and status, both between "able-bodied" and disabled people and among socioeconomic classes.

The New Deal incorporated this dichotomy, simultaneously proposing the WPA and the Social Security Act. The work program would assist "employables"; special-assistance relief would provide for various "unemployables": poor mothers with young children, the elderly, and "the disabled." The WPA would be federal; "the dole" would continue under state and local governments. The twin policies not only installed mechanisms to determine eligibility for the two types of public aid. They also defined two types of Americans.[53]

One could hardly exaggerate the alarm of Depression-era Americans across the political spectrum at the indignity of relief and the corrosive effects of dependency on it. In proposing the WPA, the president warned that "to dole out relief is to administer a narcotic, a subtle destroyer of the human spirit. . . . We must preserve not only the bodies of the unemployed from destitution but also their self-respect." Later he told the nation: "In this business of relief, we are dealing with properly self-respecting Americans to whom a mere dole outrages every instinct of individual independence. Most Americans want to give something for what they get. That something, in this case, honest work, is the saving barrier between them and moral disintegration. We propose to build that barrier high." Harry Hopkins also feared that handouts would demoralize the unemployed and set them apart from other Americans by stigmatizing them as charity cases. A work program, he believed, would restore their self-esteem. Many unemployed men shared this view. "You've got to be a goddamn charity case," complained some. "The relief mill has to put the stamp of a legalized pauper on your forehead." The Depression had forced "able-bodied and self-dependent" Americans who wanted work to submit to the humiliation of "baskets of groceries," "pantry snooping," "means tests," and "pauper's oaths." WPA officials worried that men who remained long on relief might "crack up." In response, government work programs not only offered unemployed men economic security but sought to restore their self-esteem, their reputations as family providers, their sense of control over their destinies. WPA jobs in fact proved a tonic to the self-image of many.[54]

New Dealers promoted the work programs by reinforcing the stigma of relief. If the programs supplied jobs partly to repair identities, those identities were young or middle-aged, white, male, and "able-bodied." And they were mended by assiduously contrasting them with the counterimage of "unemployables," "natural dependents" who presumably belonged on relief. Concerns about the need for "self-respect" through work and the danger of "moral disintegration" due to "dependency" on the dole applied only to "employables." As a result, complained the league, New York's Emergency Works Program labeled handicapped applicants "indiscriminately as 'unemployables,'" while the New York WPA rejected them. Many state WPAs officially barred handicapped job seekers. Like able-bodied workers, league picketers declared, "WE PROTEST THE PAUPER'S OATH," yet they were opposing, not temporary, but permanent relegation to the demeaning status of relief. Likewise, the Deaf community sought work-relief jobs, not only abhorring and resisting poor relief but also at first opposing even Social Security for Deaf people. Both groups implicitly fought being used by New Dealers as a negative counterimage to revalidate the "normal."[55]

In practice the work programs contradicted the alleged gulf between employables and unemployables. Despite New Dealers' intentions, WPA workers were tarred with the stigma of relief, while "able-bodied" applicants whose skills did "not fit into the WPA work program"—that is, into currently available WPA jobs—might be categorized as "unemployable." Contradictions in New Deal policy about the employability of handicapped people further muddled the vaunted dichotomy. A presidential executive order directed that "no one whose age or physical condition is such as to make his employment dangerous to his health or safety, or to the health and safety of others, may be employed on any work project." It added, however, that "this paragraph shall not be construed to work against the employment of physically handicapped persons, otherwise employable, where such persons may be safely assigned to work which they can ably perform." Despite this directive, the WPA classified all handicapped persons as "unemployable." Another policy prohibited recipients of Aid to the Blind (ATB) from taking WPA jobs, but blind persons not on ATB or living in areas without a federally approved ATB program might be certified for WPA employment if they were determined to have "the required skills and training which qualify them for employment and the problem is one of unemployment rather than of blindness." Federal policies operated from conflicting definitions of disability and employability.[56]

Disabled people pushed on one side of that contradiction. Handicapped and Deaf activists used FDR's executive order as leverage to gain access to WPA jobs. The league's "Thesis" cited it as "a ruling forbidding discrimination on account of physical disability." Deaf associations invoked it to protest WPA discrimination against their members. Meanwhile, numerous individuals with disabilities got around the WPA policies and won jobs. Studies found that while many handicapped applicants were rejected, more than a fifth of WPA workers had disabilities. Across the country, Deaf, physically handicapped, and blind people gained jobs with the WPA and other work programs.[57]

The inconsistency about disability and employability arose again when the WPA responded to the activists' campaigns by setting up special jobs and projects, despite the activists' opposition to such projects. During periods of retrenchment, special-projects workers were among the first laid off. Administrators sought to bar handicapped workers from regular WPA jobs because they believed those workers unsuited for the regular positions' temporary transitional employment. They assumed that most handicapped people could not meet private employers' stringent hiring and employment requirements and so could never transfer to the private sector. New Dealers failed to question the reasonableness or fairness of the practices activists criticized as disability-based discrimination.[58]

The WPA's inconsistent policies and practices typified the confusion about the nature of "disability" in twentieth-century policy. Social welfare policies defined "the disabled" as incapacitated for productive work, unemployable, and therefore legitimate recipients of home relief. Such policies sought to enforce an either/or definition of disability. This uncomplicated formula had the advantages of simplifying welfare administration, restricting access to benefits, and limiting expenditures. But it ignored the variability of disability in particular social milieus. Far from being fixed and objective, disability is fluid, dynamic, complicated, and significantly shaped by context. While some individuals needed public aid in order to retire from the job market, others demanded government backing to make their way in it. Opposing the dominant dichotomous policy thinking, leaders of many disability movements through much of the twentieth century called for nonstigmatizing and adequate welfare, effective vocational rehabilitation, and an end to both public and private job discrimination. The league and the nascent "organized blind" movement advocated those measures during the 1930s and 1940s, while Deaf associations backed some of those steps and employment bureaus as well. Later movements continued to battle against a definition of disability that, they believed, reinforced the economic and social marginalization of people with disabilities. In the league's opinion and contrary to recent scholars, categorization as unemployable did not charitably exempt them from having to work. It deliberately excluded them. They believed that label simultaneously stigmatized and segregated them, codifying job market discrimination into law. Overturning conventional notions of cripples' worthiness for poor relief, league activists redefined themselves as "handicapped people" "worthy" of getting work. The persistent perspectives of disabled activists about public policies suggest a new angle from which to examine policy history.[59]

The league also challenged gender bias in policy. New Deal work programs aimed to provide a family wage that would restore husbands as breadwinners and keep wives out of the labor force. A WPA rule limited its jobs to a family's "principal breadwinner," who was presumedly male. But if a husband were deemed "unemployable," his wife might qualify. A study of female WPA workers in rural Missouri counted 40 percent of subjects as married women with sick, disabled, or elderly husbands. Disability had thrust on these wives the male role, making them eligible for WPA work. Thus, though the WPA hired some women, its policies reinforced traditional notions of both gender and disability. Labor activists too upheld traditional gender roles, advocating jobs for men rather than for women. In contrast, the league, with significant numbers of female members, sought work for both sexes. The prominence of women in both the Jewish community and leftist political groups probably promoted women's active role in the league, but gendered ideas about disability were undoubtably a key factor. Physically disabled women have often been stigmatized as unsuited for the traditional wife-and-mother role. Some women growing up with physical disabilities have, with parental urging, sought to establish alternative valid identities through school and career. Sylvia Flexer's mother wanted her to go to college and become a pharmacist or lawyer so she could "earn her own living, whether she ever gets married or doesn't get married." The perceived failure of physically disabled women to meet conventional gender standards and the consequent parental emphasis on school and career may help explain the prominence of women in movements of physically disabled people. Sylvia Flexer became the league's president. Finding themselves defined as both unmarriageable and unemployable, dozens of other young handicapped women joined the league to demand jobs. At the intersection of gender and disability, their activism moved beyond the limits of both reform policy and labor radicalism.[60]

If the league challenged conventional thinking about hiring physically handicapped workers, it failed to probe disability's function in labor-management and, more deeply, socioeconomic class relations. Protean deployment of the disability concept appeared not only in social-service and work-relief policies, but in employment practices, industrial insurance plans, workers' compensation programs, even medical research and practice. For example, in their pathbreaking *Deadly Dust: Silicosis and the Politics of Occupational Disease in Twentieth-Century America*, David Rosner and Gerald Markowitz recount debates over definitions of disease and disability by industry, insurance, and labor leaders, politicians and government officials, medical doctors and researchers. In shaping that discourse, business interests successfully shifted silicosis—a lung disease caused by the inhalation of silica dust—from the political arena to the purview of doctors and scientists, many of whom had direct ties to the industries that produce such dust. Those medical professionals explained silicosis in ways that reduced the scope of the problem and the liability of the companies. Yet insurers mandated medical examinations that screened out, not only workers with early symptoms of silicosis, but also those with other diseases and disabilities that might eventually incur costs to both the insurers and the manufacturers. Workers identified as having those conditions were often discharged. Tagged as diseased or disabled, they had great difficulty finding other work. In another stratagem to reduce employers' liability and to remove occupational disease from the political realm by putting it in the hands of experts, business interests promoted coverage of silicosis by state workers' compensation programs, but under such restrictive eligibility requirements that few workers with silicosis could qualify for benefits. Thus, compensation programs denied them classification as disabled because many were still physically able to work, even while employers refused to hire them because they were labeled as diseased. The discourses of disability in the politics of silicosis, as in the politics of home and work relief, alert us to the material interests and the political content underlying medicalized speech. If the league's attempt to politicize disability discourse fell short, it implicitly points to the importance of medical constructions of disability in class relations under modern capitalism.[61]

FDR never adopted the league's analysis or advice. He apparently never even responded to its "Thesis." Instead he presided over the beginnings of a federal-state welfare system that sequestered growing numbers of handicapped Americans as "unemployable" and a medical-vocational rehabilitation system that prescribed individual corrective treatments as the only means for them to achieve employability and social integration. The divergence of perspective between the league and FDR grew out of differing disability identities and ideologies. It is best explicated by contrasting it with the contemporaneous political experiences of African Americans and women.

Within the New Deal, networks of black and female appointees emerged to advocate the interests of African Americans and women. The "Black Cabinet," composed of an unprecedented number of African American administrators, pressed the concerns of the constituency it both represented and helped to generate. This circle, along with civil-rights organizations, mobilized protests against federal and private job discrimination and forged a black voting bloc that became a key component of the Democratic party coalition. Eleanor Roosevelt's support gained black administrators access to the president. She stood even more prominently at the apex of the New Deal's network of female reform-

ers who had defined women's and children's issues as their special domain. They became personally influential in Democratic politics but
avoided political feminism or directly addressing gender discrimination.
While the black constituency made notable though limited political
gains that paved the way for postwar activism, the female reformers' suc-
cesses were not institutionalized. Still, both networks prodded the president and key white male officials to make the work programs more re-
sponsive to the needs of unemployed African Americans and women by
hiring black and female workers and by putting black and female administrators in charge of special WPA outreach efforts.[62]

The political experience of handicapped people differed markedly.
Though a handicapped man headed the New Deal and handicapped
men held WPA executive positions, no network of politicized disabled
advocates emerged. In late 1935, as Jack Isaacs, who had lost one leg to
amputation, led the picketing at New York WPA headquarters, Orrick
Johns, also a one-leg amputee, headed the WPA Writers Project in New
York. Johns apparently neither identified with nor supported the demonstrators. Meanwhile New York City WPA administrator Victor Ridder,
who wore a "built-up shoe" to compensate for a shortened leg, publicly
clashed with the disabled activists, calling them "mentally as well as physically handicapped." Insulted by their charge that he was "callous to the
needs" of handicapped persons, he declared that his own "infirmity"
made him "particularly considerate of others afflicted."[63]

Ridder's hostility and Johns's apparent apathy toward handicapped
activism reflected experiences that contrasted with those of league members. Though Ridder, Johns, and FDR differed from one another eth-
nically, religiously, and politically, all came from higher-status and more
affluent backgrounds than league activists and were a generation older.[64]
Most league members were in their twenties, children of working-class
immigrants, and Jewish; labor and leftist backgrounds had predisposed
some toward radical politics. The affluent older men and the activists differed also in their connections with other handicapped people. Johns's
autobiography never mentions relationships with other disabled people. Whether Ridder had affiliations with other disabled people is unknown. FDR's connections occurred in the context of medical rehabilitation or charity fund-raising. The core league leaders had formed
friendships in special-education classes, basement clubs, summer camps,
and recreation centers.

These differing experiences probably fostered diverging disability identities and ideologies. Roosevelt, Ridder, and Johns likely viewed disability as a private tragedy best dealt with by sympathetic public support for individuals striving to overcome adversity. League members' similar backgrounds and shared experiences fostered a group identity that generated an oppositional political consciousness. Their social network provided opportunities to discuss common experiences of job discrimination, to express and bolster shared indignation toward employer and government biases, and to fashion strategies for challenging those practices and policies. They came to regard disability as a social and political, more than a medical and moral, condition, one that required collective political action on their part and redress of discrimination by the government.

The contrast between the identities and ideologies of the league members and those of the three older men highlights the need to examine the historic varieties of disability experience as they interacted with class, ethnicity, education, age/generation, and types of association among people with disabilities. The evolution of a network of handicapped friends into a political action organization also exemplifies a motif in nineteenth- and twentieth-century U.S. disability history. Graduates of residential schools for Deaf or blind people formed alumni associations and social clubs to perpetuate friendships and provide mutual support. Over time those organizations began to address vocational, economic, and policy issues that affected their members. They became politicized. Deaf community organizations defended the use of sign language against the "oralist" campaign to suppress it. They lobbied state and federal governments for Deaf vocational bureaus, against denial of driver's licenses, and against discrimination in civil-service and work-relief hiring. Blind associations opposed means-tested poor relief and segregation in sheltered workshops. All of those groups resisted professional domination. All opposed reigning cultural stereotypes of blindness, deafness, and physical handicap. By the mid-1930s, the Deaf associations had developed into an increasingly well organized and well connected national network. The organized blind movement was poised to emerge at the national level. And some physically handicapped people were just beginning to mobilize at the local level. Educational and service institutions founded by nonhandicapped benefactors inadvertently enabled people with disabilities to overcome their natural geographical dispersion and lack of generational continuity and to create informal social networks and formal self-directed organizations. Those structures ultimately became sites of oppositional consciousness and political resistance to culturally dominant ideas about disability.[65]

Spurred by that new outlook, members of the league agitated to protect their hard-won WPA jobs. Into fall 1936, they continued to charge the New York WPA with failing to give handicapped persons "sufficient consideration." In September, Ridder's successor, Col. Brehon B. Somervell, promised that handicapped workers would receive a minimum 7 percent of future WPA jobs. But the following spring, WPA offices nationwide began massive layoffs. The league claimed that Somervell had pledged to dismiss no more than forty-eight handicapped workers locally, but more than six hundred lost their jobs. On June 29, the leaders telegraphed Harry Hopkins, threatening "drastic actions unless all cuts [were] stopped and dismissed persons reinstated." The firings continued. In mid-August, thirty-three delegates took a bus to Washington hoping to see Hopkins or Roosevelt. With only twenty dollars for food and lodging, they camped out on a small lawn in front of the WPA and at the Washington Monument. A conversation with two of Hopkins's deputies and a meeting with Hopkins himself, obtained through the intercession of Workers Alliance of America president David Lasser, yielded nothing. The delegates left for home, pledging to "return in larger numbers within a short time." It seems, however, that league activists never came back to the capital.[66]

Though the league failed to redirect federal policies, it continued to oppose job discrimination in New York City and to open the public sector to workers with disabilities. At its peak, its militant tactics forced the WPA to hire nearly fifteen hundred New Yorkers with disabilities, an impressive achievement for a small band of handicapped activists in the depths of the Depression. The most active leaders moved from the WPA into civil-service careers. Successful employment, along with internal political differences, soon led to the league's demise.[67]

League officers from leftist backgrounds were probably the organization's sparkplugs, but, as with many working-class white and black Americans in the 1930s, league members followed such leaders pragmatically and only for a time. The rank and file pursued specific objectives militantly rather than seeking to transform the system radically. They welcomed support from the Young Communists of America, the Communist-controlled Unemployed Councils, and the Socialist-Communist hybrid Workers Alliance of America. The American Civil Liberties Union and the Communist-backed International Labor Defense, usually antagonistic toward each other, together defended them in court. The greatest influence on their political thinking and strategizing was the Depression-era climate of crisis and desperate activism. Most league members, like most working-class Americans, were not committed radicals. They too sought, not societal transformation, but limited personal goals. They too wanted the economic security, social validity, and personal control of their destinies that they expected jobs to ensure.[68]

In emulating and pragmatically borrowing from other activist groups, the league exemplified another pattern in disability-based political movements. League leaders battled disability discrimination by adopting ideas and tactics from labor and leftist organizers. Likewise, blind leaders in the 1940s and disabled activists from the 1970s on adapted to their own situation the critical analyses and militant tactics of contemporaneous social-change movements. In the 1940s and 1950s, National Federation of the Blind president Jacobus ten Broek drew support for his organization from labor unions, asserting a parallel between the two. Later activists became involved with or inspired by the black civil-rights, feminist, antiwar, and labor movements. All disability movements have borrowed and adapted the analyses and tactics of contemporaneous movements. Whatever the sources of influence, those movements have typically espoused liberal reformist, rather than radical transformative, political agendas.[69]

The shared experience of discrimination had united league members, spurring their militancy. Employment made some more cautious and then fearful of their compatriots' leftist politics. Looking back, league veterans found it too painful or too threatening to talk freely about the fierce political disagreements. Sylvia Bassoff said: "I think there was some Red-baiting going on, and we got cold feet. It's easy to get cold feet when you've sort of won what you want for yourself." Disagreements over tactics and ideology degenerated into divisiveness. The "Red-baiting" mirrored the wave of such charges in other movements in the late 1930s, as the New Deal commitment to reform unraveled.[70]

The league also illustrated recurrent difficulties of American reform campaigns and patterns typical of disability-based political movements. It advocated piecemeal gains—jobs, effective vocational rehabilitation, adequate home relief—rather than systematic reconstruction of disability policies and programs, let alone of society. Likewise, its analysis touched only the surface of the problem of disability in twentieth-century policies. It never probed disability's function in modern society and culture as the counterimage of "normality" to aid in managing social, and especially class, relations. In that era, few Americans shared even the league's exposition of disability in institutional and political, rather than individual and pathological, terms. As an outsider group, it simply lacked the public voice to reshape the terms of public discourse. Finally, the league did not try to fashion a larger disability-based political coalition. The handful of handicapped people who joined forces in activist groups enlisted in disability-specific advocacy organizations. The Deaf associations and the organized blind protested job discrimination too, but none of these groups identified or allied with the others. Later disability-specific political groups continued to organize around issues of concern to those with their members' particular disabilities. This pattern reflected the perceived interests, the focused agendas, and the collective identities of those groups. Late-twentieth-century disability politics departed from this pattern as cross-disability coalitions formed to promote universalistic disability rights legislation such as the Americans with Disabilities Act. Such confederated efforts asserted that all people with disabilities, confronting a common set of cultural prejudices and social hazards, should act in political solidarity. That inclusive definition of interests and identity embraced a more diverse constituency than those of disability-specific groups, prompting attention to a much wider range of issues. By the 1980s, a cross-disability minority group consciousness had emerged among a younger generation. As a political result, networks of disabled appointees finally appeared in the Bush and Clinton administrations.[71]

In the late 1930s, those long-term developments in identity, ideology, and agenda were neither foreseeable nor inevitable. Whereas the labor, African American, and women's movements laid the groundwork for later efforts, the league failed to establish an institutional base upon which to build further activism by physically handicapped people. Former members stayed in touch as friends, but few ever joined another disability rights group. There was no direct line of descent, no institutional or even individual continuity, from the league to any later activist organization. It appears that sometime in 1938 the League of the Physically Handicapped dissolved.[72]

The brief episode of the League of the Physically Handicapped highlights major themes of modern disability history, with its complicated interactions among institutional, group, and individual actors and its complex interplay of public policies, professional practices, and cultural values. The league's history should prompt scholars to shift from medical to sociocultural and political definitions of disability. We need also to broaden our focus to add the views of people with disabilities to those of policy makers and professionals. Though disabled people usually wielded significantly less power than other historical agents, they were not passive. Nor were their experiences homogeneous. There were varieties of disability experience, identity, and ideology. We must also explore the role of disability, not only in the many fields of history where it has appeared, but as central to modern history. Finally, historians should learn to handle disability as a necessary tool of historical analysis. Perhaps the final accomplishment of these long-forgotten activists will be to help spur a new history of disability.

Notes

Acknowledgments: The authors thank the World Institute on Disability, Oakland, California, and in particular Judy Heumann and Steven Brown, former executives there, for a travel grant that enabled David Goldberger to do research in the National Archives. Drafts benefited greatly from the comments of Edward Berkowitz, Robert Cherny, William Issel, Mark Leff, Barbara Loomis, Robert Rubin, Lauri Umansky, two anonymous readers for the *Journal of American History*, the U.S. History Workshop at Stanford University, and the World Institute on Disability Staff Forum. Brooke Wirtschafter and Barbara Berglund did additional research in New York City newspapers. Most important, we thank the members of the League of the Physically Handicapped who shared their recollections. In addition, Florence Haskell supplied newspaper clippings, photos, and referrals; Sylvia Flexer Bassoff provided clippings; and Frederica Goldsmith sent a photocopy of the "Thesis on Conditions of Physically Handicapped." We thank Dr. Samuel Anderson and Frieda Zames of Disabled in Action of New York for providing audiotapes of two oral-history interviews.

1. *New York Post*, May 31, 1935, 2; *New York Herald Tribune*, May 31, 1935, 26; Frances Fox Piven and Richard A. Cloward, *Poor People's Movements: Why They Succeed, How They Fail* (New York, 1979), 41–95.

2. The term "disabled" is currently preferred by most disability rights activists. During the 1930s, the individuals who formed the League of the Physically Handicapped, along with many other people with physical disabilities, preferred "handicapped." For that reason, we often use "handicapped" when discussing the events of that era. This essay draws extensively on oral-history interviews with members of the League of the Physically Handicapped. Like all forms of evidence, oral-history data has limitations, but, as Ronald Grele has noted, the usefulness of any source depends on the kind of information one is seeking and the sort of questions one

wants to answer. Contrary to the frequent criticism that somehow written documents provide more reliable evidence, the difficulty with oral testimony is not the fallibility of memory. The English scholar R. R. James concluded that "memories are very fallible as a rule on specific events, very illuminating on character and on atmosphere, matters on which documents are inadequate." Confirming James's observation, our league informants' recollection of the details of events was often uncertain, inaccurate, or completely lost, but their memories of motivation and mood were strong. Newspapers and other contemporaneous documents frequently corroborated those elements of their oral testimony, indicating a surprising degree of consistency across time regarding the explanations league members offered for their activities and the meanings they attributed to them. Not that they delivered the objective truth about the league. Whether formed in 1935 or 1991, their perceptions were, of course, subjective. But one aim of this study was to capture the subjective experience of a group of historical actors. Yet we did not want simply to recount that subjective experience credulously. Here oral history, unlike other methods, enables researchers to cross-question their sources, probing memories and "unpacking" their deeper layers of meaning. As Peter Friedlander found in studying the formation of a United Auto Workers local in the 1930s, the limitations of the documentary evidence meant not only that the necessary information was unavailable outside participants' memories, but also that the historically most useful memories emerged only through a "critical dialogue" between the historian and his principal informant. Likewise, much of the evidence presented here on the league was jointly created by the interaction, sometimes vigorous, between the investigators and the historical participants. Ronald J. Grele, "Movement Without Aim: Methodological and Theoretical Problems in Oral History," in Grele, ed., *Envelopes of Sound: Six Practitioners Discuss the Method, Theory, and Practice of Oral History and Oral Testimony* (Chicago, 1975), 131–37; R. R. James quoted in Paul Thompson, *The Voice of the Past* (New York, 1978, revised edition, 1988), 136; Peter Friedlander, "Theory, Method, and Oral History," in David Dunaway and Willa Baum, eds, *Oral History: An Interdisciplinary Anthology* (Nashville, 1984), 132.

3. For critiques of these omissions, see Paul K. Longmore and Lauri Umansky, "Disability History, from the Margins to the Mainstream," in Paul K. Longmore and Lauri Umansky, eds., *The New Disability History: American Perspectives* (New York, 2001), 1–29; Douglas Baynton, "Disability and the Justification of Inequality in American History," in Longmore and Umansky, eds., *New Disability History* 33–57; John Williams-Searle, "Courting Risk: Disability, Masculinity, and Liability on Iowa's Railroads, 1868–1900," *Annals of Iowa* 58 (Winter 1999), 27–77, esp. 28–31; Douglas Baynton, "Defectives in the Land: Disability and Federal Immigration Policy, 1882–1924," paper presented at the annual meeting of the American Historical Association, Seattle, January 1998; and Karen Hirsch and Jerrold Hirsch, "Paternalism and Disability: Rethinking the History of the Southern Mill Village Community," paper presented at the annual meeting of the American Historical Association, Seattle, January 1998. For recent research, see Longmore and Umansky, eds., *New Disability History;* Douglas Baynton, *Forbidden Signs: American Culture and the Campaign Against Sign Language* (Chicago, 1996); Robert Bogdan, *Freak Show: Presenting Human Oddities for Amusement and Profit* (Chicago, 1988); Robert M.

Buchanan, *Illusions of Equality: Deaf Americans in School and Factory, 1850–1950* (Washington, D.C., 1999); Hugh Gallagher, *FDR's Splendid Deception* (New York, 1985); Nora Groce, *Everyone Here Spoke Sign Language: Hereditary Deafness on Martha's Vineyard* (Cambridge, Mass., 1985); Harlan Lane, *When the Mind Hears: A History of the Deaf* (New York, 1985); Claire H. Liachowitz, *Disability as a Social Construct: Legislative Roots* (Philadelphia, 1988); Paul K. Longmore, "The Life of Randolph Bourne and the Need for a History of Disabled People," *Reviews in American History* 13 (December 1985), 581–87; Paul K. Longmore, "Uncovering the Hidden History of Disabled People," *Reviews in American History* 15 (September 1987), 355–64; James W. Trent, Jr., *Inventing the Feeble Mind: A History of Mental Retardation in the United States* (Berkeley, 1994); Peter L. Tyor and Leland V. Bell, *Caring for the Retarded in America: A History* (Westport, 1985); John Vickrey Van Cleve, ed., *Deaf History Unveiled: Interpretations from the New Scholarship* (Washington, D.C., 1993); and John Vickrey Van Cleve and Barry Crouch, *A Place of Their Own: Creating the Deaf Community in America* (Washington, D.C., 1989).

    4. On reactions to disability, see Harlan Hahn, "The Politics of Physical Differences: Disability and Discrimination," *Journal of Social Issues* 44:1 (1988), 39–47; Gary L. Albrecht, Vivian G. Walker, and Judith A. Levy, "Social Distance from the Stigmatized: A Test of Two Theories," *Social Science Medicine* 16:13 (1982), 1319–27; Karen Dion, Ellen Berscheid, and Elaine Walster, "What Is Beautiful Is Good," *Journal of Personality and Social Psychology* 24 (December 1972), 285–90; R. William English, "Correlates of Stigma Towards Physically Disabled Persons," *Rehabilitation Research and Practice Review* 2 (Fall 1971), 1–17; Erving Goffman, *Stigma: Notes on the Management of Spoiled Identity* (Englewood Cliffs, 1963); Marcia D. Horne and Jerry L. Ricciardo, "Hierarchy of Response to Handicaps," *Psychological Reports* 62 (February 1988), 83–86; Reginald L. Jones, "The Hierarchical Structure of Attitudes Toward the Exceptional," *Exceptional Children* 40 (March 1974), 430–35; Robert Kleck, Hiroshi Ono, and Albert H. Hastorf, "The Effects of Physical Deviance upon Face-to-Face Interaction," *Human Relations* 19 (November 1966), 425–36; Rhoda Olkin and Leslie J. Howson, "Attitudes Toward and Images of Physical Disability," *Journal of Social Behavior and Personality* 9:5 (1994), 81–96; Clifford R. Schneider and Wayne Anderson, "Attitudes Toward the Stigmatized: Some Insights from Recent Research," *Rehabilitation Counseling Bulletin* 23 (June 1980), 299–313; John L. Tringo, "The Hierarchy of Preference Toward Disability Groups," *Journal of Special Education* 4 (Summer–Fall 1970), 295–306; and Harold E. Yuker, ed., *Attitudes Toward Persons with Disabilities* (New York, 1988).

    5. For revisionist approaches in medical, public health, and occupational-disease history, see Roy Porter, "The Patient's View: Doing Medical History from Below," *Theory and Society* 14 (March 1985), 175–98; Susan Reverby and David Rosner, eds., *Health Care in America: Essays in Social History* (Philadelphia, 1979); Charles E. Rosenberg and Janet Golden, eds., *Framing Disease: Studies in Cultural History* (New Brunswick, 1992); Morris J. Vogel, "Patrons, Practitioners, and Patients: The Voluntary Hospital in Mid-Victorian Boston," in Daniel Walker Howe, ed., *Victorian America* (Philadelphia, 1976), 121–40; Morris J. Vogel and Charles Rosenberg, eds., *The Therapeutic Revolution: Essays in the Social History of American Medicine* (Philadelphia, 1979); and David Rosner and Gerald Markowitz, eds., *"Slaves of the Depression":*

Workers' Letters about Life on the Job (Ithaca, 1987), 115–20, 141, 148. On job discrimination, see David Rosner and Gerald Markowitz, *Deadly Dust: Silicosis and the Politics of Occupational Disease in Twentieth-Century America* (Princeton, 1991), 74–75, 79–80, 96, 113, 130, 146, 165.

6. Van Cleve, *Deaf History Unveiled*, ix; Floyd Matson, *Walking Alone and Marching Together: A History of the Organized Blind Movement in the United States, 1940–1990* (Baltimore, 1990), iii–iv; Edward D. Berkowitz, *Disabled Policy: America's Programs for the Handicapped* (New York, 1987); Liachowitz, *Disability as a Social Construct*; Theda Skocpol, *Protecting Soldiers and Mothers: The Political Origins of Social Policy in the United States* (Cambridge, Mass., 1992); Deborah Stone, *Disabled State* (Philadelphia, 1986). For exceptions to the usual policy historiography, see Richard K. Scotch and Edward D. Berkowitz, "One Comprehensive System? A Historical Perspective on Federal Disability Policy," *Journal of Disability Policy Studies* 1 (Fall 1990), 1–19; and K. Walter Hickel, "Medicine, Bureaucracy, and Social Welfare: The Politics of Disability Compensation for American Veterans of World War I," in Longmore and Umansky, eds., *New Disability History*, 236–67.

7. Douglas C. Baynton, "Disability: A Useful Category of Historical Analysis," *Disability Studies Quarterly* 17 (Spring 1997), 82; Longmore and Umansky, "Disability History."

8. Herman Joseph interviewed Sylvia Flexer Bassoff and Florence Haskell for Disabled in Action of New York City. Sylvia Flexer Bassoff interview by Herman Joseph, December 7, 1985, audiotape, side 1; Florence Haskell interview by Joseph, March 29, 1986, audiotape, side 1; Florence Haskell telephone interview by Paul K. Longmore and David Goldberger, March 2, 1991, side 1; Sylvia Flexer Bassoff and Isadore Bassoff interview by Goldberger, June 21, 1991, side 2; Sara Lasoff Applebaum telephone interview by Longmore and Goldberger, May 26, 1991, side 1; Sylvia Fishman telephone interview by Longmore and Goldberger, June 9, 1991, side 1; Bob Brown, "March of the Cripples," *New Masses*, November 26, 1935, 10; Frances Lide, "Girl Leader of Cripples Asks Plan to End 'Discrimination,'" *Washington Star*, May 11, 1936. In the following notes, both maiden and married names are used for Sara Lasoff Applebaum and Sylvia Flexer Bassoff.

9. Rosner and Markowitz, *Deadly Dust*, 86, 87–89, 118–20, 179–80; Hickel, "Medicine, Bureaucracy, and Social Welfare." On the medical, social, and minority group paradigms and their applications, see Paul Abberley, "The Concept of Oppression and the Development of a Social Theory of Disability," *Disability, Handicap, and Society* 2:1 (1987), 5–21; Colin Barnes, Geof Mercer, and Tom Shakespeare, *Exploring Disability: A Sociological Introduction* (London, 1999); Len Barton, Keith Ballard, and Gillian Fulcher, *Disability and the Necessity for a Socio-Political Perspective* (Durham, N.H., 1992); Lennard Davis, *Enforcing Normalcy: Disability, Deafness, and the Body* (New York, 1996); Michelle Fine and Adrienne Asch, "Disability Beyond Stigma: Social Interaction, Discrimination, and Activism," *Journal of Social Issues* 44:1 (1988), 3–21; Victor Finkelstein, *Attitudes and Disabled People: Issues for Discussion* (New York, 1982); B. J. Gleeson, "Disability Studies: A Historical Materialist View," *Disability and Society* 12:2 (1997), 179–202; John Gliedman and William Roth, *The Unexpected Minority: Handicapped Children in America* (New York, 1978); Harlan Hahn, "Disability Policy and the Problem of Discrimination," *American Behav-*

ioral Scientist 8 (January–February 1985), 293–318; Simi Linton, *Claiming Disability: Knowledge and Identity* (New York, 1998); Longmore, "Life of Randolph Bourne"; Longmore, "Uncovering the Hidden History"; Michael Oliver, *The Politics of Disablement: A Sociological Approach* (New York, 1990); William Roth, "Handicap as a Social Construct," *Society* 20 (March–April 1983), 56–61; and Tom Shakespeare, ed., *The Disability Reader: Social Science Perspectives* (London, 1998). For examples of early recognition that "disability" is artificially constructed and that prejudice frames the experience of disability, see Roger G. Barker, et al., *Adjustment to Physical Handicap and Illness: A Survey of the Social Psychology of Physique and Disability* (New York, 1953), and Jacobus ten Broek and Floyd W. Matson, "The Disabled and the Law of Welfare," in William R. F. Phillips and Janet Rosenberg, eds., *Changing Patterns of Law: The Courts and the Handicapped* (New York, 1980), 811–16.

10. Stone, *Disabled State*; ten Broek and Matson, "Disabled and the Law of Welfare," 811; Martha L. Edwards, "Infanticide in the Classical Greek World and Two Disability Studies Models," paper presented at the annual meeting of the American Historical Association, Seattle, January 1998.

11. Marvin Lazerson, "The Origins of Special Education," in Jay G. Chambers and William T. Hartman, eds., *Special Education Policies: Their History, Implementation, and Finance* (Philadelphia, 1983), 34–39; Brad Byrom, "A Pupil and a Patient: Hospital-Schools in Progressive America," in Longmore and Umansky, eds., *New Disability History*; Berkowitz, *Disabled Policy*, 184; Barbara P. Ianacone, "Historical Overview: From Charity to Rights," in Phillips and Rosenberg, eds., *Changing Patterns of Law*, 957; Marcia Pearce Burgdorf and Robert L. Burgdorf, Jr., "A History of Unequal Treatment: The Qualifications of Handicapped Persons as a 'Suspect Class' under the Equal Protection Clause," in Phillips and Rosenberg, eds., *Changing Patterns of Law*, 865; Jacobus ten Broek, "The Right to Live in the World: The Disabled and the Law of Torts," *California Law Review* 54 (May 1966), 885–94. On the public schooling of physically handicapped children, see David Hinshaw, *Take Up Thy Bed and Walk* (1948; New York, 1980), 18–19, 11. New York City's Charity Organization Society kept a "Directory of Cripples" to help the police distinguish legitimate from illegitimate beggars. The Chicago ordinance warned: "No person who is diseased, maimed, mutilated, or in any way deformed so as to be an unsightly or disgusting object or improper person to be allowed in or on the public ways or other public places in this city, shall therein or thereon expose himself to public view." It was finally repealed in 1974, but in that same year a disabled man was arrested under a similar law in Omaha. Brad Byrom, "Of Backrooms, Basements, and Beggars: Mendicancy and Disability in Late-Nineteenth-Century America," unpublished paper, but 1999, 4; Burgdorf and Burgdorf, "History of Unequal Treatment," 863–64.

12. Immigration Act of February 20, 1907, ch. 1134, 34 Stat. 898 (1907); Baynton, "Defectives in the Land."

13. *The Black Stork*, director W. R. Strafford (1916), retitled *Are You Fit to Marry?* (1918; Quality Amusement Corporation, 1927); Ianacone, "Historical Overview," 955; Robert L. Burgdorf, Jr., and Marcia Pearce Burgdorf, "The Wicked Witch Is Almost Dead: *Buck v. Bell* and the Sterilization of Handicapped Persons," in Phillips and Rosenberg, eds., *Changing Patterns of Law*, 1000; Martin S. Pernick, *The Black*

Stork: Eugenics and the Death of "Defective" Babies in American Medicine and Motion Pictures since 1915 (New York, 1996), esp. 72–73, 238n17; Flexer Bassoff and Bassoff, side 1; Fishman interview, side 1, tape 1; Haskell interview by Longmore and Goldberger, side 1, tape 1. Photos supplied by Florence Haskell.

14. For examples of movies from the 1930s that portray characters with disabilities similar to those of most league members as vengeful, manipulative, cruel, or weak, see *The Mad Genius*, director Michael Curtiz (Warner, 1931); *West of Zanzibar*, director Todd Browning (MGM, 1928); *Kongo*, director William Cowen (MGM, 1932); *The Mystery of the Wax Museum*, director Michael Curtiz (Warner, 1933); *Have a Heart*, director David Butler (MGM, 1934); *Of Human Bondage*, director John Cromwell (RKO, 1934); and *Dick Tracy*, director Alan James and Ray Taylor (Republic, 1937). On the dichotomy between disabled and "normate" figures in American culture and literature, see Rosemarie Garland Thomson, *Extraordinary Bodies: Figuring Physical Disability in American Culture and Literature* (New York, 1997), esp. 7–9, 34.

15. Scott M. Cutlip, *Fundraising in the United States: Its Role in America's Philanthropy* (New Brunswick, 1965), 351–87; *New York Post*, June 3, 1935, 6; Flexer Bassoff and Bassoff interview, side 2. As if to point out that "the old custom" was still in practice, the *Daily News* reported: "Rain yesterday failed to dampen the spirits of 5,000 crippled and orphan children" taken to Coney Island by the Long Island Automobile Club. *New York Daily News*, June 5, 1935, Brooklyn section, 6.

16. John Hockenberry, *Moving Violations: War Zones, Wheelchairs, and Declarations of Independence* (New York, 1995), 64–66; Flexer Bassoff and Bassoff interview, side 2; Frederica Goldsmith telephone interview by Longmore and Goldberger, May 27, 1991, side 1; Lou Razler telephone interview by Longmore and Goldberger, June 8, 1991, side 1. For another example of a physically disabled individual distancing himself from other cripples, see Leonard Kriegel, *The Long Walk Home* (New York, 1964), 45–46, 119, 121–22, 203–12.

17. Tennessee Williams drew upon his sister's post-polio disability in his semi-autobiographical play. Tennessee Williams, *The Glass Menagerie: A Play* (New York, 1945). Haskell interview by Longmore and Goldberger, side 1, tape 1; Flexer Bassoff and Bassoff interview, side 2, tape 1. Sara Roosevelt's friend is quoted in Gallagher, *FDR's Splendid Deception*, 28.

18. Gallagher, *FDR's Splendid Deception*; Franklin D. Roosevelt, *The Public Papers and Addresses of Franklin D. Roosevelt*, comp. Samuel Rosenman (13 vols., New York, 1938), I, 334; Franklin D. Roosevelt, "Why Bother with the Crippled Child?" *Crippled Child* 5:6 (1928), 140–43. We thank Brad Byrom for the last reference. On the ideology and history of overcoming, see Byrom, "Pupil and a Patient"; David Gerber, "Anger and Affability: The Rise and Representation of a Repertory of Self-Presentation Skills in a WWII Disabled Veteran," *Journal of Social History* 27 (Fall 1993), 5–27; Daniel J. Wilson, "Crippled Manhood: Infantile Paralysis and the Construction of Masculinity," *Medical Humanities Review* 12 (Fall 1998), 9–28; and Kriegel, *Long Walk Home*, esp. 56–58, 72–75, 107–8, 127, 130–33, 150–64. Kriegel refers to himself as a "cripple," but his strategy for constructing a new "self," a new identity, is a classic instance of overcoming. *Long Walk Home*, 212–13.

19. Flexer Bassoff and Bassoff interview, side 1; Fishman interview, side 1.

20. Haskell interview by Joseph, side 1; Lide, "Girl Leader of Cripples." Flexer Bassoff interview, side 1. Emphasis to indicate Sylvia Flexer Bassoff's verbal inflection.

21. Razler interview, side 1; Brown, "March of the Cripples," 10–12. Wage discrimination against workers with disabilities persisted into the late twentieth century. William G. Johnson and James Lambrinos, "Wage Discrimination Against Handicapped Men and Women," *Journal of Human Resources* 20 (1985), 264–77; Joseph Shapiro, *No Pity: People with Disabilities Forging a New Civil Rights Movement* (New York, 1993), 28–29.

22. Roosevelt, *Public Papers and Addresses*, IV, 19–20; Edward D. Berkowitz, *America's Welfare State: From Roosevelt to Reagan* (Baltimore, 1991), 91–92; William E. Leuchtenburg, *Franklin D. Roosevelt and the New Deal, 1932–1940* (New York, 1963), 124–25; Arthur M. Schlesinger, Jr., *The Age of Roosevelt*, vol. II: *The Coming of the New Deal* (Boston, 1959), 296; "What Happens to 'Unemployables,'" *New Masses*, October 1, 1935, 6; *New York Herald Tribune*, June 4, 1935, 20; *New York Post*, May 11, 1936, 4.

23. Lizabeth Cohen, *Making a New Deal: Industrial Workers in Chicago, 1919–1939* (New York, 1990), 1–10, 251–89, 361–68.

24. Flexer Bassoff and Bassoff interview, side 1.

25. The historian Lizabeth Cohen reports that basement clubs were common among the young in Chicago's working-class ethnic communities. Flexer Bassoff interview, side 1; Flexer Bassoff and Bassoff interview, side 1; Haskell interview by Joseph, side 1; Haskell interview by Longmore and Goldberger, side 1; Lasoff Applebaum interview, side 1; Fishman interview, side 1; Brown, "March of the Cripples," 10; Lide, "Girl Leader of Cripples"; Cohen, *Making a New Deal*, 145. In a novel written in the 1930s, Jewish boys just out of high school in 1920s Chicago establish a basement club and invite local girls to it. Meyer Levin, *The Old Bunch* (New York, 1937), 4, 5–9, 18–26.

26. Flexer Bassoff interview, side 1; Flexer Bassoff and Bassoff interview, side 1; Haskell interview by Joseph, side 1; Haskell interview by Longmore and Goldberger, side 1; *New York Post*, May 31, 1935, 2; *New York Herald Tribune*, May 31, 1935, 26, 1.

27. Flexer Bassoff interview, side 1; Haskell interview by Joseph, side 1; Haskell interview by Longmore and Goldberger, side 1; *New York Post*, May 31, 1935, 2; *New York Herald Tribune*, May 31, 1935, 26, 1.

28. *Daily Worker*, May 31, 1935, 1; *Daily Worker*, June 1, 1935, 8; *New York Herald Tribune*, May 31, 1935, 1, 26; *Washington Post*, May 31, 1935, 10; *New York Post*, May 31, 1935, 2; *Daily Worker*, May 31, 1935, 1. Although Hyman Abramowitz claimed that the league had "200 members," Sylvia Flexer Bassoff remembered the original group as comprising only 35–40 members. But Abramowitz may not have been exaggerating greatly when he said the membership included "pharmacists, lawyers, clerks and stenographers." One newspaper identified Sara Lasoff Applebaum, Florence Haskell, and Pauline Portugalo respectively as a file clerk, a typist, and a clerical worker and listed Harry Friedman as a chemist, Morris Dolinsky as a pharmacist, and Abramowitz as a watchmaker. *Washington Post*, May 31, 1935, 10; Flexer Bassoff interview, side 1; *Washington Post*, May 31, 1935, 10; *New York Her-*

ald Tribune, May 31, 1935, 26. It is unclear exactly when the league was officially organized. Haskell recalled formal organization coming soon after the initial protest. See Haskell interview by Joseph. Throughout that action, newspapers referred to the organization by various names. The group had probably not yet organized formally; perhaps different protesters were interviewed by various reporters, each protester giving a different name to their group. *Washington Post,* May 31, 1935, 10; *New York Herald Tribune,* May 31, 1935, 1; *Daily Worker,* May 31, 1935, 1.

29. *Washington Post,* May 31, 1935, 10; *New York Herald Tribune,* May 31, 1935, 1, 26; *New York Post,* May 31, 1935, 2; *New York American,* June 1, 1935, regular edition, 3; *New York American,* June 1, 1935, evening edition, 3; *New York Post,* June 1, 1935, 3; *New York Herald Tribune,* June 1, 1935, 2.

30. *New York Post,* June 1, 1935, 3; *New York American,* June 2, 1935, 3; *New York Herald Tribune,* June 2, 1935, 9; *Daily Worker,* June 3, 1935, 2; "Crippled Jobless Hold Firm Despite Tremendous Odds," *Daily Worker,* June 4, 1935; Razler interview, side 1; Lasoff Applebaum interview, side 1; Flexer Bassoff interview, side 1.

31. *New York Herald Tribune,* June 4, 1935, 20; *New York Post,* June 3, 1935, 6. Abramowitz demanded a wage higher than the New York WPA would pay its employees but in line both with the demands of Mayor LaGuardia and labor leaders and with the cost of living. Barbara Blumberg, *The New Deal and the Unemployed: The View from New York City* (Lewisburg, 1979), 52–54, 226.

32. *New York Herald Tribune,* June 21, 1935, 1, 13; *New York Times,* June 27, 1935, 14; "Harris Convicts Crippled Pickets," *New York Times,* June 29, 1935; *New York American,* June 7, 1935, 1; *New York Herald Tribune,* June 7, 1935, 19; *New York Daily News,* June 7, 1935, 18B; "Jobless Cripples Storm Air Station as Knauth Speaks," *New York Post,* June 7, 1935; "Fourth of July 1935," *Labor Defender* 9 (July 1935), 3.

33. *New York American,* June 8, 1935, 6; *New York American,* June 9, 1935, 2L; *New York Post,* June 8, 1935, 2.

34. The defense attorneys were Lee Hazen of the American Civil Liberties Union and Harry Alexander, Isadore Bassoff, and Samuel Goldberg from the International Labor Defense. Bassoff had defended Abramowitz on a previous charge resulting from his action at a Brooklyn relief office. Flexer Bassoff and Bassoff interview, sides 1–2; Haskell interview by Joseph, side 1; Razler interview, side 1; *New York Times,* June 20, 1935, 4; *Bronx and Manhattan Home News,* June 20, 1935, 3; *New York Times,* June 21, 1935, 21; *New York Daily News,* June 20, 1935, 27; *New York Daily News,* June 21, 1935, 2, 9; *New York Herald Tribune,* June 21, 1935, 1, 13; *New York Herald Tribune,* June 20, 1935, 6; *New York Herald Tribune,* June 21, 1935, 1, 13; *New York Herald Tribune,* June 22, 1935, p. 30; "Crippled Pickets Released on Writ," *New York Times,* June 22, 1935; "Crippled Pickets Are Paroled Again," *New York Times,* June 23, 1935; *New York Herald Tribune,* June 23, 1935, 13; "Harris Convicts Crippled Pickets," *New York Times,* June 29, 1935; *New York Herald Tribune,* June 29, 1935, 28.

35. The authorities evidently feared another "riot" at the city hall demonstration. "To maintain peace . . . there were 120 uniformed patrolmen" and 20 mounted officers. *New York Herald Tribune,* June 29, 1935, 28. See also *New York Herald Tribune,* June 2, 1935, 9; and *New York American,* June 2, 1935, 3. The *Herald Tribune* and the *Daily News* had already declared the strike "Communist-supported": *New*

York Herald Tribune, June 1, 1935, 2; *New York Daily News,* June 1, 1935, final edition, 4. *New York Herald Tribune,* June 21, 1935, 1, 13; *New York Times,* June 27, 1935, 14; "Harris Convicts Crippled Pickets"; *Bronx and Manhattan Home News,* June 7, 1935, 3; *New York American,* June 7, 1935, 1; *New York Herald Tribune,* June 7, 1935, 19; *New York Daily News,* June 7, 1935, 18B; *New York Post,* June 8, 1935, 2.

36. Jack Isaacs had lost his leg in a factory accident, but he was not part of the sit-in. *Daily Worker,* May 31, 1935, 1; "Crippled Jobless Hold Firm"; *New York American,* June 7, 1935, 1; "Fourth of July 1935," 3; *New York Herald Tribune,* June 7, 1935, 19; *New York Times,* June 20, 1935, 4; *Daily Worker,* June 7, 1935, 2; *Daily Worker,* June 8, 1935, 8; Flexer Bassoff interview, side 1. See also *Daily Worker,* November 19, 1935, 6.

37. Even the *New Masses* invoked these demeaning stereotypes. See Brown, "March of the Cripples." The *Daily Worker* veered back and forth between "crippled" and "handicapped." Herbert Benjamin, the Communist Party of the United States of America's principal organizer of unemployed and WPA workers, urged, "Fight discrimination against handicapped workers." Herbert Benjamin, *A Handbook for Project Workers* (New York, 1936), 23. Flexer Bassoff and Bassoff interview, side 2; Haskell interview by Longmore and Goldberger, side 1.

38. Gallagher, *FDR's Splendid Deception;* Flexer Bassoff interview by Joseph, side 1; Haskell interview by Joseph, side 1. For examples of other disability activist groups engaging in "identity politics," see Renee R. Anspach, "From Stigma to Identity Politics: Political Activism among the Physically Disabled and Former Mental Patients," *Social Science and Medicine* 13A (November 1979), 765–73; and Matson, *Walking Alone and Marching Together,* 36–38, 40–41, 44–45.

39. Flexer Bassoff and Bassoff interview, side 1; Goldsmith interview, side 2; Lasoff Applebaum interview, side 1; Haskell interview by Joseph, side 1; Haskell interview by Longmore and Goldberger, side 1.

40. Blumberg, *New Deal and the Unemployed,* 49; Brown, "March of the Cripples," 11–12.

41. *New York Times,* November 30, 1935, 13; Blumberg, *New Deal and the Unemployed,* 71; *New York Post,* May 13, 1936, 6; *New York Times,* December 6, 1935, 18; Razler interview, side 1; Haskell interview by Joseph, sides 1–2; *Washington Evening Star,* May 11, 1936, A1.

42. The Emergency Relief Bureau reported a total of twelve thousand handicapped persons on its rolls. *New York Times,* April 6, 1936, 16; *Daily Worker,* May 6, 1936, 6; Sylvia Flexer Bassoff to Harry Hopkins, April 23, 1936, folder L, box 2157, Complaints 1935–42, NYC, 69.3–69.3.1 (Records of the Federal Emergency Relief Administration), WPA Central Files: State, Records of the Work Projects Administration, RG 69 (National Archives, Washington, D.C.). See also League Secretary Sylvia Weissman to FDR, April 23, 1936, folder L, box 2157, Complaints 1935–42, NYC, 69.3–69.3.1, WPA Central Files: State, RG 69 (National Archives, Washington, D.C.); Weissman to Senator Royal S. Copeland of New York, April 23, 1936, folder J–Z, box 2034, Labor Complaints, Requests, Quota, etc., 1935–43, NYC, 641,WPA Central Files: State, RG 69 (National Archives, Washington, D.C.).

43. Weissman to Copeland, April 23, 1936; Flexer Bassoff to Hopkins, April 23, 1936; League of the Physically Handicapped to Hopkins, May 5, 1936; Flexer Bas-

soff to Thad Holt, telegram [May 1936]; Holt to Flexer Bassoff, May 8, 1936, last four items in folder L, box 2157, Complaints 1935–42, NYC, 69.3–69.3.1 (Records of the Federal Emergency Relief Administration), WPA Central Files: State; *Daily Worker,* May 6, 1936, 6; Flexer Bassoff interview, side 1; Flexer Bassoff and Bassoff interview, side 1; *Washington Post,* May 10, 1936, 4; *Washington Sunday Star,* May 10, 1936, A1, A2; *Washington Evening Star,* May 11, 1936, 1, 2; *New York Times,* May 10, 1936, 42; Lide, "Girl Leader of Cripples," *Daily Worker,* May 12, 1936, 2; *Washington Post,* May 11, 1936, 1, photo p. 9.

44. *Washington Post,* May 12, 1936, 1, 14; *Washington Evening Star,* May 12, 1936, A2; *Daily Worker,* May 12, 1936, 2; *Daily Worker,* May 13, 1936, 2.

45. "Thesis on Conditions of Physically Handicapped," undated typescript, 1. The memorandum is likely from early August 1936, as it matches an account of a league "memorandum" in *New York Times,* August 10, 1936, 2.

46. "Thesis on Conditions of Physically Handicapped," 1–2; Buchanan, *Illusions of Equality,* 92–95. The argument about "illogical and unnecessary physical qualifications" anticipated by half a century the Americans with Disabilities Act's prohibition against denial of employment if a disabled person could perform the "essential functions" of a job. The terms "deaf" and "Deaf" are used by scholars to distinguish between persons who merely have impaired hearing and those who are "culturally Deaf," that is, belong to the Deaf community and use a sign language as their primary language.

47. "Thesis on Conditions of Physically Handicapped," 3.

48. "Thesis on Conditions of Physically Handicapped," 3–4, 5–6, 9–10; Haskell interview by Joseph, side 2; Flexer Bassoff interview, side 1. On the Red Cross Institute, see Douglas C. McMurtrie, *The Organization, Work and Method of the Red Cross Institute for Crippled and Disabled Men* (New York, 1918); Douglas C. McMurtrie, *Rehabilitation of the War Crippled* (New York, 1918); John Culbert Faries, *Three Years of Work for Handicapped Men: A Report of the Activities of the Institute for Crippled and Disabled Men* (New York, 1920); and Hinshaw, *Take Up Thy Bed and Walk,* 63, 71–72, 77–79, 226–29. On subminimum wages, see Hinshaw, *Take Up Thy Bed and Walk,* 76–77; *New York Times,* July 23, 1934, 26; Lewis Mayers, ed., *A Handbook of NRA* (New York, 1934), 219–21; U.S. Department of Labor, Bureau of Labor Statistics, "Handicapped Workers under Public Contracts Act," *Monthly Labor Review* 55 (October 1942), 843–44; Jacobus ten Broek and Floyd Matson, *Hope Deferred: Public Welfare and the Blind* (Berkeley, 1959), 224–68; C. Edwin Vaughan, *The Struggle of Blind People for Self Determination, the Dependency-Rehabilitation Conflict: Empowerment in the Blindness Community* (Springfield, Ill.,1993), 67–69, 165, 173–79, 198–201; Buchanan, *Illusions of Equality,* 95–96; William Branigin, "Subminimum Wage among Issues as Advocates Convene," *Washington Post,* December 12, 1999. On tension between advocates and professionals, see Berkowitz, *Disabled Policy,* 187–89; James I. Charlton, *Nothing about Us Without Us: Disability, Oppression, and Empowerment* (Berkeley, 1998); Gliedman and Roth, *Unexpected Minority,* 35; Hockenberry, *Moving Violations,* 112–14, 116–17; Lane, *Mask of Benevolence,* 43–49; Matson, *Walking Alone and Marching Together,* 15, 27–28, 32, 41; William Roth, "The Politics of Disability: Future Trends as Shaped by Current Realities," in Leonard G. Perlman and Gary F. Austin, eds., *Social Influences in Rehabilitation Planning: Blue-*

print for 21st Century: A Report of the Ninth Mary E. Switzer Memorial Seminar (Alexandria, 1985), 45–46; Shapiro, *No Pity*, 50–52, 72–73, 127–39; Randy Shaw, *Activist Handbook* (Berkeley, 1996), 235–50; Karen G. Stone, *Awakening to Disability: Nothing about Us Without Us* (n.p., 1997); and Vaughan, *Struggle of Blind People*, 5–7, 17–56, 120–30, 144–59, 172–210.

49. "Thesis on Conditions of Physically Handicapped," 4–5.

50. "Thesis on Conditions of Physically Handicapped," 4–7; Edward D. Berkowitz and Kim McQuaid, *Creating the Welfare State: The Political Economy of Twentieth-Century Reform* (Lawrence, 1992), 125–26; Scotch and Berkowitz, "One Comprehensive System?" 9–11; Matson, *Walking Alone and Marching Together*, 9–10, 14, 17–23, 27.

51. "Thesis on Conditions of Physically Handicapped," 9–10.

52. Stone, *Disabled State*, 15–28, 42–54, 119–20. On the historical formulation of the disability category, see also Frances Fox Piven and Richard A. Cloward, *Regulating the Poor: The Functions of Public Welfare* (New York, 1971), xvi–xvii, 3–5; Mark Priestley, "The Origins of a Legislative Disability Category in England: A Speculative History," *Disability Studies Quarterly* 17 (Spring 1997), 87–94. On "disability" as a privileged status, see Berkowitz, *America's Welfare State*, 98; Berkowitz, *Disabled Policy*, 230; Scotch and Berkowitz, "One Comprehensive System?" 2–3, 6; Stone, *Disabled State*, 28, 172–73. For an analysis of the function of "disability" in welfare programs that departs from the common scholarly view to offer one similar to that presented here, see Piven and Cloward, *Regulating the Poor*, 3–4, 33–34, 147–48. To compare the intrusive and humiliating investigations of women receiving Aid to Families with Dependent Children with case workers' investigations of disabled people, see Berkowitz, *America's Welfare State*, 103–6; Piven and Cloward, *Regulating the Poor*, 165–71; and ten Broek and Matson, "Disabled and the Law of Welfare," 830–33.

53. Anthony J. Badger, *The New Deal: The Depression Years, 1933–40* (New York, 1989), 201; Robert H. Bremner, "The New Deal and Social Welfare," in Harvard Sitkoff, ed., *Fifty Years Later: The New Deal Evaluated* (Philadelphia, 1985), 73; James T. Patterson, *The New Deal and the States: Federalism in Transition* (Princeton, 1969), 41, 74–80, 84, 99; Piven and Cloward, *Regulating the Poor*, 94–97.

54. Roosevelt, *Public Papers and Addresses*, iv, 19–20; Donald S. Howard, *The WPA and Federal Relief Policy* (New York, 1943), 779, 785–86, 805–13, 826–29; Berkowitz, *America's Welfare State*, 91–92; Leuchtenburg, *Franklin D. Roosevelt and the New Deal*, 124–25, 130; Schlesinger, *Coming of the New Deal*, 296; Harry L. Hopkins, *Spending to Save: The Complete Story of Relief* (New York, 1936), 109–11, 114, 160–61, 163–64, 182–83; Badger, *New Deal*, 32–37, 201–3, 210–11; F. Charles Searle, *Minister of Relief: Harry Hopkins and the Depression* (Syracuse, 1963), 128; Blumberg, *New Deal and the Unemployed*, 22–23, 37–41, 282–86; Forrest A. Walker, *The Civil Works Administration: An Experiment in Federal Work Relief, 1933–1934* (New York, 1979), 27–28; Terry A. Cooney, *Balancing Act: American Thought and Culture in the 1930s* (New York, 1995), 1–2, 185. Earlier work programs had the same goals. Walker, *Civil Works Administration*, 45–46, 65.

55. WPA policies also often excluded mothers with dependent children and older workers. Hopkins, *Spending to Save*, 110, 139, 180–81; Howard, *WPA and Federal*

Relief Policy, 271–77, 425–34, 457–59, 463–64, 778, 806, 808–9, 829, 834; Bremner, "New Deal and Social Welfare," 89; G. John Ikenberry and Theda Skocpol, "Expanding Social Benefits: The Role of Social Security," *Political Science Quarterly* 102 (Fall 1987), 414; "Thesis on Conditions of Physically Handicapped," 6–7; Brown, "March of the Cripples," 11–12; Buchanan, *Illusions of Equality,* 91–101.

56. In 1940, Congress determined that ATB recipients could temporarily substitute WPA employment for ATB. But Congress blocked recipients of Old Age Assistance and mothers getting Aid to Dependent Children from doing the same. Badger, *New Deal,* 208–13; Blumberg, *New Deal and the Unemployed,* 45–47, 222–26; Bremner, "New Deal and Social Welfare," 75–76; Charles, *Minister of Relief,* 225–26; Howard, *WPA and Federal Relief Policy,* 228–36, 432, 448–52, 463–64, 466; Patterson, *New Deal and the States,* 74–76; Exec. Order No. 7046 (1935), in *Presidential Executive Orders, Numbers 1–7403 (1845–June 1936)* (microfilm, 11 reels, Trans-Media Publications Microfilms, 1983), reel 11. For a classic example of hostility to WPA workers, as well as class bias, that uses disabled figures to make its case, see John Faulkner's novel *Men Working* (New York, 1940).

57. "Thesis on Conditions of Physically Handicapped," 1–2, 6–7; Buchanan, *Illusions of Equality,* 94–5; Buchanan, "Deaf Students and Workers," 376–97; Susan Burch, "Biding the Time: American Deaf Cultural History, 1900 to World War II" (Ph.D. diss., Georgetown University, 1999), 166–73; Badger, *New Deal,* 212, 218, 221; Blumberg, *New Deal and the Unemployed,* 62–63; Howard, *WPA and Federal Relief Policy,* 459–62, 464–65; William F. McDonald, *Federal Relief Administration and the Arts* (Columbus, 1969), 569.

58. The special jobs included work done by guards, watchmen, checkers, and timekeepers. Howard, *WPA and Federal Relief Policy,* 99–101, 462–65; Buchanan, "Deaf Students and Workers," 381–83. In his thorough review of the WPA, Donald Howard questioned private employers' practices toward handicapped job seekers. Howard, *WPA and Federal Relief Policy,* 469.

59. Scotch and Berkowitz, "One Comprehensive System?"; Matson, *Walking Alone and Marching Together,* 9–10, 14, 17–23, 27, 32–33, 38–42; Berkowitz, *Disabled Policy,* 77–78, 186, 230–36; Buchanan, *Illusions of Equality,* 96–101; Flexer Bassoff interview, side 1; Flexer Bassoff and Bassoff interview, side 1; *New York Herald Tribune,* June 7, 1935, 19. For an early example of blind advocates challenging state relief and rehabilitation policies and programs see Thomas A. Krainz, "Implementing Poor Relief: Colorado's Progressive-Era Welfare State" (Ph.D. diss., University of Colorado, 2000).

60. The proportion of female WPA workers, 1935–1941, fluctuated between 12.1 percent and 19.2 percent. The Louisiana WPA declared that "a woman with an employable husband is not eligible for referral, as her husband is the logical head of the family." Howard, *WPA and Federal Relief Policy,* 280–83; Badger, *New Deal,* 204–8; Blumberg, *New Deal and the Unemployed,* 77–78; Lois Scharf, *To Work and to Wed: Female Employment, Feminism, and the Great Depression* (Westport, 1980), 123, 126; Susan Ware, *Beyond Suffrage: Women in the New Deal* (Cambridge, Mass., 1981), 110–11; Susan Ware, *Holding Their Own: American Women in the 1930s* (Boston, 1982), 21–37; Adrienne Asch and Michelle Fine, eds., *Women with Disabilities: Essays in Psychology, Culture, and Politics* (Philadelphia, 1988), 24–25, 132, 148–62, 307;

Flexer Bassoff interview, side 1. At least one other woman in the league had grown up with similar prompting. Fishman interview, side 1. In contrast, male domination of Deaf and blindness organizations may have been linked to deaf and blind women's closer approximation to gender norms and tendency to assume more traditional female roles. Burch, "Biding the Time," 284–98; Catherine J. Kudlick, "The Outlook of *The Problem* and the Problem with *The Outlook:* Two Advocacy Journals Reinvent Blind People in Turn-of-the-Century America," and Susan Burch, "Reading Between the Signs," both in Longmore and Umansky, eds., *New Disability History*, 191, 201–7, 215, 218, 219–21. If disablement has often been regarded as feminizing men, at other times, depending on the type and extent of disability and particularly on the manner in which it was acquired, it has been perceived as a masculine "red badge of courage." That complex moral economy of disability and gender requires investigation. Wilson, "Crippled Manhood"; Hockenberry, *Moving Violations*, 110; Williams-Searle, "Courting Risk," esp. 40–45.

61. See Rosner and Markowitz, *Deadly Dust*, esp. 86–89, 118–20, 125–34, 148–49, 179–80. See also Rosner and Markowitz, *"Slaves of the Depression,"* 115–20, 141, 148. On disability and the politics of medical speech, see Roth, "Handicap as a Social Construct"; William Roth, "Almsgiving in the 1980s: Social, Political, and Policy Aspects of Being Disabled in an Able-Bodied World," *Pediatric Social Work* 2:4 (1982), 106.

62. Badger, *New Deal*, 203–8, 254–60, 305; Blumberg, *New Deal and the Unemployed*, 78–83; Patterson, *New Deal and the States*, 197–98; Harvard Sitkoff, *A New Deal for Blacks: The Emergence of Civil Rights as a National Issue*, vol. I: *The Depression Decade* (New York, 1978), 52, 59–79, 84–97, 247–50, 254–67; Ware, *Beyond Suffrage;* Ware, *Holding Their Own*, 89–101.

63. Orrick Johns, *Time of Our Lives: The Story of My Father and Myself* (New York, 1937), 119–30, 167, 219, 342–51; Badger, *New Deal*, 223; *Washington Evening Star,* May 12, 1936, A2; *New York Post*, May 13, 1936, 6; *New York Times*, June 5, 1936, 2; Brown, "March of the Cripples," 10; Blumberg, *New Deal and the Unemployed*, 70.

64. Ridder was a German American, Catholic, conservative, Republican newspaper publisher; Johns a Scottish American, former Presbyterian, sometime Communist, journalist and writer; and FDR a Dutch American, Episcopalian, liberal Democrat. Blumberg, *New Deal and the Unemployed*, 70; Johns, *Time of Our Lives.*

65. Alan B. Spitzer, "The Historical Problem of Generations," *American Historical Review* 78 (December 1973), 1353–85; Van Cleve and Crouch, *Place of Their Own*, 47, 60–61, 87–103; Robert Buchanan, "The *Silent Worker* Newspaper and the Building of a Deaf Community, 1890–1929," in Van Cleve, ed., *Deaf History Unveiled*, 172–97; Buchanan, *Illusions of Equality;* Burch, "Biding the Time"; Michael Reis, "Student Life at the Indiana School for the Deaf During the Depression Years," in Van Cleve, ed., *Deaf History Unveiled*, 198–223; Kudlick, "Outlook of *The Problem*"; Matson, *Walking Alone and Marching Together,* 4–10; Sharon A. Groch, "Oppositional Consciousness: Its Manifestations and Development—The Case of People with Disabilities," *Sociological Inquiry* 64 (November 1994), 369–95.

66. *New York Times*, June 5, 1936, 2; *New York Times*, June 21, 1936, sec. 2, 1; *New York Times*, June 22, 1936, 19; *New York Times*, August 25, 1936, 21; *New York Times*, September 13, 1936, sec. 2, 10; *New York Herald Tribune*, September 13, 1936,

20; League of the Physically Handicapped to Hopkins, June 28, 1937, and David R. Niles to League of the Physically Handicapped, June 30, 1937, both in folder L, box 2164, Complaints 1935–42, NYC, 69.3–69.3.1 (Records of the Federal Emergency Relief Administration), WPA Central Files: State; *New York Times*, August 15, 1937, 24; *New York Herald Tribune*, August 15, 1937, 15; *Washington Sunday Star*, August 15, 1937, B2; *Washington Evening Star*, August 16, 1937, A1; *New York Times*, August 17, 1937, 7; *Daily Worker*, national edition, August 17, 1937, 3; *Washington Evening Star*, August 18, 1937, B1; *New York Times*, August 20, 1937, 8; *Washington Post*, August 22, 1937, 2.

67. Haskell interview by Joseph, side 1.

68. The phrase "sparkplug" is Anthony Badger's. Badger, *New Deal*, 38–41, 138–40, 288–89; Cohen, *Making a New Deal*, 261–67; Cooney, *Balancing Act*, 57; James R. Green, *The World of the Worker: Labor in Twentieth-Century America* (New York, 1980), 137; Robin D. G. Kelley, *Hammer and Hoe: Alabama Communists During the Great Depression* (Chapel Hill, 1990), xi–xii, 92–108; Harvey Klehr and John Earl Haynes, *The American Communist Movement: Storming Heaven Itself* (New York, 1992), 81–83, 89; Mark Naison, *Communists in Harlem During the Depression* (Urbana, 1983), xvi, 140–48, 187–88, 194–95, 257–59, 279–81; Robert H. Zieger, *American Workers, American Unions* (Baltimore, 1994), 15–19; Flexer Bassoff and Bassoff interview, side 1; Blumberg, *New Deal and the Unemployed*, 90–95, 228–35; Harvey Klehr, *The Heyday of American Communism: The Depression Decade* (New York, 1984), 6, 82–86, 104–5, 292–303; Marc S. Miller, ed., *Working Lives, the Southern Exposure: A History of Labor in the South* (New York, 1974), 44–45. We have been unable to determine the precise relationship of any league member to any other political or labor group. During the league's November 1935 picketing of the New York WPA Port Authority headquarters, a writer for *New Masses* reported that "though the pickets aren't in the Party yet, they are getting great training." Brown, "March of the Cripples," 10. An inquiry into the Federal Bureau of Investigation's central records system under the Freedom of Information Act yielded no record of the league or its leading members. J. Kevin O'Brien to Paul K. Longmore, August 1, 1991.

69. Matson, *Walking Alone and Marching Together*, 33–34; Richard K. Scotch, *From Good Will to Civil Rights: Transforming Federal Disability Policy* (Philadelphia, 1985), 35, 41, 141, 152–53; Shapiro, *No Pity*, 47; Shaw, *Activist Handbook*, 239, 246.

70. Badger, *New Deal*, 140; Klehr, *Heyday of American Communism*, 106; Haskell interview by Joseph, side 2; Flexer Bassoff and Bassoff interview, side 2; Lasoff Applebaum interview, side 2.

71. Flexer Bassoff interview, side 1; Haskell interview by Joseph, side 2; Anspach, "From Stigma to Identity Politics," 765–73; Buchanan, *Illusions of Equality*, 102–26; Burch, "Biding the Time," 166–73; Jack Gannon, *The Week the World Heard Gallaudet* (Washington, 1989); Lane, *Mask of Benevolence*; Matson, *Walking Alone and Marching Together*; Vaughn, *Struggle of Blind People*; Scotch, *From Good Will to Civil Rights*, 31–34, 55–56, 82–85, 111–16; Shapiro, *No Pity*, 10, 24–25, 52–53, 67–69, 105–41; Shaw, *Activist Handbook*, 235–50; National Council on Disability, *Equality of Opportunity: The Making of the Americans with Disabilities Act* (Washington, 1998). A 1986 survey of adults with disabilities documented the emergence of a younger genera-

tion that identified as a cross-disability minority. Louis Harris and Associates for the International Center for the Disabled, *ICD Survey* (New York, 1986), 112–15; Robert J. Funk, "Lou Harris Reached Out and Touched the Disabled Community," *Mainstream* 11 (May 1986), 18. For a literary account of this new minority consciousness, see Jean Stewart, *The Body's Memory* (New York, 1989), 249–52, 258, 262–63, 271–73.

72. In the 1980s and 1990s, Florence Haskell belonged to Disabled in Action of New York (DIA) but was not an active member. Haskell interview by Longmore and Goldberger, side 1. Sylvia Flexer Bassoff was an advocate for transportation for elderly disabled persons. Flexer Bassoff interview, side 2. When leaders of DIA learned about the league in the late 1980s, they arranged interviews with Haskell and Flexer Bassoff.

5

The Disability Rights Moment
Activism in the 1970s and Beyond

Two of the brief pieces that follow recount important episodes in
the late-twentieth-century disability rights movement. The third
examines the ideology of one contingent of that campaign, the
Independent Living Movement. The first article was commis-
sioned by the editors of the scholarly journal *Radical History
Review*. The second piece is based on a talk my San Francisco
State University colleague Bill Issel asked me to give as part of a
symposium he organized on the politics of inclusion in the Bay
Area. The third article was requested by the editors of a reference
encyclopedia on U.S. civil rights. Solicitation of these pieces represents an emerging recognition of the importance of disability
history and the need to integrate it into U.S. history in general
and with the histories of U.S. minorities and social-justice movements in particular.

The section "Richard Nixon and the Disability Rights Movement: An Unintended Legacy"
was originally published in slightly different form in *Radical History Review* 60 (Fall 1994),
175–77. The section "The 504 Sit-in of April 1977: The Disability Rights Movement Comes
of Age" was originally delivered as a talk entitled "Frontiers of Activism: The Bay Area's Leadership Role in the Disability Rights Movement" at the San Francisco Public Library Symposium "The Politics of Inclusion," January 24, 1997, organized by my colleague Professor
William Issel. Both of these first two sections draw extensively on Richard K. Scotch, *From
Good Will to Civil Rights: Transforming Federal Disability Policy* (Philadelphia: Temple University Press, 1985); Joseph P. Shapiro, *No Pity: People with Disabilities Forging a New Civil Rights
Movement* (New York: Times Books/Random House, 1993); and Randy Shaw, *Activist Handbook* (Berkeley: University of California Press, 1996), "'Stop Stealing Our Civil Rights'—Direct
Action for Disability Rights," 235–50. The section "The Independent Living Movement" is
extensively revised from an article originally published in Waldo E. Martin and Patricia Sullivan, eds., *Civil Rights in the United States* (New York: Macmillan Reference, 1999).

Richard Nixon and the Disability Rights Movement: An Unintended Legacy

Richard M. Nixon and the early disability rights movement encountered one another in 1972 and 1973. In the fall of 1972, Congress passed a bill to reauthorize federal funding of state vocational rehabilitation programs. But the legislation mandated radical changes in VR. It sought to reverse the long-standing pragmatic professional practice of "creaming" the least disabled prospective clients, those who might be run through the system most quickly and counted as successful rehabilitants, closed cases. Priority should be given instead, said Congress, to persons with significant disabilities. And the goal need not necessarily be employment, but preparation and assistance to live in the larger community rather than in nursing homes or institutions. To facilitate both residence in the community and employment for significantly disabled persons, the bill authorized funding for "independent-living centers."

The concept of such centers had originated with disabled activists. They conceived independent-living centers as community-based, "consumer"-oriented, and "consumer"-run agencies that would provide services (e.g., wheelchair repair), referrals (accessible housing, personal-assistance providers), training (managing money or personal-assistance service providers), and advocacy (particularly in dealing with government bureaucracies). The first Center for Independent Living (CIL) was founded that same year of 1972 in Berkeley, California, by a group of disabled activists. As students in the late 1960s, they had persuaded the University of California to establish a disabled-student services program. It had included personal assistance to significantly disabled students, enabling them to live in campus housing. Transferring their ideas and strategies to the off-campus community, the group helped to launch the Independent Living Movement that would soon emerge also in Los Angeles, Houston, Boston, and the rest of the country. Their central goal, self-directed living in the community supported by centers like CIL, was adopted by Congress in the vocational rehabilitation act. (Senator Alan Cranston of California was a coauthor.)

But 1972 was also, of course, an election year, and President Nixon defied conventional political wisdom never to oppose "do-good" legislation, such as a bill to "aid . . . the crippled," as one Congress member put it who supported the proposed law but misunderstood its implications. Nixon pocket vetoed the bill, rejecting it on two grounds. First, it would make federal funding of state vocational rehabilitation programs contingent on compliance with the new priorities. He regarded that requirement as excessive federal interference in state government. His other objection concerned federal spending on social programs. Independent living services would cost too much and, he feared, would "seriously jeopardize" the vocational goals of rehabilitation.

Nixon's veto of the rehabilitation act provoked sharp criticism from the emerging generation of disability rights activists. In New York City, a recently formed cross-disability alliance called Disabled in Action (DIA) demonstrated against the president's decision. In Washington, D.C., disabled activists held an all-night vigil at the Lincoln Memorial. The latter protest involved younger and more militant delegates to the annual meeting of the generally conservative-to-moderate President's Committee for Employment of the Handicapped (PCEH). In 1973, when Nixon again vetoed virtually identical legislation, many of the same delegates to the PCEH meeting paraded down Connecticut Avenue in protest. But Nixon's two vetoes spurred younger activists to do more than demonstrate. The vetoes also prodded them to form political alliances across traditionally competitive disability categories. In effect, Nixon provided the nascent disability rights movement with a focus, a unifying target. He became one of its early enemies.

In September 1973, Nixon at last signed a third version of the Rehabilitation Act. Congress retained the important new priority regarding persons with significant disabilities, but it reduced the amount of spending authorized. The final act also omitted the mandate for independent-living centers to which Nixon had objected. It would require another half-decade of lobbying by disability rights advocates to secure federal support of independent living. Even then President Jimmy Carter would sign the legislation reluctantly, like Nixon fearing its cost.

Nixon's two vetoes and his subsequent signing of the Rehabilitation Act of 1973 involved one historical irony. All three versions of the act contained Section 504, the concluding provision, that prohibited discrimination against persons with disabilities in federally funded programs or activities. This potentially far-reaching requirement had been drafted by Senate staffers with little or no experience of disability issues, who nonetheless recognized that prejudice was a problem for disabled Americans and that resulting discrimination could thwart the aims of vocational rehabilitation. Nixon and his advisers overlooked 504. Indeed, it escaped the notice of virtually everyone. If disabled activists were aware of 504, they as yet lacked the organization to lobby for it or the act. The lone and significant exception was the National Federation of the Blind (NFB), which for decades had had a vigorous lobby in Washington and had taken a consistent civil rights–oriented approach to disability issues. Testifying in favor of the act, the NFB's director took note of Section 504 and stressed its importance to citizens with disabilities. Though disabled activists played only a limited role in passage of the act, they worked energetically in the coming years for issuance of the long-delayed regulations implementing Section 504.

By then, Richard Nixon was long departed. But he had left Americans with disabilities an unintended legacy, a legal weapon he had been unaware of and surely would have opposed as too expensive. In one of American history's ironies, Richard Nixon had signed into law a major civil rights statute that the new generation of disabled people would use to fight discrimination, perhaps most importantly in higher education, and to gain equal access to American society.

The 504 Sit-in of April 1977: The Disability Rights Movement Comes of Age

On April 5, 1977, disability rights activists occupied federal offices around the United States. They demanded implementation of Section 504 of the 1973 Rehabilitation Act. Passed primarily to support state vocational rehabilitation programs, that act included an unprecedented civil-rights provision. The act's final section, 504, mandated: "No otherwise qualified handicapped individual . . . shall . . . be excluded from participation in, be denied the benefits of, or be subjected to discrimination under any program or activity receiving federal financial assistance." That single sentence, the first federal anti-discrimination protection for disabled citizens, had been drafted and adopted without any lobbying or public campaign, for in the early 1970s disability rights activism was still a fledgling movement. Though limited to federally funded entities, 504 offered a potentially powerful weapon against disability-based discrimination. But it would take effect only when implementing regulations were issued.

Some critics have noted that Congress could pass this grand gesture without actually having to see to its enforcement. Meanwhile opponents, such as hospitals and universities, could avoid publicly battling a civil-rights bill but still block it by delaying the regulations. The Department of Health, Education, and Welfare, designated as lead agency in developing those rules, bore out the critics' concerns. For three years, HEW made no progress toward issuing the regulations. Finally in July 1976, disability rights groups persuaded a federal court to order the agency to promulgate the final regulations forthwith. Instead, the Ford administration threw up more delays. Then just eight days before leaving office in January 1977, HEW secretary David Mathews asked Congress if the rules should include alcoholics and drug addicts. Seeing this as yet another delaying tactic, advocates immediately got a federal court to again direct HEW to issue the rules at once, but the agency appealed the order.

Advocates expected favorable action from the incoming Carter administration. In a speech at Warm Springs, Georgia, in September of 1976, candidate Jimmy Carter had criticized the Ford administration for stalling on the implementing regulations. But disability rights activists had drafted that speech. It apparently did not reflect a strong commitment by Carter to disability rights enforcement. To the activists' dismay, HEW secretary-designate Joseph Califano said he needed time to study the proposed rules. More alarming, he set up a review task force that included no disabled members or representatives of disability organizations. It also met behind closed doors. Disability rights leaders got word that the panel planned to weaken 504. For example, while the draft regulations would mandate integration of disabled schoolchildren, the task force would allow "separate but equal" education.

Disability advocates organized the American Coalition of Citizens with Disabilities to spearhead the 504 struggle. ACCD made a shrewd preemptive move. Before the task force could announce its recommended changes, the coalition publicly warned Califano that if he did not sign the regulations unaltered by April 4, 1977, activists would stage nationwide demonstrations.

ACCD planned protests at HEW headquarters in Washington and eight regional HEW offices. But the protests would last just one day. After that, Califano would be free from pressure to sign 504. The strategic answer was to sit in until he issued the regulations. Organizing a prolonged protest by people with disabilities, though, would involve extensive logistical preparation.

On April 5, protestors occupied HEW offices in nine cities. In Denver, HEW officials had to put up with the demonstrators because, according to the local press, "even the jails of Denver are inaccessible." In Washington, more than seventy-five activists occupied HEW headquarters overnight. There and in New York, HEW quickly starved the protestors out by refusing to allow food to be brought in. But in San Francisco at the climax of the rally, Judy Heumann, of Berkeley's Center for Independent Living, called on the crowd to "go and tell Mr. Maldonado [the HEW regional administrator] that the federal government cannot steal our civil rights." Hundreds followed her into Maldonado's office. Uninformed about Califano's stance and thus unable to defend it, Maldonado stood like a deer caught in the headlights of the television news cameras. To cap the confrontation, Heumann declared that the protestors would not leave until Califano signed the 504 rules unchanged. Two hundred activists, most of them disabled, spent that night sleeping in the offices and hallways. Some 120 would stay on for the next three and a half weeks.

The organizers had quietly prepared for long-term occupation of HEW's offices by developing a support network of community organizations. The recent disability rights movement had seemingly operated separately from other social justice campaigns or been shunned by them. The 504 sit-in strategy returned to the practice of some earlier disability-based political movements of seeking alliance with nondisability organizations. Thus, unlike the 504 protests in other cities, the San Francisco sit-in won both broad-based political support and practical assistance. A network of volunteers from such groups as the Black Panthers and the Delancey Street Foundation would risk arrest to bring the protestors food donated not just by churches and unions, but even by Safeway and McDonald's. HEW officials in Washington quickly saw that if they tried to starve out the demonstrators, they might provoke a larger protest involving many other groups. Shrewd planning and alliance building established the political and logistical basis for a prolonged sit-in.

On day four, Ed Roberts, a founder of the Center for Independent Living in Berkeley and now the director of the California Department of Rehabilitation, came and endorsed the sit-in. "We are not even second-class citizens, we're third-class citizens," he said. "We have got to keep up the pressure." Federal officials, said Roberts, have "underestimated the commitment of this group."

On day six, Representative Phillip Burton, a liberal Democrat who represented San Francisco, demanded that HEW allow delivery of food to the protesters and installation of free pay phones. Meanwhile, protesters used other means to get their message out of the building. They unfurled banners from the windows, while Deaf demonstrators passed information using American Sign Language. The Butterfly Brigade, a patrol against anti-gay violence, snuck in walkie-talkies. Several federal employees who continued to work in the building even offered covert aid. Some smuggled food. One wore a ceramic pin with a snake on it. He told protest leaders that if Maldonado decided to call in the police, he would alert them by turning the pin upside-down. San Francisco mayor George Moscone had twenty air mattresses and hoses with showerheads delivered. José Maldonado complained, "We are not running a hotel here."

On day twelve, Representative Burton and George Miller, the latter another liberal Democrat from the Bay Area, held a hearing on disability discrimination, taking testimony from the demonstrators occupying the building. In another dramatic moment caught on TV, Burton, listening to the disabled activists, wept. Meanwhile Califano, still refusing to sign the implementing regulations unchanged, made an astonishing political blunder. He sent a low-ranking assistant, Gene Eiderberg, to explain to Burton and Miller why twenty-two changes had to be made to the draft regulations. Eiderberg reported that these would include exemptions from the requirement of ramps and other access features in hospitals and schools. He also announced that rather than mainstreaming disabled schoolchildren, HEW planned to place some in what he called "separate but equal" facilities. As the news cameras rolled, Heumann exploded at him: "We will not accept more segregation. When you erect buildings that are not accessible to the handicapped, you enforce segregation. There will be more sit-ins until the government understands this." The drama continued as Eiderberg, finishing his testimony, retreated into an office and locked the door. The incensed Burton, demanding that Califano's representative listen to the disabled activists, ran to the office and began kicking the door.

As Randy Shaw has explained in his shrewd analysis of this sit-in, relations with the media and adoption of the civil-rights movement's tactics enabled the sit-in organizers to define the issues. HEW, supported by the major national news media, tried to depict 504 as a legislative provision that had generated confusing bureaucratic regulations. The demonstrators framed the issue as a problem of discrimination and civil rights. Bay Area media and then national news outlets covering the sit-in day after day disseminated images of disabled people engaged in civil disobedience in quest of their rights. Stories profiled individual protestors, thereby exposing the public to disabled people's experience of discrimination and explaining why they were demanding legal protection. The coverage defeated HEW's efforts to shape the public discourse on 504. The activists successfully got most of the news media to present their cause as a civil-rights issue, as a struggle between ordinary disabled people and federal bureaucrats and politicians who were "trying to steal our civil rights."

But the sit-in could not go on indefinitely. On the one hand, it posed for the protestors physical inconvenience, pain, even health risks. On the other, political support and media coverage would sooner or later fade. The leaders knew they had to prod Califano to sign the 504 regulations. Two weeks into the sit-in, several flew to Washington. Again they built useful political alliances, gaining assistance from the International Association of Machinists and backing from two powerful Democratic senators, Alan Cranston of California and Harrison Williams of New Jersey. They also dogged Califano and President Carter, picketing the latter's church and the former's house while singing "We Want 504" to the tune of "We Shall Overcome." At last they got a meeting with Carter's top domestic adviser, Stuart Eizenstat. Soon after, Califano capitulated. He would issue the 504 regulations virtually unchanged.

Journalist Joseph Shapiro has called the 504 sit-in "the political coming of age of the disability rights movement." Four features distinguish that event as a turning point.

First, more powerfully and effectively than ever before, the protest redefined the problems faced by people with disabilities. It framed them as mainly social, not medical. It marked as the most serious obstacle pervasive prejudice and discrimination. It presented as the appropriate solution civil-rights protection, as exemplified in Section 504.

Second, in pursuit of that political objective, the organizers, as noted, built coalitions with other social-change movements.

Third, the leaders simultaneously fashioned ties across disability lines. "Disability" is not a homogeneous or monolithic class. Disability groups have typically formed around disability-specific categories and often competed for scarce material resources. At times they have practiced the same prejudices as the larger society toward people with disabilities different from their own. In contrast, the 504 sit-in leaders espoused an inclusive ideology of disability and cross-disability activism. The ACCD involved an alliance among hitherto often competing disability organizations. The San Francisco sit-in enacted that coalition both politically and personally. One protestor, Mary Jane Owen, explained later: "People went into that building with some kind of idealism, but they didn't have much knowledge of other disabilities. Up to that point, we had blind organizations, organizations for deaf people, for wheelchair users, for people with spina bifida, or people with mental retardation." On the sixth floor of the federal building in downtown San Francisco, the demonstrators for the moment set aside disability parochialism. They proclaimed an ecumenical ideology of disability: all people with disabilities, whatever their particular conditions, confronted a common set of stigmatizing values and social hazards. This inclusive ideology would not continuously hold the cross-disability alliance together. Contending disability-specific political interests and agendas would persist. But from then on, they would operate in tension with a universalistic approach to disability rights.

Finally, if the sit-in formally pursued a politics of issues, it also produced an unplanned politics of identity. One leader, Kitty Cone, told reporters: "Nobody gave us anything. We showed we could wage a struggle at the highest level of government and win." Her proud claim did not just represent a declaration of political victory. It also affirmed a positive disability identity. By risking arrest and even their health, the protestors countered the devaluing cultural assessment of disabled people as weak and dependent. By adopting the militant tactics of other social movements, they showed society—and themselves—that people with disabilities were not feeble but strong, not incompetent but skillful, not helpless but powerful.

The protesters also began creating a positive disability identity in other ways. They had come together around the issue of second-class citizenship, but as they assisted one another during the prolonged sit-in, as they lived together, they formed themselves into a community of people with disabilities. Late into the nights, they talked and listened and learned about one another's lives and experiences. They came to recognize their commonalities. Without their intending it, the discussions became a process of collective, as well as individual, redefinition of their identities. They came to see themselves differently. During one late-night conversation, each individual in a circle expressed what he or she would ask for if given one wish. One young woman said: "I used to know what I would wish for. I wanted to be beautiful. I wanted to stop being a cripple. But now I know I am beautiful." Mary Jane Owen recalled: "We all felt beautiful. We all felt powerful. It didn't matter if you were mentally retarded, blind, or deaf. Everybody who came out felt, we are beautiful. We are powerful. We are strong. We are important." Their activism enabled many of the protestors to assume the authority to define themselves, not *despite* their disabilities, but, in a positive way, *as* people with disabilities. That was at least as radical as their claim that disability was a civil-rights issue.

On April 28, 1977, Secretary Califano signed the implementing regulations, making Section 504 an enforceable law. Two days later, the protestors in San Francisco triumphantly paraded out singing "We *Have* Overcome." Their twenty-five-day sit-in remains the longest occupation of a federal building by political protestors in U.S. history.

The Independent Living Movement

The Disability Rights Movement is not a homogeneous or unitary effort. Rather, it is an assemblage of disability-based political movements that sometimes cooperate and sometimes compete. Those movements have arisen among disability-specific constituencies, for example, the organized blind, the culturally Deaf, associations of psychiatric survivors, the developmental disabilities community, and the campaign on behalf of people with learning disabilities. Each of these movements has addressed issues and pursued agendas particular to its constituency. Yet at the same time, they have operated from strikingly—and increasingly— similar principles, often in quest of comparable objectives. The many parallels warrant speaking of these various movements as components of a larger Disability Rights Movement. The ideology and agenda of the Independent Living Movement (ILM) epitomizes many of the ideas, issues, and themes that characterized all of the late-twentieth-century disability-based political movements. A brief review of the ILM's history and principles can stand as a summary of the paradigmatic features of recent disability rights movements.

The Independent Living Movement has focused on ensuring people with significant disabilities the means to achieve self-directed community-based living. In the early 1970s, the first independent-living centers were organized in Berkeley, Houston, and Boston by and for physically disabled young adults, most of them white and middle class, many of them recent or current college students. By the 1990s, the centers had expanded their clienteles to include adults with sensory, developmental, and emotional disabilities of all ages and various ethnic minorities, though most still belonged to the original constituency. In important respects, the ILM paralleled the deinstitutionalization movements for people with psychiatric and developmental disabilities. Ultimately it forged links with them.

As early as 1959, rehabilitation professionals had unsuccessfully lobbied Congress to fund independent living for individuals for whom employment was not a practical objective. By the late 1970s, advances in medicine and rehabilitation technology along with the computer revolution had rendered obsolete the dichotomy between independent living and work. In 1978, Congress authorized federal grants for independent-living centers. By the 1990s, the federal-state vocational rehabilitation system funded some four hundred.

Adapting some concepts and objectives from the civil-rights, consumer, and self-help movements while formulating an analysis and agenda distinctive to disability rights campaigns, the Independent Living Movement has developed a comprehensive ideology of disability and disability rights. Most fundamental, the ILM has redefined the nature of "disability" and the problems people with disabilities confront. It regards disability as primarily a social, rather than a medical, issue. The limitations people with disabilities confront in social and vocational functioning are not the inevitable result of physiological difference but are largely caused by inaccessibility in the built environment, "disincentives" in public policies, domination of disabled people by bureaucrats and professionals, prejudice in the culture, and institutionalized discrimination.

That reframing of the problem facing disabled people leads to different solutions than those traditionally pursued by the medical and vocational rehabilitation systems. Those institutions have promoted physical self-sufficiency, independent mobility (for example, walking), and paid employment. In contrast, the ILM has supported those goals if they are practical objectives for particular individuals. But it regards as more important, indeed central, personal self-determination backed by independent-living support services.

Most radical in terms of U.S. civil-rights theory, the ILM asserts that people with disabilities have a right to the means necessary for them to participate in the community. These means include legal protection from discrimination; the right to receive quality treatment or services; the right to refuse such treatment or services; due process in all professional or governmental decision making that affects them; equal access to public transportation and accommodations; and, most central to the

ILM's objectives, the rights to deinstitutionalization and support services for independent living. In the realm of public policy, the ILM has pursued two major goals. It has sought elimination of work disincentives from federal income-maintenance and health-insurance programs, while calling for federally mandated funding for independent-living services. The ILM has identified personal-assistance services as the key support. Those services are defined as one person assisting another with tasks the individual would ordinarily do for him or herself if he or she did not have a disability. The services include aid with such activities as personal maintenance and hygiene; mobility; household chores such as cooking, cleaning, and child care; cognitive tasks such as money management; and communications access such as interpreting and reading. In the early 1990s, an estimated 9.6 million Americans needed some form of personal assistance. Some 7.8 million of them already lived in the community, but only 10 percent of those individuals had access to paid personal assistance. Viewed from the standpoint of civil rights theory, these claims by the ILM combined civil rights with benefit entitlements. Thereby it redefined services and assistive devices as alternative modes of functioning, not as means of caring for those who are fundamentally dependent. It also made them matters of right, not charity.

It should come as no surprise that in espousing these principles and pursuing these goals the Independent Living Movement has often clashed with medical and rehabilitation professionals. Directly confronting that conflict, the ILM has viewed encounters and relationships between professionals and consumers as frequently adversarial, with power tilted to the professionals' side. In addition, it has criticized manufacturers, vendors, and service providers as often serving their own financial and status interests at the expense of disabled people's best interests. In response to these disparities of power and conflicting interests, independent-living centers established advocacy departments, while also offering personal self-advocacy and systems-change training.

Complementing its promotion of individual self-determination and self-advocacy, the Independent Living Movement has also called for collective empowerment and self-direction by communities of disabled people. ILM activists have insisted that people with disabilities must have majority power in designing and running the programs that affect them. Medical and social-service professionals initially had a limited role in the ILM as independent-living leaders challenged the dominant ideologies of the rehabilitation/social-service system and contested professionals' power. But by the early 1980s, nondisabled professionals were taking an increasingly prominent role in running the centers. This paralleled a shift from activism to service provision in response to criticism by political conservatives and threats to withdraw federal funding. In consequence, during the 1980s disability rights advocacy moved outside the centers. In the 1990s, federal law came to require that 50 percent of centers' boards of directors and staffs be people with disabilities. Following that policy shift, a growing number of centers began to return to systems-change advocacy and political activism.

The principles and objectives that have characterized the Independent Living Movement have parallels in virtually every other recent disability-based political movement:

- the reframing of "disability" as a social and political, rather than simply a medical and rehabilitative, problem;
- the shift in priorities from correcting individuals to reforming society;
- the assertion that the necessary means for social participation and integration, whether devices and services or access and accommodations, should be enforceable civil rights rather than dispensations of charity;
- the contests for power with professionals and bureaucrats;
- the quest for both individual and collective empowerment and self-determination.

These common concepts and comparable agendas link the various disability-based political movements. They indicate that these disability-specific campaigns have simultaneously operated—and continue to operate—as contingents of a larger Disability Rights Movement. They also reflect the emergence of a sense of cross-disability identification, if not of cross-disability identity. Those senses of identification and of possible identity have often jostled uneasily with disability-specific interests and identities. Still, the ongoing effort to address that tension, indeed, the necessity of regularly dealing with it, evidences not only the presence of a universalistic disability identity, but also its historical significance. Cross-disability identification and identity reflect a transformation in consciousness among people with disabilities. At the same time, they serve as organizing tools spurring that change. Paralleling developments in consciousness and identity, the correspondence of concepts and agendas among disability-based political movements points to the formulation of an ecumenical ideology of disability and disability rights.

That ideology supplies the specific content of disability rights advocacy as it contests ideologies that oppose both civil rights in general and disability rights in particular.

These ways of thinking about people with disabilities had their genesis during and after World War II. But they reached critical social and political mass only in the last third of the twentieth century. Their achievement of historical weight during those two generations justifies referring to the recent era as the Disability Rights Moment.

TWO

IMAGES AND REFLECTIONS

6

Film Reviews

Over the decades, thousands upon thousands of characters with disabilities have appeared on movie and television screens. Three artistically powerful and culturally significant films of the 1980s— *Whose Life Is It, Anyway?*, *Mask*, and *My Left Foot*—not only revolved around a disabled character, but centered on issues of disability. Yet, to my way of thinking, the mainstream movie critics whose reviews I read almost completely misunderstood these stories. Hence the three reviews that follow.

Answer to *Whose Life Is It, Anyway?*

The motion picture *Whose Life Is It Anyway?* argues for the right to die by showing that severely disabled people have nothing worth living for and would be better off dead. Richard Dreyfuss plays Ken Harrison, a brilliant young sculptor paralyzed from the neck down in an auto accident. He decides that suicide is preferable to life as a quadriplegic who needs dialysis. Persuasively, even eloquently, the film makes the case for his death. But that case is totally one-sided, distorting the alternatives and thereby defaming the value of the lives of people with severe disabilities.

The section "Answer to *Whose Life Is It, Anyway?*" was originally published in slightly different form in the *Los Angeles Times Sunday Calendar*, March 14, 1982, 45–46. "*Mask*: A Revealing Portrayal" was originally published in the *Los Angeles Times Sunday Calendar*, May 5, 1985, 22–23. "The Glorious Rage of Christy Brown" was written in 1989 at the request of my friend and colleague Tari Susan Hartman to be included in a publicity kit promoting this film to the U.S. disability community. Among other periodicals, it was published in *Disability Studies Quarterly* 10:4 (Fall 1990), 23–24, and *Mainstream* 14:7 (March 1990), 11–14.

Ken spends an unbelievable six months in intensive care before his doctors decide to move him to a rehabilitation hospital. By that time most spinal-cord-injured quadriplegics have finished rehabilitation. Just as improbable, only then does he ask if he will recover and only then do his physicians tell him that his condition is permanent.

Naturally, he feels that this catastrophe has left his life in ruins. His doctors glibly tell him that he will feel differently once he starts rehabilitation. But rehabilitation never begins. He and we never catch a glimpse of the adaptive methods and special equipment available to severely disabled people. A social worker weakly suggests that he may be able to use a reading machine and a special typewriter, but she never shows him those devices.

The movie's press kit brags about the panoply of up-to-date medical hardware. With all of that gadgetry, couldn't they find a power wheelchair anywhere? Instead, an orderly pushes Ken around in a manual chair. Ken travels throughout the hospital and even out-of-doors, his very mobility weakening the case for his death. If he operated a power chair himself, that would further undermine the false impression of his utter helplessness.

Ken is obsessed with sex because he is sure he can never have sex with a woman again. He breaks off his relationship with his lover and bitterly laments that he is "not a man anymore." His despair about the loss of physical love helps propel him toward suicide.

A real medical specialist in spinal-cord injury, knowing that 70 percent of men with this sort of quadriplegia can have genital intercourse, would have explored Ken's sexual capabilities. Also, there are other satisfying ways to make love, as the disabled veteran played by Jon Voight showed in *Coming Home*. By ignoring these possibilities *Whose Life* reinforces the popular misconception of the asexuality of disabled people.

Ken argues that sculpting was his life and that he cannot simply switch to another art form. Someone who cares would mourn with him the loss of the thing he held most dear but would insist that as with everything else in his situation there are alternatives. His gift expressed itself through his fingers, but it originated in his brain.

This sardonic sculptor asserts himself with admirable defiance. But disturbingly the writers have him use his biting wit only to express contempt of himself as a disabled person.

This man of such passion and intelligence calls himself "a vegetable." And no one in the film disputes him! That term formerly referred to permanently comatose patients. The makers of *Whose Life . . .* coin a new definition: anyone with a severe disability is a "vegetable," in other words, subhuman. But many of us have lived for years with serious physical handicaps and have enjoyed our lives "anyway."

Ken cries that he is "dead already." Anyone who has endured a disabling accident or illness can empathize with these feelings. The point is that most people successfully negotiate this necessary painful passage through the stages of grief to accept themselves as persons with disabilities.

They make it partly because the people around them, family and friends and professionals, help them to learn new ways of living and to establish a new identity. Ken's doctors fail him, not by "arrogantly" trying to keep him alive, but by inadequately and half-heartedly showing him *how* he can live.

A competent physician would have another severely disabled person visit Ken to sympathize with his current feelings of despair and to demonstrate to him that there is hope. Unfortunately in *Whose Life . . .* other quadriplegics are absent.

The writers have tried to stack the deck against Ken. We know that he needs dialysis, but viewers unfamiliar with medical jargon will remain unaware that both of his kidneys and his spleen were removed. This makes his condition more difficult over the long term. Never has a movie straw man been more skillfully constructed, crippled, and persuaded to commit suicide.

Still, contrary to the impression given in the film, the latest developments would permit Ken to live at home and receive dialysis there. This would further weaken the case against taking his life.

This picture chiefly makes that case by an emotion-manipulating appeal to unspoken, even unconscious, fears and prejudices. During the movie, members of the audience in which I sat audibly agreed when Ken expressed his contempt of himself in his present condition and demanded to be allowed to die. I and disabled friends have had people say to us, "If I were you I'd kill myself."

Many nondisabled people think that those of us with serious physical handicaps are incapable of managing our lives or living meaningfully. I know respiratory quadriplegics more severely disabled than Ken who have resided in their homes and raised families.

This film also traffics in the current political mood that is dangerously cutting back vital aid to severely disabled citizens. In one scene a character complains that "we are spending thousands of dollars a week to keep [Ken] alive," when for a few pennies we could save the lives of African children by vaccinating them against measles. How dare they force us to choose between our lives and those of Third World children! Money is wasted, not in keeping him alive, but in keeping him hospitalized when he could live safely and at far less cost in the community.

Frighteningly, this picture reflects not just an opinion, but a way of dealing with severely disabled people that is rapidly gaining acceptance. A philosopher recently recommended to a federal commission that doctors be permitted to practice euthanasia on severely disabled infants if supporting them would involve great expense for their families or society. The *Hartford Courant* reported that doctors at the Yale–New Haven Hospital routinely offer parents of severely disabled newborn children the option of "mercy" killing.

In California, the parents of a deaf four-year-old are suing a doctor for failing to warn them of her disability. Deafness is such a terrible handicap, contends their attorney, that the child would have been better off had she never been born. Other "wrongful life" suits also propose that nonexistence is preferable to life with a disability.

Last year a television film told of a man who had shot to death his brother at the brother's request shortly after an accident left him a quadriplegic. Instead of portraying the tragedy of a man who ended his life before he discovered the possibilities of rebuilding it, the story confirmed his and the audience's death-dealing misconceptions. Sadly some people do commit suicide, because they have been taught that life is worthless if you are severely disabled. *Whose Life Is It, Anyway?* perpetuates the self-same false ideas that keep killing people.

Having decided to present a drama about an important contemporary social and ethical dilemma, the makers of this movie had a moral obligation to examine the issues fairly, factually, and thoroughly. The film they have produced is irresponsible.

For Richard Dreyfuss this was only acting. For us—to answer the question posed in this picture's title—it is *our* lives.

Mask: A Revealing Portrayal

The current movie *Mask* tells the offbeat, real-life tale of Rocky Dennis, a teenager with a rare facially disfiguring disorder who grows up amid a hard-riding, hard-living, tough and tender "family" of bikers.

For disabled people the picture has particular appeal because it significantly departs from typical screen images of us. Characters with severe disfigurements or "deformities" like Rocky's rarely appear outside horror films. Those movies portray them as dangerous, subhuman "monsters."

Likewise, motion pictures and fictional television frequently depict handicapped people as bitter and self-pitying. Whether a blind woman or an amputee surgeon on *The Love Boat*, a wheelchair-using mechanic on *Happy Days*, a blind farmer's son or Elmonzo Wilder recovering from a stroke on *Little House on the Prairie*, or a paraplegic former gymnast on *Diff'rent Strokes*, disabled people are inevitably shown to be angry and obnoxious, wallowing in self-pity and unwilling to take responsibility for themselves.

Producers and script writers consistently take a paternalistic, condescending approach by climaxing their "disabled stories" by having nondisabled characters confront the maladjusted "cripples" and tell them to stop feeling sorry for themselves. In these movie and TV treatments, disability is usually a matter of psychological adjustment, of individual character and coping. Social prejudice rarely intrudes.

Mask is a welcome departure. It shifts the source of the problem from the disabled individual to society. Emotionally, Rocky is clearly the healthiest, most mature, and most self-assured person in the film—a genuine rarity on screen for a disabled character. The greatest obstacles he must "overcome" are not within himself, but in the biases of other people. As one disability rights activist put it, "It's not Rocky's head that needs to change, but other people's."

Mask shows that disability is not primarily a medical condition, but rather a stigmatized social identity. Rocky Dennis's disability may be unusual, but his experience of devaluation and rejection is common to people with disabilities. If anything, the movie understates the discrimination handicapped people encounter daily: fear, revulsion, hostility, assumptions of inferiority, the transformation from social pariah to inspirational hero while still never being regarded as a "normal" person.

Importantly, Rocky finds himself accepted by the motorcycle gang "family," people stigmatized by society as social "misfits." The bikers also embrace and protect another handicapped person, B. D. (Bulldozer) Collins, a brawling, tender, mountainous man with a severe speech impairment. *Mask* also subtly makes the connection between different forms of prejudice when a black woman teacher wordlessly but knowingly welcomes Rocky as a student in her class. All of these people understand and receive one another out of their common experience of prejudice.

The film authentically depicts the extraordinary efforts expended by a disabled person to make nondisabled people comfortable with him. With every new situation, with every new school, with every new individual, Rocky must start all over again. Repeatedly he must summon the emotional stamina to deal with impertinent questions, insensitive remarks, paternalistic reactions. His mother may try to reassure him about his incredible and genuine skills in handling such situations. But some days he feels that he cannot once more confront the prejudice that persists despite his winning personality.

Mask is most honest in showing that social stigma results in romantic rejection. With few exceptions, television programs and movies depict disabled people shunning romantic possibilities because of low self-esteem. From the amputee veteran in the film classic *The Best Years of Our Lives* to a quadriplegic accountant in this season's *Highway to Heaven*, handicapped characters typically cannot believe that anyone could love them with their disabilities. Saintly nondisabled characters in these stories, having no fears or biases, must prove to the disabled persons that they are loveable as they are.

Rocky Dennis squarely faces the truth, an awful truth his mother would avoid: in a culture obsessed with appearance, disabled people, looking different or functioning differently, are often rejected as romantic partners. It is a blind girl, another outsider, who "sees" past the disability to the person Rocky is.

Additionally, *Mask* indirectly touches upon pressing public issues of concern to disabled Americans. In one hilarious scene, Rocky's mother chews out an arrogant young physician who has told her that her son has only a few months to live. Parents have often heard such doctors unequivocally and authoritatively declare that their handicapped children would live miserably and die soon.

In real life, children with conditions more treatable than Rocky's are too often allowed to die because someone decides that their "quality of life" is low and that they would be better off dead. This is why disability rights activists insist on medical treatment as a civil right of disabled persons. Could anyone meet Rocky Dennis and conclude that his life was not worth living?

Mask also reflects the growing militancy in the disability community. Like many parents of handicapped children, Rocky Dennis's mother is ready to fight for her son's right of equal access to public education. He does not need segregated special schooling, she maintains. He needs algebra and English, just like everyone else.

After repeated slurs and insults, Rocky at last explodes, slamming a biased student up against a locker and cussing him out for his bigotry. In that moment, he acts out the indignation apparent in growing numbers of disabled people. One need only attend meetings of disability rights organizations to see this political anger developing.

Finally, and perhaps most fascinating, Rocky displays what the magazine *The Disability Rag* calls "disability cool." He carries himself with easy self-assurance and pride. The people who reject him are not only prejudiced; they are uncool.

A new generation of disabled young adults is showing this same style. They too are "disability cool." They are proud and determined to insure their right of equal access to all areas of society. They declare that a society that devalues them is itself deformed. They assert that a community that would keep them out is crippled. They intend to unmask prejudice and to fashion for themselves a new and positive identity. For them, Rocky Dennis will be a hero.

The Glorious Rage of Christy Brown

At last a movie hero utterly true to our experience as disabled people. *My Left Foot* dramatizes the life of the Irish painter and novelist Christy Brown. Born in 1932 with cerebral palsy into a poor, brawling, tight-knit Dublin family, he had severely impaired speech and was nearly quadriplegic, but could use his left foot and leg.

Critics and the film's makers have said that this story is about family and growing up and being working-class Irish and striving to make oneself known and about an artist's struggle to express himself. It is not about "disablement," they have all assured us. They seem to fear that if prospective viewers think *My Left Foot*'s subject is the experience of disability, we will expect it to be depressing or saccharine and will stay away.

This film is about all of the things they describe, but most of all, despite what they say, it is about growing up disabled. And for once we get the story from our point of view, the perspective of disabled people, even down to the camera angles. We witness Christy Brown, boy and man, furiously fighting to break free of other people's devaluing biases and paternalistic domination, to control his own life, to define himself, to slake his yearning desires. The emotional dynamic that propels this film is his glorious disabled rage.

Though the reviewers enthusiastically praise the film, they misunderstand much that is in it because they know little of the experience of disabled people and, in fact, share many of society's biases about us.

We have had movie and TV tales beyond measure about angry handicapped people, all of them succumbers to self-pity. They are not angry about prejudice or discrimination. They are simply bitter about being disabled, and they need, we are told, some nondisabled person to shake them by the shoulders and snap them out of their childishness.

A few films have depicted prejudice. In *The Elephant Man*, John Merrick is simply its passive victim. In *Mask*, although the disfigured Rocky Dennis slams a taunting youth up against a school locker, he mostly quietly endures bias and tries to win people over with his warmth. The translators of *Children of a Lesser God* from stage to screen pretty much sanitized Deaf people's anger about hearing people's prejudice.

But now comes Christy Brown, funny and passionate and fierce in his refusal to tolerate even a moment's condescension. When a temporary attendant addresses him in a tone he considers patronizing, he snaps that he doesn't need a psychology lesson, he needs his cigarette lighted. When he is persuaded to go to a clinic for physical therapy, he finds himself packed together with handicapped children. Feeling infantilized, he quickly decides to go home.

Like so many disabled people, Christy aches to express his capacity for love and romance and sexuality and knows that he is devalued because of his disability. Even movie reviewers have expressed that bias. Vincent Canby of the *New York Times* calls a priest's warning to the severely disabled Christy about "the evils of the flesh" "funny-terrible." He concludes that Brown's "mind was . . . it seems, surprisingly romantic." It is surprising only if one regards people with disabilities as asexual and incapable of romantic love. Mr. Canby, it seems, wonders if the filmmakers fictionalized our Christy's romanticism.

The difference between Christy Brown and most disabled people is that he confronts romantic rejection head on. He senses that Mary (Ruth McCabe), the woman he will one day marry, is both attracted to him and anxious about feeling attracted to a severely disabled man, so he tells her straight out that she is afraid of him and of herself. What attracts Mary is not just Christy's wit and charm, but even more his emotional directness and strength and vulnerability. Capturing those qualities of his and Mary's ambivalent reaction to him is part of this movie's fidelity to the experience of people with disabilities.

Every nonhandicapped professional who works around handicapped people should study the way Dr. Eileen Cole (Fiona Shaw), a speech therapist, relates to the young adult Christy. Even while she helps him, she inflicts deep hurt. She flirts with him. She lounges seductively on his bed. At his first art gallery show, she drapes herself over him like a lover. Then when he summons the courage to tell her he loves her, she springs the news of her wedding engagement.

I have seen professionals play this kind of seductive game with disabled people. Not just women like Eileen playing with disabled men and boys. Males, too, flirting with disabled women and girls. It is cruel and dangerous, not because Christy's sexual and romantic feelings could never be fulfilled, but because people like Eileen evoke such feelings but have no intention of satisfying them.

No wonder Christy erupts with rage. When Eileen reveals her relationship with the gallery director, Christy boils and then explodes, finally grabbing a tablecloth in his teeth and dragging it and everything on it to the floor of a fancy restaurant. *Los Angeles Times* film critic Sheila Benson calls this "the tyrannical side of Christy's disablement." She thoroughly misunderstands his fury. He is enraged by what he now recognizes as Eileen's toying with him. Eileen undoubtably does not manipulate him consciously, but her behavior is certainly insensitive, wanton, and contemptuous of his feelings.

Christy is also incensed in this scene by the attempt of his embarrassed nondisabled companions to stifle his anger. One woman repeatedly tells the man next to her to take Christy's drink away from him. Eileen's fiancé tries to pull his wheelchair out of the restaurant. For Christy, this is simply nondisabled people trying to silence and control him by physically overpowering him. That is what provokes him to rip the cloth from the table. To her credit, Eileen lets him rage.

The film's reviewers have indulged in the usual devaluing language and attitudes. Canby finds Daniel Day-Lewis's rendition of Christy at first hard to evaluate. "It's never easy," he says, "judging the work of actors in such singular and grotesque circumstances." Benson refers to Brown as "wheelchair-bound" and Canby calls him "almost completely immobilized." This is a boy we see rescue his injured mother by hurling himself to the bedroom floor, scooting across it and down the hall, kicking his right foot with his left to unwedge it in the narrow hallway, sliding down the stairs, and pounding on the front door with that marvelous left foot. This is a young man we see playing football in the alley, blocking one field goal with his head and kicking another while lying on his side. Christy Brown immobilized? My left foot!

Like Christy's neighbors, the critics will not credit him with the talent and the drive that enable his achievements. "Through the uninhibited, unself-conscious love of his family," Canby tells us, "and the patience of his doctors, Christy learned how to be understood when he talked and to express himself first as a painter and then as a writer." There is only one "doctor," Eileen, and she is a speech therapist, not a physician. This comment reveals that Canby, like many nondisabled people, thinks of people with disabilities as patients who primarily need medical treatment.

What Brown primarily needs is to get an education. Canby makes Eileen "largely responsible" for that education. Benson says Christy "will be reached through" her. In real life too, disabled people's achievements are often chalked up to someone nondisabled who allegedly "reached" us. The film plainly shows that Brown himself is "largely responsible" for his education. He teaches himself to paint. Then he decides he is not really a painter after all and starts to write. The film omits that he wrote *Down All the Days*, one of the great modern Irish novels. To be sure, Christy needs and gets the help and support of his family and Eileen and, most important, his mother, but his accomplishments belong to him.

Canby calls *My Left Foot* a "triumph-over-adversity" film. That is exactly the sort of film this is not. Christy finds himself regarded as helpless and incompetent. From the first we are made to see that this bias infuriates him, so he confronts nondisabled people, forces them to deal with him. Sometimes he uses wit and charm, sometimes temper. Whatever his tactics, he will allow no one to dismiss him.

We witness the devalued boy become the leader of his brothers and the virtual head of his family. How many of us with physical disabilities have found nonhandicapped people at first condescending to us and at last relying on our brains and common sense? This is emphatically not a "triumph-over-adversity" tale. It is the story of a disabled man's life-long struggle against prejudice.

And the tone is far from triumphal. Prejudice deeply wounds Christy Brown. He aches with the loneliness, the sense of being excluded by social stigma, that many disabled people feel. He becomes alcoholic. He almost kills himself. If we find his rudeness at times unpleasant, we find his pain all but unbearable. The audience I saw the picture with audibly sighed with relief when we learned at the story's end that Christy eventually married Mary. Never before has a film so relentlessly demanded that its viewers feel the prejudice inflicted on a disabled person.

The raves about Daniel Day-Lewis's overpowering performance as Christy Brown go beyond the merely technical brilliance of his impersonation. He gets inside the mind of this disabled man. To achieve this he stayed in character as much as possible off the set. He used a wheelchair. He was lifted in and out of cars. He spoke the way a person with severe cerebral palsy would speak. He had someone feed him. He even dined in character in some of Dublin's best restaurants.

By living the role of a disabled man, Day-Lewis experienced something of the social reality of our lives. "It's strange what happens," he says, "regardless of the conceit, even though everybody knew who I was and what I was doing. When people see someone in a wheelchair, their attitudes change. People's voices change, they start treating you like a child." They talked around him as though he were not there, as though he were invisible.

Without knowing it, Day-Lewis had taken on a clearly defined social identity, the Crippled Role. As soon as he assumed the physical appearance of a "cripple," nonhandicapped people started treating him as one of us. They devalued him. They patronized him. They regarded him as a nonperson.

Any person with a disability could have predicted Day-Lewis's reaction to this prejudice. He says he felt "incessant rage." That is how he came to understand emotionally the mind and heart of Christy Brown. That is how and why he can give us this searing performance. That is how and why he and his colleagues can present this document of a disabled man's life, this fiercely honest, grim, funny, powerful and empowering mirror of our lives as people with disabilities.

Most of us who have disabilities hate the word "inspiring." We hate being told we are "inspirations." We know it is usually a way of devalu-

ing us by defining us as heroic oddities. It is a weapon to blame handicapped people who have not proved their worth by cheerfully "overcoming" their disabilities. It is a way of distracting attention from the
reality of the prejudice and discrimination and inaccessibility that thwart
the lives of millions of us.

Sometimes, though, the word "inspiring" fits. People with disabilities do need heroes, not uncomplaining overcomers, but real disabled
heroes who fight bias and battle for control of their lives and insist that
they will make their mark in the world. Christy Brown, difficult and
dangerous as he is, is such a hero. He embodies the consciousness of a
new generation of people with disabilities who assert that for the overwhelming majority of us prejudice is a far greater problem than any impairment, discrimination is a bigger obstacle than disability. He reflects
our demands for full human dignity, self-determination, and equal access to society and to life. Christy Brown is a hero of our struggle. We
will be inspired by his glorious disabled rage.

1

Screening Stereotypes
Images of Disabled People in Television and Motion Pictures

The film reviews in chapter 6 inspected several individual productions in detail. The following essay attempted to explicate
some of the major recurring themes about disability and characterizations of people with disabilities in motion pictures and television. Though many of the examples date from the period when
this article was written, the same themes and characterizations,
the same stereotypes, have persisted up to the present.

When one examines images of people with disabilities in television and
film, one encounters two striking facts. First, one discovers hundreds of
characters with all sorts of disabilities: handicapped horror "monsters";
"crippled" criminals; disabled war veterans, from *The Big Parade* (1925)
to *The Best Years of Our Lives* (1946) to *Coming Home* (1978); central characters of television series temporarily disabled for one episode; blind detectives; disabled victims of villains; animated characters like stuttering
Porky Pig, speech-impaired Elmer Fudd, near-sighted Mr. Magoo, and
mentally retarded Dopey.

The second striking fact is how much we overlook the prevalence of
disability and the frequent presence of disabled characters. Why are

Alan Gartner requested that I write this piece, which was originally published in slightly different form in *Social Policy* 16 (Summer 1985), 31–37, and reprinted in Alan Gartner and Tom
Joe, eds., *Images of the Disabled/Disabling Images* (New York: Praeger, 1986), 65–78, and in
Christopher E. Smit and Anthony Enns, eds., *Screening Disability: Essays on Cinema and Disability* (Lanham: University Press of America, 2001), 1–18. Courtesy of *Social Policy*.

there so many disabled characters, and why do we overlook them so much of the time? Why do television and film so frequently screen disabled characters for us to see, and why do we usually screen them out of our consciousness even as we absorb those images?

The critic Michael Wood has some useful observations that apply here. "All movies mirror reality in some way or other," he writes.

> There are no escapes, even in the most escapist pictures. . . . Movies bring out [our] worries without letting them loose and without forcing us to look at them too closely. . . . It doesn't appear to be necessary for a movie to solve anything, however fictitiously. It seems to be enough for us if a movie simply dramatizes our semi-secret concerns and contradictions in a story, allows them their brief, thinly disguised parade. . . . Entertainment is not, as we often think, a full-scale flight from our problems, not a means of forgetting them completely, but rather a rearrangement of our problems into shapes which tame them, which disperse them to the margins of our attention.[1]

Often, as Wood says, film and television programs do touch upon our areas of concern without explicitly acknowledging or exploring them. At other times, for instance in the "social problem" dramas seen during the 1970s and 1980s, the subjects of our worries were addressed, but without deep examination. In such cases, television and film supply quick and simple solutions. They tell us that the problem is not as painful or as overwhelming as we fear, that it is manageable, or that it is not really our problem at all, but someone else's.

Disability happens around us more often than we generally recognize or care to notice, and we harbor unspoken anxieties about the possibility of disablement, to us or to someone close to us. What we fear, we often stigmatize and shun and sometimes seek to destroy. Popular entertainments depicting disabled characters allude to these fears and prejudices, or address them obliquely or fragmentarily, seeking to reassure us about ourselves.

What follows is a brief consideration of the most common screen images of people with physical, sensory, and developmental disabilities and some thoughts about their underlying social and psychological meaning. This article by no means exhausts the range of images or their significance; although it concentrates on live-action fictional depictions, it also compares them to nonfictional images in order to illuminate further the social and cultural attitudes and concerns they reflect and express. Further, it is important to show the connections between recent changes in those characterizations and the emergence of a new sociopolitical consciousness about disability, particularly among disabled people themselves.

Disability has often been used as a melodramatic device not only in popular entertainments, but in literature as well. Among the most persistent is the association of disability with malevolence. Deformity of body symbolizes deformity of soul. Physical handicaps are made the emblems of evil.

Richard the Third's hunchback and Captain Ahab's peg leg immediately come to mind, but "bad guys" still frequently have handicaps. Doctor No and Doctor Strangelove both have forearms and hands encased in black leather. The overpowering evil embodied in Strangelove's leather-wrapped hand nearly makes him strangle himself. He is also "confined to a wheelchair." The disabilities of both doctors apparently resulted from foul-ups in their nefarious experiments. They are "crippled" as a consequence of their evil.

One of the most popular adversaries of the TV adventure series *Wild, Wild West* was the criminal genius, yet another doctor, Miguelito P. Loveless, a "hunch-backed dwarf." Michael Dunn, a marvelous and talented actor, spent much of his career relegated to such horrific roles. In one episode, Dr. Loveless says to the story's hero: "I grow weary of you, Mr. West. I weary of the sight of your strong, straight body." This brilliant villain repeatedly hatches grandiose schemes to wreak havoc and overthrow the U.S. government, with an obvious motive: he wants revenge on the world, presumably the able-bodied world. Disabled villains, raging against their "fate" and hating those who have escaped such "affliction," often seek to retaliate against "normals."

Other criminal characters may operate on a less magnificent scale, but act from the same animus. In the "Hookman" (1973) episode of *Hawaii Five-O*, a double-amputee sniper who had lost both hands in a foiled bank robbery blamed the series's hero and pledged to avenge his "maiming" by killing the police detective. Or consider the "one-armed man," the real murderer in one of the most popular series in television history, *The Fugitive*. (Bill Raisch was another handicapped actor confined to criminal roles because of his disability.)

The connection between criminality and disability continues. In 1984, the short-lived series *Hot Pursuit* unsuccessfully tried a variation on the "fugitive" formula. This time an innocent woman accused of murder was chased by the real killer, a one-*eyed* hit man. Another recent series, a modern-day western, *The Yellow Rose* (1983–1984), featured Chuck

Connors as Hollister, a greedy and vengeful oilman who walks with a limp, supporting himself with a cane. The scene introducing this character made clear the connection between his nastiness and his handicap. An establishing long shot showed him "hobbling" toward the camera, with a cut to a close-up of the "bad" leg and the cane.

Another recent disabled villain—not a criminal, but a "bad guy" just the same—appeared in the popular British miniseries *The Jewel in the Crown* (broadcast on American public television in 1984–1985). This dramatization of the last years of British colonial rule in India revolved around one Ronald Merrick, a police investigator and army intelligence officer who is arrogant, deceitful, and viciously racist. As the result of a battle injury, the left side of his face is disfigured and he loses his left arm. Like Doctor No, Doctor Strangelove, and a number of other maimed or amputee bad guys, he acquires a black leather–covered prosthetic limb. This dramatic device recurs frequently enough that one begins to wonder about the psychosexual significance of the connection between blackness, badness, amputation, and artificial arms.

Giving disabilities to villainous characters reflects and reinforces, albeit in exaggerated fashion, three common prejudices against handicapped people: disability is a punishment for evil; disabled people are embittered by their "fate"; disabled people resent the nondisabled and would, if they could, destroy them. In historic and contemporary social fact, it is, of course, nondisabled people who have at times endeavored to destroy people with disabilities. As with popular portrayals of other minorities, the unacknowledged hostile fantasies of the stigmatizers are transferred to the stigmatized. The nondisabled audience is allowed to disown its fears and biases by "blaming the victims," making them responsible for their own ostracism and destruction.

Closely related to the criminal characterization, but distinct from it, is the depiction in horror stories of the disabled person as "monster." The subtext of many horror films is fear and loathing of people with disabilities. As with the equation of disability and criminality, the horrific characterization long antedates television and persists most frequently in horror films made for theatrical release. Still, television perpetuates the "monster" image not only by broadcasting these theatrical films, but also by producing new versions of horror classics. The most prominent recent examples are the TV movie remakes of those perennial favorites *The Hunchback of Notre Dame* (1981) and *The Phantom of the Opera* (1983).

The most obvious feature of "monster" characterizations is their extremism. The physical disabilities typically involve disfigurement of the face and head and gross deformity of the body. As with the criminal characterization, these visible traits express disfigurement of personality and deformity of soul. Once again, disability may be represented as the cause of evildoing, punishment for it, or both.

Further, the depiction of the disabled person as "monster" and the criminal characterization both express to varying degrees the notion that disability involves the loss of an essential part of one's humanity. Depending on the extent of disability, the individual is perceived as more or less subhuman. These images reflect what Erving Goffman describes as the fundamental nature of stigma: the stigmatized person is regarded as "somehow less than human." Such depictions also exemplify the "spread effect" of prejudice. The stigmatized trait assumedly taints every aspect of the person, pervasively spoiling social identity.[2]

That "spread effect" is evident in an extension of the notion of loss of humanity, the idea that disability results in loss of self-control. The disabled character thus endangers the rest of society. The dangerous disabled person is not necessarily a criminal or a malevolent monster, but may be a tragic victim of fate, as with Lenny in the nonhorror story *Of Mice and Men* (1939, 1969, 1981, 1992). Whatever the specific nature of the disability, it unleashes violent propensities that "normally" would be kept in check by internal mechanisms of self-control.

Violent loss of self-control results in the exclusion of the disabled person from human community. Often in horror stories, and virtually always in criminal characterizations, it is the disability itself and the resultant dangerous behavior that separates and isolates the disabled character from the rest of society. But in some "monster" stories, for instance *The Hunchback of Notre Dame*, the disabled person is excluded because of the fear and contempt of the nondisabled majority. Still, even when the handicapped character is presented sympathetically as a victim of bigotry, it remains clear that severe disability makes social integration impossible. While viewers are urged to pity Quasimodo or Lenny, we are let off the hook by being shown that disability or bias or both must forever ostracize severely disabled persons from society.

For both monstrous and criminal disabled characters, the final and only possible solution is often death. In most cases, it is fitting and just punishment. For sympathetic "monsters," death is the tragic but inevitable, necessary, and merciful outcome. Again we can "sympathize" with the mentally retarded Lenny, while avoiding our fears and biases about him, and escape the dilemma of his social accommodation and integration.

During the 1970s and 1980s, another depiction of persons with severe disabilities emerged: the severely physically disabled character who seeks suicide as a release from the living death of catastrophic disablement. This was the theme of the play and motion picture *Whose Life Is It, Anyway?*, the TV movie *An Act of Love*, and the theatrical drama *Nevis Mountain Dew*. In the first two stories, recently spinal cord–injured quadriplegics request assisted suicide, and in the last, a postpolio respiratory quadriplegic asks his family to unplug his iron lung. The ostensible subject of the first and second dramas is the arrogance and oppressive power of a medical establishment gone wild, which at exorbitant expense keeps alive suffering people who would be better off dead. But just beneath the surface of all of these tales runs a second unacknowledged theme, the horror of a presumed "vegetable-like" existence following severe disablement.

These stories present distinct parallels with the "monster" characterization. Disability again means loss of one's humanity. The witty, combative central character in *Whose Life Is It, Anyway?* refers to himself as a "vegetable" and says that he is "not a man" anymore. The disabled persons in the other two dramas make similar statements of themselves. Severe disability also means loss of control. Unlike the criminal and "monster" characterizations, it does not mean loss of moral self-control, since the disabled would-be suicides clearly have a moral sensibility superior to those who would force them to live. Rather, disability means a total physical dependency that deprives the individual of autonomy and self-determination.

Disability again results in separation from the community. This exclusion is not presented as necessary to protect society from danger, as with the monstrous disabled character. Nor is it the result of discrimination or inaccessibility. It is portrayed as the inevitable consequence of a serious physical impairment that prevents normal functioning, normal relationships, and normal productivity. All of these dramas distort or ignore the possibilities of rehabilitation and modern assistive technology. They also totally avoid considering what effects the enforcement of antidiscrimination and accessibility laws would have on the activities, identities, and sense of self-worth of disabled individuals.

Finally, as with the "monster" and criminal characterizations, these dramas present death as the only logical and humane solution. But instead of eliminating the disabled person who is a violent threat, it relieves both the individual viewer and society of the impossible emotional, moral, and financial burden of severe disability. The disabled characters choose death themselves, beg for it as release from their insupportable existence. The nondisabled characters resist this decision, but then reluctantly bow to it as necessary and merciful. Once again, the nondisabled audience is allowed to avoid confronting its own fears and prejudices. It is urged to compliment itself for its compassion in supporting death as the only sensible solution to the problems of people with severe disabilities.

Even when bigotry is presented as a fundamental problem confronting severely disabled persons, as in *The Elephant Man* (1980), the final solution, the choice of the disabled character himself, is suicide. Whether because of prejudice or paralysis, disability makes membership in the community and meaningful life itself impossible; death is preferable. Better dead than disabled.

The most prevalent image in film and especially in television during the past several decades has been the maladjusted disabled person. These stories involve characters with physical or sensory, rather than mental, handicaps. The plots follow a consistent pattern: the disabled central characters are bitter and self-pitying because, however long they have been disabled, they have never adjusted to their handicaps, have never accepted themselves as they are. Consequently, they treat nondisabled family and friends angrily and manipulatively. At first, the nondisabled characters, feeling sorry for them, coddle them, but eventually they realize that in order to help the disabled individuals adjust and cope they must "get tough." The stories climax in a confrontation scene in which a nondisabled character gives the disabled individual an emotional "slap in the face" and tells the disabled person to stop feeling sorry for him or herself. Accepting the rebuke, the disabled characters quit complaining and become well-adjusted adults.

These portrayals suggest that disability is a problem of psychological self-acceptance, of emotional adjustment. Social prejudice rarely intrudes. In fact, the nondisabled main characters have no trouble accepting the individuals with disabilities. Moreover, they understand better than the handicapped characters the true nature of the problem.

Typically, disabled characters lack insight about themselves and other people, and require emotional education, usually by a nondisabled character. In the end, nondisabled persons supply the solution: they compel the disabled individuals to confront themselves.

The drama of adjustment seems to have developed in the aftermath of World War II, probably in response to the large numbers of disabled veterans returning from that conflict. Note, for instance, that two of the most powerful examples appeared in the films *The Best Years of Our Lives* (1946) and *The Men* (1950). This genre became a staple of television in the 1960s, 1970s, and 1980s.

Paradoxically, this depiction represents progress in the portrayal of disabled persons. The criminal and "monster" characterizations show that disability deprives its victims of an essential part of their humanity, separates them from the community, and ultimately requires that they be put to death. In contrast, the dramas of adjustment say that disability does not inherently prevent deaf, blind, or physically handicapped people from living meaningfully and productively and from having normal friendships and romantic relationships. But these stories put the responsibility for any problems squarely and almost exclusively on the disabled individual. If they are socially isolated, it is not because the disability inevitably has cut them off from the community or because society has rejected them. Refusing to accept themselves with their handicaps, they have chosen isolation.

A recurring explicit or implicit secondary theme of many stories of adjustment is the idea of compensation. God or nature or life compensates handicapped people for their loss, and the compensation is spiritual, moral, mental, and emotional. In an episode of *Little House on the Prairie*, "Town Party, Country Party" (1974), about a "lame" schoolgirl, Charles, the father, says that many "cripples" seem to have "special gifts." Laura, his daughter, asks if those gifts include "gumption." Yes, he answers, and goodness of heart too. Other stories represent blind people with special insights into human nature (for instance, the blind old black man in *Boone*, a short-lived 1983 TV series) or paraplegic detectives with superior skills (*Ironside*). Far from contradicting the image of the maladjusted disabled person, the notion of compensation reiterates it in yet another way. Compensation comes to those who cope. It is a "gift" to handicapped individuals who responsibly deal with their "afflictions."

Nonfictional television programs, particularly magazine shows such as *That's Incredible, Real People,* and *Ripley's Believe It or Not,* frequently present handicapped individuals who are the opposite of the fictional "maladjusted" disabled person. Repeatedly they recount stories of achievement and success, of heroic overcoming. Over and over they display inspiring blind carpenters, paraplegic physicians, and "handicapable" athletes. These "real-life" stories of striving and courage seem the antithesis of the bitter and self-pitying "cripples" in dramas of adjustment, but both stem from the same perception of the nature of disability: disability is primarily a problem of emotional coping, of personal acceptance. It is not a problem of social stigma and discrimination. It is a matter of individuals overcoming not only the physical impairments of their own bodies but, more important, the emotional consequences of such impairments. Both fictional and nonfictional stories convey the message that success or failure in living with a disability results almost solely from the emotional choices, courage, and character of the individual.

Both the dramas of adjustment and the nonfictional presentations of people with disabilities stem from the common notion that with the proper attitude one can cope with and conquer any situation or condition, turning it into a positive growth experience. Nothing can defeat us; only we can defeat ourselves. This belief in the power of a positive mental outlook, so widely and successfully marketed in therapies, psychologies, and sects, not only currently but throughout American history, suggests a primary reason for the popularity of stories about disabled people adjusting and overcoming. It points to one of the social and cultural functions of that image and to one of the primary social roles expected of people with disabilities: in a culture that attributes success or failure primarily to individual character, "successful" handicapped people serve as models of personal adjustment, striving, and achievement. In the end, accomplishment or defeat depends only on one's attitude toward oneself and toward life. If someone so tragically "crippled" can overcome the obstacles confronting them, think what you, without such a "handicap," can do.

Another obvious social function of the psychologized image of physical and sensory disability is to make it an individual rather than a social problem. Prejudice and discrimination rarely enter into either fictional or nonfictional stories, and then only as a secondary issue. In fictional productions, nondisabled persons usually treat disabled people badly, not because of bias, but out of insensitivity and lack of understanding. It becomes the responsibility of the disabled individual to "educate" them, to allay their anxieties and make them feel comfortable. For instance, in an episode of *Little House on the Prairie*, "No Beast So Fierce" (1982), a boy who stutters is told that he must patiently help the other children to accept him and then they will stop ridiculing him.

Nonfictional programs also generally avoid or obscure the issue of prejudice. In an interview on *Hour Magazine*, a paraplegic teenage fashion model briefly mentioned repeated professional rejection and discrimination because of her disability. Diverting her from that subject, the interviewer concentrated his questions on her strenuous efforts to learn to walk. (By then she was up to twelve steps.) Presumably, walking would make her a more acceptable and attractive model than using a wheelchair.

Segments about disabled people on magazine shows and news broadcasts frequently focus on medical and technological advances. They also often present "human interest" stories about individuals with disabilities performing some physical feat to demonstrate that they are not "handicapped," only "physically challenged." One could argue that these features demonstrate that medical and technological innovations are increasingly neutralizing physical impairments and that they and the "human interest" stories show that attitudes rather than disabilities limit people. But simultaneously they reinforce the notion that disability is fundamentally a physical problem requiring a medical or mechanical fix. They also suggest that disabled people can best prove their social acceptability, their worthiness of social integration, by displaying some physical capability. Finally, these features also reiterate, with the active complicity of the disabled participants themselves, the view that disability is a problem of individual emotional coping and physical overcoming, rather than an issue of social discrimination against a stigmatized minority.

The reactions of disabled people themselves to "human interest" stories are particularly illuminating. Some praise these features for showing that "physically inconvenienced" folks are as able as so-called "normals." Others criticize such "super-crip" segments for continuing to portray handicapped people as "incredible," extraordinary, or freakish. Both responses, it would seem, stem from the same concern and aim: increasingly and in various ways, for instance, in the debate over the language of disability, people with disabilities are rejecting the stigmatized social identity imposed upon them.[3] They are struggling to fashion for themselves a positive personal and public identity. Whether or not "human interest" stories in fact promote an alternative image, handicapped people themselves clearly intend to oppose stigma and discrimination. Stigma and discrimination are still especially powerful regarding sexuality and romance. In a sexually supercharged culture that places almost obsessive emphasis on attractiveness, people with various disabilities are often perceived as sexually deviant and even dangerous, asexual, or sexually incapacitated either physically or emotionally. Film and television stereotypes reflect and reinforce these common biases.

Criminal disabled male characters convey a kinky, leering lust for sex with gorgeous "normal" women. Dr. Loveless, the hunch-backed dwarf super-criminal in *Wild, Wild West*, surrounds himself with luscious women. The Nazi dwarf in the film comedy *The Black Bird* (1974) displays a voracious appetite for sex with statuesque beauties. Dr. Strangelove salivates over the prospect of having his share of nubile young women to perpetuate the human race in underground caverns following a nuclear holocaust. "Monster" disabled characters menace beautiful women who would ordinarily reject them. The disfigured phantom of the opera kidnaps a woman who reminds him of his dead wife. Quasimodo, the hunchback of Notre Dame, rescues and tenderly cares for a woman with whom he has obviously fallen in love. But there is always an undertone of sexual tension, of sexual danger. We are never quite sure what he might do to her.

Mentally retarded adult men also at times appear as sexually menacing figures, partly because of their supposed inability to control their emotions, to gauge their own strength, and to restrain a propensity toward violence. Thus, George mercifully kills his friend Lenny *(Of Mice and Men)* after Lenny accidentally breaks the neck of a beautiful young woman. Sexual menace, deviancy, and danger stem from the loss of control often represented as inherent in the experience of disability .

In other stories, physical paralysis results in asexuality or sexual incapacitation. The quadriplegic characters in *Whose Life Is It, Anyway?*, *An Act of Love*, and *Nevis Mountain Dew* opt for suicide partly because they believe they have lost the ability to function sexually. Neither of the first two films examines the reality of sexual physiology among people with spinal-cord injuries, or the possibilities of sexual rehabilitation. *Nevis Mountain Dew* inaccurately represents sensory deprivation and sexual dysfunction as consequences of polio. But these individuals, and characters with less severe physical disabilities in other stories, have lost something more important than the physical capacity to function sexually. Disability has deprived them of an essential part of their humanness: their identities as sexual beings. More than one male character with a disability refers to himself as "only half a man."

Even when a disability does not limit sexual functioning, it may impair the person emotionally. Disabled characters may be quite capable of physical lovemaking but spurn opportunities for romance because of a lack of self-acceptance, a disbelief that anyone could love them with their "imperfections." Nondisabled characters have no trouble finding the disabled persons attractive or falling in love with them, and have no difficulty in accepting them with their disabilities. From the double-amputee veteran in *The Best Years of Our Lives* (1946) to a quadriplegic accountant in "A Marriage Made in Heaven," an episode of *Highway to Heaven* (1985), disabled characters require convincing that they are loveable and that a romantic relationship is workable despite their disabilities. These depictions fly in the face of the real-life experiences of many handicapped men and women who find that even the most minor impairments result in romantic rejection. Once again, popular entertainments invert social reality and allow the nondisabled audience to disown its anxieties and prejudices about disabled people. The source of the "problem" is shifted to the stigmatized person himself or herself, in another version of blaming the victim.

In the past, most stories presenting a positive image of disabled people and romance have involved blind characters. Recently, a few productions have presented people with physical disabilities as attractive and sexual. Most prominent among these are Jon Voight's paraplegic Vietnam veteran in *Coming Home* and an episode of the TV situation comedy *Facts of Life* starring Geri Jewell, an actress with cerebral palsy. What distinguishes these and a handful of other portrayals is the self-assurance of the disabled characters regarding their own sexuality and romantic value. They enter relationships out of the strength of their own identities as persons with disabilities.

These romantic portrayals and other new characterizations have slowly begun to appear, partly as a result of the increasing impact of the disability civil-rights movement and the growing media awareness of the disability community. Even while previous stereotypes have persisted, a few productions have struggled to "read" these evolving events and to respond to a developing sociopolitical consciousness about disabled people. The resulting images are fascinatingly contradictory. Elements of a minority group view of disabled people jostle uncomfortably with the themes of the drama of adjustment.

This complicated trend first appeared in *The Other Side of the Mountain* (1977) and *The Other Side of the Mountain, Part II* (1979). This film biography of Jill Kinmont turned her story into a traditional account of overcoming severe disability, while almost completely ignoring her struggle to combat discrimination in education and employment. However, one important scene showed her confronting prejudice when a professor praises her as an "inspiration" while declaring that she will never get a teaching job. Subsequently, the TV movie *The Ordeal of Bill Carney* (1981) dramatized the "real-life" landmark legal battle of a quadriplegic father to gain custody of his two sons. The characterization of Carney, according to Carney himself, distorted his personal life by fitting it into the stereotype of coping, showing him as frequently bitter and depressed, and particularly maladjusted in a sexual and romantic relationship. In contrast, his paraplegic lawyer was portrayed as having an emotionally and sexually healthy relationship with his wife. More important, the film showed the attorney militantly defending Carney's legal right to raise his children and the lawyer's own right of physical access to public places.

Contradictions of characterization and theme have also appeared in episodic television. The *T. J. Hooker* segment "Blind Justice" (1983) presented a blind woman in physical danger because she had witnessed a murder. Here is a recurring stereotype: a blind person in jeopardy, usually a woman, who tells of the terror of "living in darkness." But in this instance, the stereotype was mitigated and complicated because the woman was also presented as an advocate of the rights of handicapped people, and Hooker was given a speech about the need to end bias against people with disabilities. Similarly, an episode of *Quincy*, "Give Me Your Weak" (1983), showed hundreds of politically active disabled people demonstrating in favor of the "Orphan Drugs Bill" pending in Congress. But the story also followed the descent into self-pity of a woman who succumbed to her disability until her husband rebuked her and demanded that she act responsibly again. An installment of *Alice* (1984) focused on accessibility for wheelchair users, clearly a response to that pressing social and policy question. But it treated accessibility as an act of generosity that the nondisabled should perform to make things easier for "the handicapped," rather than an issue of the civil and legal rights of disabled people.

A few recent productions have directly dealt with the issue of prejudice. *The Elephant Man* showed the dehumanizing exploitation and bigotry inflicted on a severely disabled man; "Little Lou," an episode of *Little House on the Prairie* (1983), told of a short-statured man denied employment because of discrimination. Unfortunately, instead of showing such bias as widespread, this story had only one prejudiced character, the cartoonishly obnoxious and snobbish Mrs. Oleson. The weakness of both dramas was their indulgence in melodramatic sentimentality.

More realistic was the powerful "For Love of Joshua" on *Quincy* (1983), which examined the denial of medical treatment and nutrition to developmentally disabled newborns and showed the possibilities of independent living for intellectually handicapped people. The story climaxed with an eloquent courtroom speech by a teenager with Down's syndrome protesting prejudice against mentally retarded people. In the theatrical film *Mask* (1985), a teenager with a rare facially disfiguring disease confronts discrimination in education, social ostracism, and romantic rejection. He and his mother militantly resist prejudice. Unfortunately, as in *The Elephant Man*, the movie lets the audience off the hook when the youth dies. It is easier to regret prejudice if its victims won't be around.

If stereotyping of handicapped persons has prevailed in both fictional and nonfictional television programming, the problem in TV commercials has been the total exclusion, until recently, of people with disabilities. Sponsors have feared that the presence of individuals with visible handicaps would alienate consumers from their products. They also have failed to recognize the substantial population of disabled Americans as potential customers. Additionally, they have asserted, not without reason, that by casting performers with disabilities in their commercials they would incur the charge of exploitation. As a result, past efforts to integrate commercials have met with massive resistance.

In 1983, 1984, and early 1985, commercials using handicapped performers began to appear. Departing significantly from past practices, these spots may signal a trend. In mid-1983, CBS broadcast a series of promos for its fall schedule. One showed a paraplegic wheelchair racer. Another had a deaf couple signing, "I love you." "I love you too." Significantly, these commercials garnered not only praise from the disability community, but also criticism from at least one nondisabled TV critic who implied that CBS was exploiting handicapped people. More important breakthroughs came in 1984. Levi's jeans, a major sponsor of ABC's coverage of the 1984 Summer Olympics, presented jazzy spots showing hip young adults, including one with a beautiful woman walking next to a young man in a sports wheelchair who pops a wheelie and spins his chair around. Late in 1984, MacDonald's "Handwarmin'" commercial featured patrons of the restaurant chain clapping rhythmically and enjoying its food, warmth, and conviviality. One of them is a young woman seated in a wheelchair. In May 1985, network commercials for Kodak and *People Magazine* included wheelchair users, and, most important, a spot for the Plymouth Voyager prominently featured a middle-aged man on crutches praising the car.

These commercials represent a major departure in several ways. Most obvious and important, all include disabled persons in efforts to promote products, whether hamburgers, blue jeans, TV shows, magazines, cameras, or cars. They seek out handicapped Americans as a market and audience; they reject the fear that nondisabled consumers will be distressed or offended. Further, in order to sell their products, these commercials present a new image of disabled persons. They are not portrayed as helpless and dependent, but rather as attractive, active, and "with it," involved and competitive, experiencing "normal" relationships, and in the auto commercial, smart about what they buy. Ironically, these commercials offer perhaps the most positive media images of people with disabilities to date.

Positive images in commercials and other programs reflect the growing sociopolitical perception of disabled people as a minority group and the increasing impact of the disability civil-rights movement. Whether these new depictions will become an important trend depends partly on the response from the disability community itself. Advertisers and broadcasters pay close attention to the reactions of various audiences. They are more likely to expand inclusion of disabled performers in commercials and other programming if they receive positive reinforcement from the disability community. By the same token, they will avoid stereotyping and discrimination only if they know that such practices will evoke a negative reaction from handicapped viewers. It is *organized* constituencies, of whatever size, that have brought about changes in broadcasting and advertising. Although the disability community and civil-rights movement have slowly been becoming more media conscious, concerted efforts to alter media images have thus far remained on a comparatively small scale.

Meanwhile, representations of people with disabilities in television, film, literature, and the arts needs more detailed investigation. It seems probable that an analysis of not only the "monster," criminal, and maladjusted characterizations, but also other types, would reveal a hierarchy of disability, involving a complex interaction among such factors as visibility, severity, mode of functioning, and proximity to the face and head. Such studies should draw upon psychological and social-psychological explorations of the dynamics of prejudice against disabled people. That linkage would deepen our understanding of both the images themselves and the social and cultural attitudes they express. Students of those images should also examine their historical evolution. How have they changed over time? These historical developments should also be connected with the historical experience of disabled people in various societies and cultures. What was their social and economic condition? How did their societies regard and treat them? In short, we need a social and cultural history of disabled people.

The scholarly task is to uncover the hidden history of disabled people and to raise to awareness the unconscious attitudes and values embedded in media images. The political task is to liberate disabled people from the paternalistic prejudice expressed in those images and to forge a new social identity. The two are inseparable.

Notes

1. Michael Wood, *America in the Movies* (New York, 1975), 16–18.

2. Erving Goffman, *Stigma: Notes on the Management of Spoiled Identity* (Englewood Cliffs, 1963), 3; Beatrice Wright, *Physical Disability: A Psychological Approach* (New York, 1960), 8.

3. Paul K. Longmore, "A Note on Language and the Social Identity of Disabled People," *American Behavioral Scientist* 28:3 (January–February 1985), 419–23.

THREE

ETHICS AND ADVOCACY

Elizabeth Bouvia, Assisted Suicide, and Social Prejudice

In 1983, Elizabeth Bouvia, a Southern California woman with cerebral palsy, said she'd rather be dead than disabled. Public opinion generally seemed to assume that her bid to die made sense. "Right-to-die" campaigners energetically promoted her request that a doctor aid her death. The American Civil Liberties Union of Southern California reflexively and unreflectively supplied her with legal assistance to achieve that end. In order to present a disability rights perspective on the case, a group of Southern California activists organized ourselves as the Disability Rights Coordinating Council. As the movement to legalize assisted suicide pushed on over the next half decade, we too expanded our opposition. We broadened our critical analysis of the ideology of disability that has significantly shaped the pro-suicide crusade. The essay that follows was my first systematic examination of assisted suicide advocacy.

Current discussion of assisted suicide is mainly focused on terminally ill persons. In fact, the most prominent and vigorous suicide rights activists seek legalization of assisted suicide not only for those who are terminally ill, but also for an array of other socially devalued and disadvantaged persons, most notably, people with disabilities and older people. Explicitly or implicitly underlying their arguments, and the arguments of many medical cost containment advocates as well, is a gen-

Originally published in slightly different form as Paul K. Longmore, *Elizabeth Bouvia, Assisted Suicide, and Social Prejudice*, 3 ISSUES IN LAW & MED. 141 (1987). Reprinted with permission. Copyright © 1987 by the National Legal Center for the Mentally Dependent & Disabled, Inc.

erally unquestioning adoption and reinforcement of social prejudices against people with disabilities, the elderly, and even sick people. This article concentrates on the historical and contemporary experience of disabled people in relation to this issue.

A hidden but powerful component of any discussion about disabled people must be brought to the surface and addressed: the usually unacknowledged and unconscious fear and prejudice of many nonhandicapped persons toward people with disabilities. It involves bias against those who look different and function differently. It reflects hostility toward those who require and increasingly demand alternative physical and social arrangements to accommodate them and in some cases need a larger share of societal resources. It stems from the frightened belief that disability inevitably means loss of control, social isolation, loss of an essential part of one's humanity, and the related deep-seated anxiety that this could happen to me or to someone close to me. At times, these fears and prejudices burst out in violent words and deeds, but usually, and perhaps even more dangerously, they are masked by an avowed compassion, contempt cloaking itself in paternalism.

Only recently have historians begun to reconstruct the social history of persons with disabilities and the ideological history of "disability." We have learned enough to enable us to trace the contours of those histories, particularly for the modern era. Historical research is substantiating that, whatever the social setting and whatever the disability, people with disabilities have been, and are, subjected to a common set of prejudicial values and attitudes and share a common experience of discrimination.[1]

Prior to the eighteenth century, people with disabilities in Western societies were most probably regarded as locked in an immutable condition that rendered them subhuman. The emergence of a medical model in the modern era redefined disability as a biological insufficiency that could be ameliorated by what we now call professional intervention. It came to be believed that treatment could cure, or at least correct, most disabilities or their functional concomitants enough for handicapped individuals to conduct themselves in a socially acceptable manner. This paradigm became the basis of what has developed into vast systems of medical and vocational rehabilitation, special education, and social welfare. Yet, despite their optimistic ideologies, professionals in these fields and the societies in which they operated have often regarded people with disabilities as unfit to direct their own lives, to participate in society, or to live at all. Repeatedly, this has justified making them objects of professional supervision, often throughout their lives. The modern history of people with disabilities has been pervaded by professional paternalism.[2]

Recent studies of the history of deaf people and mentally retarded people have shown that, by the late nineteenth century, nonhandicapped professionals had concluded that the required degree of normalization was impossible for all but a few of their charges. More and more, people with disabilities came to be regarded as an unproductive element of society—a drain on social resources. For example, in a speech entitled "The Imbecile and Epileptic versus the Tax-payer and the Community," Martin W. Barr, a leader at the turn of the century in the field of "feeblemindedness," declared: "Of all dependent classes there are none that drain so entirely the social and financial life of the body politic as the imbecile, unless it be its close associate, the epileptic." The "feeble-minded" and people with other disabilities were viewed as a burden to themselves and to their families, so burdensome that they undermined and might destroy those families. It was even suggested by professionals that keeping some disabled people alive violated the laws and processes of nature that worked to weed out the unfit. Eugenicists considered euthanasia essential in society's battle to protect its "germ plasm and rid itself of defectives." Increasingly, in the late nineteenth and early twentieth centuries, experts not only adopted, but promoted, the pseudoscientific linkage between heredity, a wide range of social problems, and disability. For instance, mentally retarded people were often blamed for poverty, vice, and crime. Decrying the "Burden of Feeble-mindedness," the influential Walter Fernald asserted in 1912: "The adult males become the town loafers and incapables, the irresponsible pests of the neighborhood, petty thieves, purposeless destroyers of property, incendiaries, and very frequently violators of women and girls. . . . It has been truly said that feeble-mindedness is the mother of crime, pauperism and degeneracy." Medical and social-service specialists in disability now offered a "scientific" basis for the ancient prejudice linking disability with evil. Professionals such as Fernald and Barr warned of "the menace of the feeble-minded." Oralist educators of deaf people and some orthopedists who sought to correct those with physical disabilities used similar language and made parallel ascriptions. Assimilation was unthinkable. The only possible solution could be permanent sequestration of some, segregation of others. But such regulation was not enough, for the "unfit" might reproduce themselves. So eugenicists campaigned for laws to mandate sterilization of deaf people, blind people, people with developmental and other disabilities. A majority of the states adopted sterilization statutes affecting some of these groups.[3]

The arguments used by American eugenicists were also used in early-twentieth-century Germany: handicapped persons were said to have "lives without value." They were economically unproductive. They were a burden to society. The German proponents of euthanasia defined as "mentally dead" any person who was, in their terms, unproductive and needed care from another person. From 1934 on under the Nazi regime, German school children were given math problems such as the following: "A mental patient costs 4 RM [Reich Marks] each day. A crippled person costs 3.50 RM per day. . . . a) Analyse these figures on the basis of the fact that in Germany there are 300,000 mental patients in institutions. b) On the basis of 4 RM per day what is their total cost each year?"[4]

Some eugenicists also obscured the distinction between forced euthanasia at the hands of physicians and a patient's right to die. Nazi euthanasia propagandists even advocated assisted suicide. A 1941 propaganda film, *Ich Klage an* (I accuse), presented the story of a woman with multiple sclerosis who fears, not death, but prolonged suffering. A friend yields to her request that he assist her to die. The film's climactic moment at his murder trial becomes an indictment, not of him, but of a law that would condemn someone for an act of mercy. This motion picture was planned as an opening wedge to prepare the German public to accept the program to exterminate disabled people.[5]

The managers of the Nazi euthanasia program pledged that institutionalized disabled persons granted *gnadentod* (deliverance by death) would be carefully chosen through a series of examinations conducted by two doctors. In actual practice, of course, no such medical or procedural care was taken. One physician recalled making over 2,190 "life" or "death" decisions in seventeen days. People with disabilities were condemned to death in droves.[6]

The Allied prosecutors at Nuremberg preferred to avoid the issue of mass extermination of disabled persons. Chief U.S. counsel Robert H. Jackson explained the rationale for that stance when he said of one hospital where people with a variety of disabilities had been put to death: "To begin with, [the killings] involved only the incurably sick [i.e., disabled], insane and mentally deficient patients of the Institution. It was easy to see that they were a substantial burden to society, and life was probably of little comfort to them. It is not difficult to see how, religious scruples apart, a policy of easing such persons out of the world by a completely painless method could appeal to a hard-pressed and unsentimental people."[7] In other words, while genocide of Jews was a war crime, extermination of people with disabilities was a tough-minded mercy.

Some would argue that the evil of the Nazi euthanasia program was that it paved the way for the genocide of Jews and others. This misses the point. Personnel and techniques were transferred from the institutions where sick and handicapped people were killed to the death camps to carry out the genocide program. There was indeed a connection between German anti-Semitism and racism and the slaughter of people who were disabled, but another brand of prejudice operated here: virulent contempt of people with disabilities. The scheme aimed at exterminating people with physical, emotional, and developmental disabilities was first started in Germany and then extended to the occupied countries. The evil was not that the T4 euthanasia program took a step toward the Holocaust. T4 was a holocaust in and of itself, a handicapped holocaust.[8] That first holocaust grew out of a set of biased social values, subsequently rationalized in a formal ideology, that harbored deep prejudice against persons with disabilities. Those values were paralleled, complemented, and reinforced by German racism.

Many of those values continue to operate today. They appear most notably in discussions of euthanasia and assisted suicide. The point is not that anyone currently advocates a systematic policy of extermination as was implemented in Nazi Germany. Rather, now, as then, and as one finds throughout the modern history of people with disabilities, the same prejudicial social values operate to stigmatize and segregate disabled persons. This bigotry renders them socially dead and then justifies their physical deaths at the hands of representatives of their societies or by so-called voluntary suicide.

We further mislead ourselves if we regard the Nazi doctors as monsters. Many were well-intentioned, even compassionate men who were convinced that both society and people with disabilities themselves would be better off if they were relieved of their burdensome lives. These physicians acted, not usually out of a penchant for cruelty, but by carrying intense social prejudice against disabled people to its logical conclusion. To think of the Nazi doctors as depraved monsters only mesmerizes us about the continuing reality and danger of all forms of prejudice.[9]

For generations, people with disabilities and their nonhandicapped allies have fought to overcome prejudice and discrimination. Implicitly and increasingly explicitly, those efforts have rejected the medical model of disability in favor of a minority group model. This perspective defines "disability" as primarily a socially constructed and socially stigmatized identity. In the late nineteenth century, the National Association of the Deaf resisted attempts to suppress sign language and the signing community. In the 1930s and 1940s, working against considerable opposition, the National Federation of the Blind lobbied for "white cane" and "guide dog" laws, in effect, the first equal-access statutes. During the Great Depression, New York City's League of the Physically Handicapped, a civil-rights organization of young adults, protested job discrimination in the municipal government and in WPA projects. In the past generation, the civil-rights movement of Americans with disabilities has gained momentum. A minority group consciousness emerged among young adults with disabilities, while disabled adults of all ages sought legal protection from discrimination.[10] In the 1970s, the disability rights movement secured passage of federal laws prohibiting discrimination in federally funded programs, guaranteeing the right of equal access to public places and public transportation, and establishing the right of handicapped children to a public education. Disabled activists created "independent living" for those with severe physical disabilities, while the advocates for mentally retarded people, including a growing number of mentally retarded adults, pressed for independent-living or community-based group living arrangements. These groups lobbied for and won passage of government policies and programs providing the resources to achieve these ends. In the 1980s, disability rights activists have continued to press for civil-rights laws and public policies that will uphold the rights to equal access, education, medical and supportive services, employment, and family life.[11]

At every step of the way, this movement has met with massive resistance. From 1973 to 1977, the Nixon, Ford, and Carter administrations delayed implementing Section 504, the fundamental civil-rights law for disabled Americans. Finally, sit-ins by disability rights demonstrators forced the Carter administration to act. Higher education vigorously opposed complying with Section 504. Public transit authorities in all but a few cities have tenaciously battled against making their systems accessible, even though equal access would be cheaper in operation than segregated paratransit. During its first year, the Reagan administration tried to gut PL 94-142, the law guaranteeing handicapped children the right to a free and appropriate public education. The outcries of disability rights activists and parents of children with disabilities stopped that move.[12]

In the 1970s, the federal courts issued landmark rulings protecting the civil rights of Americans with disabilities.[13] Yet in the 1980s, the U.S. Supreme Court has repeatedly moved to restrict the scope of those rights, among other things, limiting disabled persons' right to education, the right of mentally retarded people to live in the community, and the right of disabled infants to receive medical treatment.[14] Regarding every one of these issues, judges, legislators, elected and appointed executives, transit bureaucrats, educators, liberals, and conservatives have all downplayed or ignored the socially constructed character of "disability" and the pervasiveness of prejudice against persons with disabilities. In many cases, they have also argued that equal access and equal rights cost too much and will yield too little in returns from an unproductive element of society.

Prejudice has also appeared elsewhere. Governor Richard Lamm of Colorado has gotten considerable public attention for his outspoken comments regarding medical cost containment measures and the appropriate times for older people to die. Applauding those who reject life-sustaining treatment, he said: "You've got a duty to die and get out of the way. Let the other society, our kids, build a reasonable life." It is no coincidence that he has also resisted integrating public transportation by making it accessible to persons with disabilities and has criticized special education as a waste of money because, after years of it, all mentally retarded people can do is "roll over." More violent bigotry has appeared in some localities, where attempts to establish small group homes for mentally retarded adults have met not only with protests and lawsuits, but with vandalism, beatings, and firebombings.[15]

This historical legacy and continuing reality of social oppression is the necessary background for any discussion of assisted suicide as it relates to persons with disabilities.

Prejudice reappeared in the legal case of Elizabeth Bouvia. Her experience epitomizes all of the devaluation and discrimination inflicted on disabled people by society. Because of cerebral palsy, Bouvia is quadriplegic. When she was five years old, her parents divorced, and her mother was given custody of her. When she was ten, her mother remarried and put her into an institution for handicapped children. For the next eight years, she was shunted from one facility to another. During all that time, her mother rarely visited her. Some parents, to escape the social shame of having a disabled child, adopt society's hostile attitude toward their children and reject them.[16]

At the age of eighteen, Bouvia decided to make a home for herself in the community. For eight years, in Riverside and then in San Diego, California, she lived independently, assisted by aides she hired to provide housekeeping services and to help her with her personal needs such as bathing, dressing, and eating. She paid for these aides through a California government program called In-Home Support Services (IHSS). Establishment of such programs has been one goal of the independent-living movement. Most states still do not have them. In those states, severely disabled adults like Elizabeth Bouvia must spend their lives confined to their families' homes or imprisoned in institutions. Because of her type of disability, Bouvia was legally entitled to the maximum amount available under IHSS. In fact, she received considerably less. State-mandated guidelines supposedly guarantee equal and uniform benefits statewide, but many counties deliberately seek to limit the amount of IHSS granted to disabled residents, sometimes even lying to them about their legal entitlements. Elizabeth Bouvia lived in two of the counties most notorious among disabled Californians for such abuses. The very agencies supposedly designed to enable severely physically handicapped adults like her to achieve independence and productivity in the community become yet another massive hurdle they must surmount, an enemy they must repeatedly battle but can never finally defeat.[17]

Elizabeth Bouvia wanted to get an education. She earned an A.A. at Riverside Community College and a B.A. at San Diego State University (SDSU). Deciding to pursue a career in social work, she enrolled in the master's program at SDSU. The course of study included fieldwork experience. The local hospital where she was initially placed for that experience refused to make the "reasonable accommodations" she needed and required by federal law under Section 504. The SDSU School of Social Work refused to back her up. They wanted to place her at a center where she would work only with other disabled people. She refused.

Reportedly, one of her professors told her she was unemployable and that, if they had known just how disabled she was, they would never have admitted her to the program. In fact, her disability in no way precluded her from fulfilling the requirements of the program or her profession. People with more severe disabilities work productively. The professor's statements were not only biased, they were discriminatory, again violating her civil rights under federal law.[18]

Apparently Bouvia was unaware of her legal rights, or perhaps she simply did not have the energy to fight a protracted legal battle against such formidable opponents, especially while she was confronting a series of crises in her personal life. Despairing that she would never achieve the productive professional career she had worked so hard for, she dropped out of school.[19]

Bouvia never got to the point of confronting the final and most difficult obstacle to work. By getting a job and earning no more than $300 per month, she would have quickly lost her government-financed disability benefits, including the In-Home Support Services which made it possible for her to go to work in the first place and would be essential to her continuing to work. This is euphemistically called a "work disincentive." It is, in fact, a penalty imposed on disabled persons who violate the pervasive social prejudice that they cannot productively contribute to the economy and community and that they should be segregated out of the job market and labor force. Richard Scott, a leading advocate of "aid in dying" and the attorney who has led the fight for Bouvia's supposed legal right to medically assisted suicide, shares that bias. "Quadriplegics," he said, "cannot work."[20]

Government work penalties have cost the lives of other disabled persons. In 1978, Lynn Thompson, a quadriplegic young woman attempting to make a life for herself in Los Angeles, found her efforts to work blocked by these same "disincentives." She had been working in unknowing violation of Social Security regulations. The Social Security Administration finally told her that she owed them an overpayment of $10,000. They also incorrectly said that her IHSS and Medi-Cal would be cut off. In despair, she left a tape-recorded suicide message describing what they had put her through. Significantly, it was this socially induced ordeal that caused her suicide, not her disability, a progressive and degenerative form of muscular dystrophy.[21]

Los Angeles disability rights activists managed to get *60 Minutes* to report the story of Lynn Thompson. Despite the negative publicity, the

Social Security Administration continued to oppose removal of work "disincentives" for eight more years. Finally, in 1986, the agency yielded to the elimination of some, though not all, "disincentives," and only for recipients of Supplemental Security Income (SSI). More than five million persons on Social Security Disability Insurance (SSDI) are still denied the right to work, except at sheltered-workshop wages. Dr. Douglas Martin, a leading authority on disability policy, estimates that, if these programs were thoroughly reformed and if accessibility and antidiscrimination laws were vigorously enforced, 90 percent of SSI and SSDI recipients could work at least part-time. What blocks the Lynn Thompsons and Elizabeth Bouvias from productive work is not disability, but discrimination.[22]

Outside school, Elizabeth Bouvia faced other severe stresses. She married Richard Bouvia but did not report this marriage to the county social-service department or the federal Social Security Administration. Had she done so, those agencies would have reduced her In-Home Support Services and Supplemental Security Income benefits. "Able and available" nonhandicapped spouses are expected to provide assistance the government would pay for if the disabled partner were unmarried. This policy prevents or undermines marriages of disabled persons. The euphemism used here is "marriage disincentive," but it too is a punishment for disabled persons who violate the common prejudice that they are unfit to be wives or husbands or lovers or parents or even members of families.[23]

Additional personal stresses struck Bouvia. Her brother drowned. She became pregnant and then suffered a miscarriage. She saw the film *Whose Life Is It, Anyway?* and became severely depressed. Meanwhile, tensions in her marriage mounted. She and her husband separated. He declared later that he sought a reconciliation, but she, despairing of their relationship, decided to seek a divorce.[24]

At this point, Elizabeth Bouvia checked herself into the psychiatric unit of Riverside County Hospital. She announced her wish to end her life and requested the hospital to assist her. When they refused, she secured the services of a team of American Civil Liberties Union lawyers to help her compel the hospital to comply with her wishes. The attorneys brought in three psychiatric professionals to provide an independent evaluation. None of them had any experience or expertise in dealing with persons with disabilities. In fact, Elizabeth Bouvia has never been examined by any psychiatric or medical professional qualified to understand her life experience. She reported to these evaluators the emotionally devastating experiences of the preceding two years. She also said that she wanted to die because of her physical disability. Ignoring all of the emotional blows and the discrimination, her examiners prejudicially concluded that because of her physical condition she would never be able to achieve her life goals, that her disability was the reason she wanted to die, and that her decision for death was reasonable. These same facts were presented to the judge who heard the case in the Riverside Superior Court. He too declared that Bouvia's physical disability was the sole reason she wished to die.[25]

The trial court judge rejected the petition for assisted suicide, but in 1986, in a second round of litigation, the California Court of Appeals, despite its tortuous legal and verbal circumlocutions to prove that it was merely upholding the right to refuse medical treatment, in effect granted her a right to a judicially sanctioned, medically assisted suicide. Typical of discussions regarding disabled people and the right to die, the appellate court ruling is pervaded with ignorance and bias. The court wrote: Bouvia "suffers from degenerative and severely crippling arthritis." In fact, she has never been formally diagnosed as having arthritis. Her "physical handicaps of palsy and quadriplegia have progressed to the point where she is completely bedridden." In fact, cerebral palsy, which is the cause of her quadriplegia, rather than a separate handicap, is not a progressive condition. "She lays flat in bed and must do so the rest of her life." Her lawyers have assiduously propagated this distortion of the reality of her disability. In fact, she was never bedridden until four years ago, when, in her depressed state, she refused to get out of bed. She has been allowed to languish there ever since. When this case began, her lawyers told the court and the public that she required constant care. In fact, her in-home aides were never on duty more than six hours a day.[26]

The appeals court held that the lower court should have considered the "quality" of the life Elizabeth Bouvia would have to lead. Yet like nearly every other nonhandicapped person connected with this case, it too decided that her physical disability was the lone and exclusive reason that she had found

the quality of her life . . . diminished to the point of hopelessness, uselessness, unenjoyability and frustration.

Although alert, bright, sensitive, perhaps even brave and feisty, she must lie immobile, unable to exist except through the physical acts of others. Her mind and spirit may be free to take great flights but she herself is imprisoned and must lie physically helpless subject to the ignominy, embarrassment, humiliation and dehumanizing aspects created by her helplessness.[27]

This is a woman who operated a power wheelchair and was on her way to a master's degree and a career in social work. This is a woman who married, made love with her husband, and planned to become a mother. This is a woman who aimed at something more significant than mere physical self-sufficiency. She struggled to attain self-determination, but she was repeatedly thwarted in her efforts by discriminatory actions on the part of her government, her teachers, her employers, her parents, and her society. Contrary to the highly prejudiced view of the appeals court, what makes life with a major physical disability ignominious, embarrassing, humiliating, and dehumanizing is not the need for extensive physical assistance, but the dehumanizing social contempt toward those who require such aid.

Justice Lynn Compton's concurring opinion contains the most ominous words in this decision: "This state and the medical profession instead of frustrating her desire, should be attempting to relieve her suffering by permitting and in fact assisting her to die with ease and dignity." He expresses the hope that this case "will cause our society to deal realistically with the plight of those unfortunate individuals to whom death beckons as a welcome respite from suffering."[28]

The implications of the Bouvia case are chilling. In a society where people with disabilities are still intensely stigmatized and largely segregated and, the most disturbing feature of this case, in a society that still refuses to acknowledge the reality of that social oppression, the right to die will inevitably become a duty to die. People with major disabilities will be pressured into "choosing" to end their lives. The prejudice underlying the opinion is unmistakable. Its message to disabled people is clear: rather than upholding your right to live productively and meaningfully, this society chooses to engineer your death.

Elizabeth Bouvia's lifelong encounter with prejudice has not yet ended. At Los Angeles County–USC Medical Center, she is on a morphine drip to relieve her pain. This is far from the standard pain therapy for arthritis. Her chief attorney admits she is now addicted to the drug. Dr. David Goldstein, her attending physician, revealed at a bioethics symposium that he is not sure she even has arthritis. He also confessed that one of his staff members had warned him Bouvia might become addicted to the drug. He had replied: "So what? I mean, she's not exactly going to break into my house and steal my stereo." This is the physician her ACLU attorneys fought to have put back on the case. And this is just the sort of contempt she has encountered all her life. What does it matter how we deal with a person whose life is worthless?[29]

Some civil libertarians claim that the prejudicial attitudes and language in the appellate court ruling (not to mention in the comments of medical "experts" like Dr. Goldstein) are separate from the legal substance of the decision. How much evidence must we pile up before we can no longer deny the causal connection between pervasive social prejudice and its deadly results?

The prejudices against disabled people evident in the Bouvia case also pervade the writings of advocates of assisted suicide. That bias is often linked with prejudice against elderly people. For instance, Mary Rose Barrington, past chair of the London-based Voluntary Euthanasia Society (since renamed EXIT—The Society for the Right to Die with Dignity), is a leading British advocate of rational suicide and "planned death." In her "Apologia for Suicide," she considers suicide not only for those who are elderly and terminally ill or severely disabled, but also proposes it for those "not in fact undergoing or expecting to undergo severe suffering," someone who "is merely an elderly relation, probably a mother, in fragile health, or partially disabled, and though not acutely ill is in need of constant care and attention." She writes: "If there is no alternative to continued living, then no choice arises, and hence there can be no possibility of an older person, who is a burden to a younger person feeling a sense of obligation to release the captive attendant from willing or unwilling bondage, no questioning of the inevitability of the older person's living out her full term. But what if there were a real choice? What if a time came when, no longer able to look after oneself, the decision to live on for the maximum number of years were considered a mark of heedless egoism."[30] One cannot imagine a more open or unapologetic expression than this of bias against persons with disabilities or of the modern Western revulsion against the elderly. And those telling phrases "probably a mother" "living out *her* full term" betray gender bias too.

Responding to critics of "planned death," Barrington argues: "It is frequently said that hard-hearted people would be encouraged to make their elderly relatives feel that they had outlived their welcome and ought to remove themselves, even if they happened to be enjoying life. No one can say categorically that nothing of the sort would happen, but the sensibility of even hard-hearted people to the possible consequences of their own unkindness seems just as likely." Barrington refers to the "possible consequences" of "unkindness" as "some undesirable fringe results."[31] This is not simply a willfully naive description of age and disability prejudice. It rationalizes its deadly results.

Rationalization of those prejudices also comes from American suicide rights activists. A March 1987 newspaper interview reported the opinion of the philosopher Margaret Pabst Battin, a leading ideological exponent of assisted suicide, that "suicide assistance . . . might be warranted for elderly people worried about the prospects of extreme old age and the possibility of being without money, food, shelter, and medication. Many elderly people are enormously afraid of being totally dependent in their final years," she said. "And it's not the business of younger people to decide if old age is a tolerable situation!" The article also reported that she believes "even teenagers—at least those with catastrophic illnesses or severe mental impairments—should be entitled to receive help in killing themselves, if they believe death would be beneficial."[32]

This advocacy of assisted suicide gives society an excuse for offering elderly people and people with disabilities only the alternatives of deprivation or death. By rationalizing suicide among these oppressed groups, it helps foster a climate that will promote it. Indeed, such a climate already exists. Worldwide suicide rates among persons over sixty, notes the Austrian authority Dr. Erwin Ringel, "are high and are steadily increasing." "This may be no surprise," he continues. "If we look at the behavior of many people toward the old and even toward the merely aging, we may begin to wonder just how sincere the wish of the community is to keep its older people alive." But Ringel concludes with the "impressive and important fact that in areas where the aged enjoy real esteem (as in certain Far Eastern countries), suicide among the old is actually a rare occurrence."[33]

Not only do suicide rights advocates join disability prejudice with age prejudice, they also lump persons with disabilities with those who are terminally ill. For instance, writing about the Bouvia case, Hemlock Society founder Derek Humphry expressed that organization's support of the right to voluntary euthanasia for "a person terminally ill, or severely handicapped and deteriorating." The open-ended term "deteriorating" can be made to mean almost anything in order to justify a disabled person's suicide, as the Bouvia case shows. Even before Bouvia was being fed through a nasogastric tube, her lawyers were distorting the nature of her disability and likening her to a terminal patient. "Were Plaintiff Bouvia an 84-year-old woman whose life was prolonged solely by various tubes and numerous machines," they argued in the Riverside Superior Court, "and she sought to end such an existence, it is doubtful that this Court would even be involved. . . . Plaintiff should not be denied that same right merely because she is 26 years of age and does not yet require a machine or machines (other than her wheelchair) to prolong her piti- ful existence." A wheelchair is not a life-prolonging machine, nor will Bouvia's cerebral palsy (or arthritis) ever require such machines. As in *Whose Life Is It, Anyway?* advocates of assisted suicide twist the facts of disability to make their case. Bouvia's attorney, Richard Scott, went even further, virtually calling her disability a terminal illness: "This is not a suicide," he said. "She's dying from the effects of her cerebral palsy, which does not permit her to feed herself." By this logic, disabled peo- ple who require help to eat are receiving medical treatment that staves off, in the words of these lawyers, "the natural process of dying."[34]

Some ethicists and physicians also confound the terminally ill with people who are merely permanently disabled. This fall, the Hastings Center issued guidelines on the termination of medical treatment. Orig- inally, these were to apply in cases of terminal illness, but then the drafters decided to include people with a "disabling condition that is severe and irreversible." In other words, those of us with permanent major disabilities are no different from people who are dying. In addi- tion, cost worthiness is to be a consideration in deciding whether to con- tinue medical treatment. No leaders from the disability community were included in the drafting of these guidelines, and only two disability rights organizations were asked to comment on them.[35]

Disturbingly, the current advocates of assisted suicide, like the pro- ponents of systematic euthanasia in Germany half a century ago, also blur the distinction between voluntary and involuntary euthanasia. In her comprehensive *Ethical Issues in Suicide*, a treatise advocating assisted suicide, Margaret Pabst Battin discusses "Suicide as the Removal of So- cial Burdens." She notes that, while a disabled elderly parent or a "birth defective, chronically ill, alcoholic, retarded, or mentally disturbed" individual might demand considerable family time, care, and financial resources, in "a great many cases" they also have "salutary effects upon the family." For example, "the Down's child may give unusual affection." "But some individuals constitute a burden which is not outweighed by benefits they confer upon the family, . . . for instance when the individ- ual is irreversibly comatose, . . . as to be incapable of any communication, or so pathologically disruptive as to constitute an unrelieved psychological hardship for the family." "Removal of the burden" might be accomplished by "institutionalization of a brain-damaged child," divorce or eviction of a disruptive spouse or dependent, or counseling for the family. "But suicide will also remove the burden. . . . If an individual does impose severe burdens upon his family, friends, or associates, then suicide, if it will relieve them, might seem to be morally appropriate."[36]

How does an "irreversibly comatose" individual "incapable of any communication" choose suicide? And who chooses suicide for "a brain-damaged child?" These are not voluntary suicides. They are involuntary euthanasia. This blurring of distinctions suggests that advocates of euthanasia, whether voluntary or involuntary, are seeking means to deal with a wide variety of persons regarded as socially burdensome.

Professor Battin continues that institutionalization, medication, or divorce may "appear preferable just because of our widespread assumption that suicide is always wrong. In fact, alternatives to suicide may serve only to relocate the burden" to the state or to "a possible future spouse, and the problem arises again. This is especially true where deep-seated psychological problems or irreversible physical conditions threaten to jeopardize any new relationship."[37] One recalls that, when Elizabeth Bouvia's mother remarried, the ten-year-old child was put in an institution. Should the mother have had the right to authorize euthanasia of the little girl? Battin's confused discussion confounding voluntary suicide with forced euthanasia would seem to leave an opening for such a practice.

The use of suicide to permanently "remove" burdensome members of society recurs throughout the suicide advocacy literature. Mary Rose Barrington indirectly suggests suicide of elderly persons with disabilities as a way to deal with overpopulation and resource scarcity. "One more in the mud-hut is not a problem in the same way as one more in a small, overcrowded urban dwelling; and the British temperament demands a privacy incompatible with the more sociable Mediterranean custom of packing a grandmother and an aunt or two in the attic."[38]

Laying aside the racism and ethnocentrism of that statement, it is simply a colorful way of saying that, in order for the younger generation to maintain its preferred way and standard of living, we must convince Granny that she really ought to do herself in. It may perhaps also be worth noting the chilling irony that Mary Rose Barrington has been the administrator of a group of almshouses for older people and honorary secretary of an animal rights group.[39]

Dr. Eliot Slater more boldly supports suicide as the means to relieve society of the economic burden of people with chronic conditions. A leading British psychiatrist, he advocates suicide for "the irretrievably psychotic patient who has repeatedly shown his determination to die." Making his case for suicide of those with a variety of chronic medical problems, Slater argues that we should not "forget the welfare of society. If a chronically sick man dies, he ceases to be a burden on himself, on his family, on the health services and on the community. . . . There is, of course, absolutely no limit to the burdens we can go on piling up, by trying to keep badly damaged individuals alive. Improving techniques and increasing effort in such directions make the very words 'health service' a misnomer."[40]

Euthanasia policies to eliminate persons with disabilities and others regarded as socially burdensome have a considerable history. Battin's discussion of the ideology behind that history is particularly revealing of the values and attitudes of assisted suicide advocates. In the late nineteenth and early twentieth centuries, she reminds us, the spread of social Darwinism promoted the view that certain "less fit" members of society posed a threat to its well-being. This perspective was "quickly infected with race, class, and age prejudice," and, most important, to add what she ignores, prejudice against people with disabilities. These views were embodied in policies such as withholding medical treatment, eugenic breeding plans, and "compulsory thrift-euthanasia." The Nazi regime implemented such proposals on a massive scale.[41]

"But although social-darwinist views led to large-scale atrocities involving massive violations of human freedom," Battin argues, "the social-darwinist view of *suicide*, as distinct from involuntary 'euthanasia,' may be less easy to defeat on moral grounds."

> Social darwinism simply holds that suicide—chosen and performed by the individual—is to be welcomed as a natural self-cleansing mechanism on the part of the species. . . . Such views need not be associated with Nazism or other extermination schemes, and they may be coupled with considerable charity and sympathy for the individuals involved.
>
> We tend to find the social-darwinist view of suicide repugnant because of its association with the forced-euthanasia programs of Nazi Germany. But when this argument is applied to genuinely *voluntary* suicide, it may seem much less so: here, the individual sincerely desires to end his life, and this coincidentally works to the benefit of society as a whole.[42]

We will find this view less repugnant only if we agree with the social Darwinist premises that people with disabilities are "less fit," burdensome to themselves and everyone else, and better off dead. Given such prejudice and the earlier blurring of voluntary suicide with involuntary euthanasia, the distinction between those two forms of death made here is meaningless.

Even more revealing is Battin's discussion of the arguments against suicide of disabled persons. One argument "maintains that the collective presence of disabled or defective individuals contributes good to society even though the individuals themselves do not perform good acts or actively do good in any other way. Here, the good contributed by such individuals inheres in the responses of others to them." This view is prevalent in a wide variety of religious and nonreligious sources. David Novak writes: "One can see a need for even the helpless and infirm. Their very presence enables us to practice the human virtues of benevolence and generosity."

Battin counters: "It may be true, that contact with debilitated, disabled, deformed, or otherwise distressed persons does intensify our moral feelings and give rise to greater sympathy, benevolence, and caring for other persons in general. Such persons may serve as inspiring models, and make us more courageous in enduring our own afflictions. But to claim that those persons have an *obligation* to live (and suffer) in order to make moral individuals more humane or courageous is ethically questionable at best."[43]

A second argument holds "that the helpless and infirm may also render good to society as subjects for medical, psychological, or other experimentation." Battin questions this proposition on the same basis that she rejects the previous argument.[44]

Both suicide rights and anti-suicide advocates express prejudice in their persistent use of intensely stigmatizing language: disabled people are defective, damaged, debilitated, deformed, distressed, afflicted, anomalous, helpless and/or infirm. In contrast, nonhandicapped persons are "normal." But the bias goes deeper than the terminology. Battin's response to the anti-suicide position is deeply disturbing. Apparently, to live with disability is to "suffer" and to suffer because of disability. There is no recognition that the greatest suffering of people with disabilities is the socially stigmatized identity inflicted upon them.

She is certainly correct though that some opponents of suicide and proponents of the right to life seem to see people with disabilities as perpetual objects of their charity. This partly explains why the right-to-life movement has very strongly and commendably supported life-sustaining medical treatment as a civil right, but has been seen as absent from disabled Americans' struggle for those rights, policies, and programs necessary for a full life. By the same token, some suicide rights advocates proclaim themselves as pioneers of the civil rights of people with disabilities. But these *soi disant* champions of disability rights have been even more noticeably absent while disabled people, including Elizabeth Bouvia, have been struggling to establish their right to live meaningfully and work productively in this society.

Both the advocates of assisted suicide and many proponents of the right to life seem to recognize only three options for disabled persons: live "as objects for our pity and moral elevation," serve as subjects of experimentation, or commit suicide. The false and biased assumption here is that people with disabilities have nothing useful to contribute to society by their own efforts.[45] More important, apart from whatever good disabled individuals might contribute to others, it seems not to have occurred to either side that they might find their lives of value to themselves.

Reading through the literature of the suicide rights activists, one is struck by their willing acceptance of prejudicial assumptions about persons with disabilities. Disability renders its "victims" helpless and dependent. It robs them of the possibility of living meaningfully. It makes them emotionally, physically, and financially burdensome to themselves, their families, and society. One wades through reams of this suicide rights advocacy without finding any real acknowledgment of the intense social stigma and discrimination that segregate people with disabilities more than any other contemporary minority, deny them opportunities for education, employment, marriage, and family, rob them of social dignity and self-esteem, and inflict on many of them what can only be called "social death." One searches in vain for even a passing reference to the civil-rights movement of disabled Americans that has been battling this discrimination for at least a generation now. One finds no mention and, one concludes, no knowledge of the independent-living movement of people with major physical disabilities. Apparently, none of this has attracted the attention or interest of suicide rights activists. Indeed, nowhere else does one encounter such a reactionary and biased view of persons with disabilities, at least not in anything published since the 1930s.

Proponents of legalizing assisted suicide for terminally ill persons argue that it need not lead inevitably down a "slippery slope" to voluntary and involuntary euthanasia of other persons. It is possible, they assert, to erect barriers to prevent the slide. This is disingenuous. The most vigorous advocates of assisted suicide oppose such barriers. They have made clear their support of assisted suicide for, not only terminally ill people, but also elderly people and people with disabilities.[46]

Given the lumping together of people with disabilities with those who are terminally ill, the blurring of voluntary assisted suicide and forced "mercy" killing, and the oppressive conditions of social devaluation and isolation, blocked opportunities, economic deprivation, and enforced social powerlessness, talk of their "rational" or "voluntary" suicide is simply Orwellian Newspeak. The advocates of assisted suicide assume a nonexistent autonomy. They offer an illusory self-determination.

It is also clear that some elements in our society are seeking a solution to what they regard as the problem of economically burdensome and socially worthless people. Their arguments for euthanasia, aid-in-dying, assisted suicide, and medical cost containment simply rationalize the ultimate act of oppression. Their efforts are an assault on the rights and lives of people who are sick, old, or disabled.

Notes

Acknowledgments: I am deeply grateful to Donna Willoughby for the enormous amount of background research she did in support of this article.

1. See generally: Harlan Lane, *When the Mind Hears: A History of the Deaf* (New York, 1984); Peter L. Tyor and Leland V. Bell, *Caring for the Retarded in America: A History* (Westport, 1985); Hugh Gregory Gallagher, *FDR's Splendid Deception* (New York, 1985); Richard K. Scotch, *From Good Will to Civil Rights: Transforming Federal Disability Policy* (Philadelphia, 1985); Frank Bowe, *Handicapping America: Barriers to Disabled People* (New York, 1978); Frank Bowe, *Rehabilitating America* (New York, 1980); Paul K. Longmore, "The Life of Randolph Bourne and the Need for a History of Disabled People," *Reviews in American History* 13:4 (December 1985), 581–87; Paul K. Longmore, "Uncovering the Hidden History of Disabled People," *Reviews in American History* 15:3 (September 1987), 355–64. Since publication of this essay, the historiography of disability has burgeoned. See especially: Douglas Baynton, *Forbidden Signs: American Culture and the Campaign Against Sign Language* (Chicago, 1996); Edward V. Berkowitz, *Disabled Policy: America's Programs for the Handicapped* (New York, 1987); Robert Bogdan, *Freak Show: Presenting Human Oddities for Amusement and Profit* (Chicago, 1988); Lois Bragg, ed., *Deaf World: A Historical Reader and Primary Sourcebook* (New York, 2001); Robert M. Buchanan, *Illusions of Equality: Deaf Americans in School and Factory* (Washington, D.C., 1999); Martha Lynn Edwards, "'Let There Be a Law that No Deformed Child Shall Be Reared': The Cultural

Context of Deformity in the Ancient Greek World," *Ancient History Bulletin* 10 (July 1997), 79–92; Martha Lynn Edwards, "Women and Disability in Ancient Greece," *Ancient World* 29 (1998); Doris Zames Fleischer and Frieda Zames, *The Disability Rights Movement: From Charity to Confrontation* (Philadelphia, 2001); Robert Garland, *The Eye of the Beholder, Deformity and Disability in the Graeco-Roman World* (Ithaca, 1995); Howard S. Erlanger and William Roth, "Disability Policy: The Parts and the Whole," *American Behavioral Scientist* 28 (1985), 319–45; Rosemarie Garland Thomson, *Extraordinary Bodies: Figuring Physical Disability in American Culture and Literature* (New York, 1997); Rosemarie Garland Thomson, ed., *Freakery: Cultural Spectacles of the Extraordinary Body* (New York, 1996); David A. Gerber, ed., *Disabled Veterans in History* (Ann Arbor, 2000); David A. Gerber, "Volition and Valorization in the Analysis of the 'Careers' of People Exhibited in Freak Shows," *Disability, Handicap and Society* 7:1 (1992), 53–69; Nora Ellen Groce, *Everyone Here Spoke Sign Language: Hereditary Deafness on Martha's Vineyard* (Cambridge, 1985); Paul K. Longmore, "Conspicuous Contribution and American Cultural Dilemmas: Telethon Rituals of Cleansing and Renewal," in David Mitchell and Sharon Snyder, eds., *Discourses of Disability: The Body and Physical Difference in the Humanities* (Ann Arbor, 1997), 134–58; Paul K. Longmore and David Goldberger, "The League of the Physically Handicapped and the Great Depression: A Case Study in the New Disability History," *Journal of American History* 87:3 (December 2000), 888–922; Paul K. Longmore and Lauri Umansky, eds., *The New Disability History: American Perspectives* (New York, 2001); Floyd Matson, *Walking Alone, Marching Together: A History of the Organized Blind Movement in the United States, 1940–1990* (Washington, D.C., 1992); Richard K. Scotch, "Politics and Policy in the History of the Disability Rights Movement," *Milbank Quarterly* 67, Supplement 2, Part 2 (1989), 380–400; Richard K. Scotch and Edward D. Berkowitz, "One Comprehensive System? A Historical Perspective on Federal Disability Policy," *Journal of Disability Policy Studies* 1:3 (Fall 1990), 1–19; Henri Jacques Stiker, *The History of Disability* (Ann Arbor, 2000); Deborah Stone, *The Disabled State* (Philadelphia, 1986); James W. Trent, Jr., *Inventing the Feeble Mind: A History of Mental Retardation in the United States* (Berkeley, 1994); Phyllis Klein Valentine, "A Nineteenth-Century Experiment in Education of the Handicapped: The American Asylum for the Deaf and Dumb," *New England Quarterly* 64 (September 1991), 355–75; John Vickrey Van Cleve, "Nebraska's Oral Law of 1911 and the Deaf Community," *Nebraska History* 65 (Summer 1984), 195–220; John Vickrey Van Cleve, ed., *Deaf History Unveiled: Interpretations From the New Scholarship* (Washington, D.C., 1993); John Vickrey Van Cleve and Barry Crouch, *A Place of Their Own: Creating the Deaf Community in America* (Washington, D.C., 1989); John Williams-Searle, "Courting Risk: Disability, Masculinity, and Liability on Iowa's Railroads, 1868–1900," *Annals of Iowa* 58 (Winter 1999), 27–77; Margret A. Winzer, *The History of Special Education: From Isolation to Integration* (Washington, D.C., 1993).

2. Wolf Wolfensberger, *The Origin and Nature of Our Institutional Models* (Syracuse, 1975), 7–13; Lane, *When the Mind Hears*, 3–19, 36–37.

3. Lane, *When the Mind Hears*, 36–37, 53–59, 68–69, 83–104, 112–14, 118–19, 407; Barr speech printed in *Proceedings of the National Conference of Charities and Corrections* (1902), 162, 163, quoted in Wolfensberger, *Origin and Nature of Our Insti-

tutional Models, 34; "The Legal, Legislative and Administrative Aspects of Sterilization," in *Report of the Committee to Study and to Report on the Best Practical Means of
Cutting Off the Defective Germ-Plasm in the American Population* (1914), 59, quoted
in Lane, *When the Mind Hears*, 115; Walter Fernald, "The Burden of Feeble-Mindedness," *Journal of Psycho-Asthenics* 17 (1912), 87, 90–92, quoted in Wolfensberger,
Origin and Nature of Our Institutional Models, 35–36; Gallagher, *FDR's Splendid Deception*, 30; Bowe, *Handicapping America*, 186; Robert L. Burgdorf, *The Legal Rights
of Handicapped Persons: Cases, Materials and Text* (Baltimore, 1980).

4. Robert Jay Lifton, *The Nazi Doctors* (New York, 1986), 46–47; Ann Finger,
"Hitler's War Against the Disabled," unpublished manuscript, 1986, 13.

5. Lifton, *Nazi Doctors*, 46–50.

6. Lifton, *Nazi Doctors*, 52–56, 65–69.

7. Finger, "Hitler's War Against the Disabled," 3.

8. Some estimate that as many as 275,000 disabled people may have been killed
in the Nazi euthanasia program. Lifton, *Nazi Doctors*, 134–39.

9. Lifton, *Nazi Doctors*, passim.

10. See references in note 1.

11. For the history of federal legislation, its enactment and enforcement, see
Scotch, *From Good Will to Civil Rights*; Bowe, *Handicapping America*; Bowe, *Rehabilitating America*; John Parry, ed., *Mental Disability Law: A Primer* (Washington, D.C.,
1984); Laura Rothstein, *Rights of Physically Handicapped Persons* (Colorado Springs,
1984; Supplement 1987). Most significant was the passage of the Rehabilitation Act
of 1973, Pub. L. No. 93-112, 87 Stat. 355 (1973) (amended 1978) (codified in scat-
tered sections of 29 U.S.C.). Section 504 of the act, often referred to as the Civil
Rights Act for disabled people, provides: "No otherwise qualified handicapped individual . . . shall, solely by reason of his handicap, be excluded from the participation in, be denied the benefits of, or be subjected to discrimination under any program or activity receiving federal financial assistance." 29 U.S.C.A. §794 (1982). In
1975, Congress passed the Developmentally Disabled Assistance and Bill of Rights
Act, Pub. L. No. 94-103, 89 Stat. 486 (1975) (codified as amended at 42 U.S.C.A.
§§6000–81 (1982 & Supp. III 1985), which established the right of developmentally
disabled citizens to appropriate treatment and habilitation, designed to maximize the
individual's potential, and to have such training and education provided in the least
restrictive environment. 42 U.S.C.A. §6010 (1982). Congress had, in 1968, enacted
legislation intended to ensure that buildings financed with federal funds were designed and constructed to be accessible to people with disabilities. Architectural
Barriers Act of 1968, Pub. L. No. 90-480, 82 Stat. 718 (1968) (codified as amended
at 42 U.S.C.A. §§4151–4157). However, it was only with the passage of the Rehabilitation Act of 1973 that a mechanism, the Architectural and Transportation Barriers Compliance Board, was established to enforce compliance with the act. Rehabilitation Act of 1973, Pub. L. No. 93-112 §502, 87 Stat. 355, 391–93 (1973)
(codified as amended at 29 U.S.C.A.). The Education for All Handicapped Children
Act of 1975, Pub. L. No. 94-142, 89 Stat. 773 (1975) (codified at 20 U.S.C.A.
§§1400–61) (1982 & Supp. III 1985), since retitled the Individuals with Disabilities
Education Act, assured "all handicapped children . . . a free appropriate public education . . . designed to meet their unique needs." 20 U.S.C.A. §792 (1982 & Supp.

111 1985). On independent living, see "Independent Living: The Right to Choose," in Myron G. Eisenberg, Cynthia Griggins, Richard J. Duval, eds., *Disabled People as Second-Class Citizens* (New York, 1982).

12. Scotch, *From Good Will to Civil Rights;* Rothstein, *Rights of Physically Handicapped Persons,* 79–108; Reed, "Equal Access to Mass Transportation for the Handicapped," *Transportation Law Journal* 9 (1977); "Summary and Analysis," *Mental Disability Law Reporter* (1981), 75–78, 302–4.

13. See, e.g., *O'Connor v. Donaldson,* 422 U.S. 563 (1975) (state cannot constitutionally confine a person who is not dangerous and who is able, with assistance from others, to live by himself); *Wyatt v. Stickney,* 325;.Supp. 781, 334 F. Supp. 1341 (M.D. Ala. 1971), 344 F. Supp. 373 (M.D. Ala. 1972), *aff'd sub. nom, Wyatt v. Aderholt,* 503 F.2d 1305 (5th Cir. 1974) (institutionalized mentally disabled people have constitutional right to adequate treatment and habilitation); *New York State ARC v. Carey,* 393 F. Supp. 715 (H.D. N.Y. 1975), *modified,* 706 F.2d 956 (2d Cir.1983) (institutionalized mentally retarded persons have a right to protection from harm and to a minimum quality of care); *Halderman v. Pennhurst State School & Hospital,* 446 F.Supp. 1295 (E.D. Pa. 1977) (mentally retarded citizens have a constitutional right to minimally adequate habilitation in the least restrictive environment, which required that they be served in community settings and that Pennhurst be closed), *modified,* 612 F.2d 84 (3d Cir. 1979) (finding a right to minimally adequate habilitation in the least restrictive environment in the Developmentally Disabled Assistance and Bill of Rights Act), *rev'd and rem'd, Pennhurst State School & Hospital v. Halderman,* 451 U.S. 1 (1981), *aff'd prior judgment on state law grounds, Halderman v. Pennhurst State School & Hosp.,* 673 F.2d 647 (3d Cir. 198), *rev'd and rem'd, Pennhurst State School & Hosp. v. Halderman,* 465 U.S. 89 (1984) (Eleventh Amendment precludes federal court from exercising jurisdiction in a suit for injunctive relief based on state law and brought against state officials); *Pennsylvania Assoc. for Retarded Children v. Pennsylvania,* 324 F.Supp. 1257 (E. D. Pa. 1971) (retarded children entitled to an "appropriate" program of education and training).

14. On education, see, e.g., *Bd. of Educ. of the Hendrick Hudson Cent. School Dist. v. Rowley,* 458 U.S. 176 (1982) (Education for All Handicapped Children Act does not entitle the student to education that will maximize her potential; rather it guarantees only an education which minimally conforms to state standards). On people with developmental disabilities, see *Pennhurst State School & Hospital v. Halderman,* 451 U.S. 1 (1981) (states receiving funds under the Developmental Disabilities Act are not thereby obligated to provide developmentally disabled citizens with treatment and habilitation in the least restrictive environment). On infants, see *Bowen v. Am. Hosp. Assoc.,* 106 S.Ct. 2101 (1986) (hospitals' withholding of necessary medical treatment from a handicapped infant does not violate §504 prohibition against discrimination on the basis of handicap when the parents have not consented to the needed medical procedure).

15. "Gov. Lamm Stirs New Furor by Calling on Aged Ill to Die," *Los Angeles Times,* March 29, 1984, part 1, 16; Keating, "The War Against the Mentally Retarded," *New York,* September 17, 1979, 87.

16. Laurie Hearn, "It's More of a Struggle to Live than to Die," *Chicago Tribune,* February 8, 1984, sec. 5, 5, hereafter cited as "Struggle to Live"; Declaration of Saul

J. Faerstein, paragraph 13, *Bouvia v. Riverside*, No. 159780 (Cal. Super. Ct., Feb. 8, 1984).

17. Laurie Hearn, "She's Had Enough Pity, Is Ready to Die," *Riverside Press-Enterprise*, October 9, 1983, B1, hereafter cited as "Enough Pity"; interviews by author with friends and associates of Bouvia.

18. "Struggle to Live"; Margaret Pabst Battin, "Ms. Bouvia Challenges Law, Medicine and Morality," *Hemlock Quarterly* 15:4 (1984), 4; interviews by author with master's program associates.

19. Battin, "Ms. Bouvia Challenges Law," 4.

20. For a discussion of "work disincentives" see Bowe, *Rehabilitating America*. Remarks of Richard Scott, attorney for plaintiff Elizabeth Bouvia, in debate with Stanley Fleishman, attorney for amicus curiae, Disability Rights Coordinating Council, at Loyola Law School, Los Angeles, 1983.

21. *60 Minutes:* "Help Wanted," broadcast on CBS, October 1, 1978; "Suicide Blamed on Threat to Cut Off Disabled Woman's Aid," *Los Angeles Times*, March 3, 1978, sec. 1, 27.

22. *60 Minutes:* "Help Wanted"; "Employment Opportunities for Disabled Americans Act of 1986," Pub. L. No. 99 643,1986 U.S. Code, *Congressional and Administrative News*, 6087; personal communication with Douglas Martin.

23. "Struggle to Live"; 42 U.S.C.A. 1382c (f)(1) (income of a nondisabled spouse is deemed to the SSI recipient whether or not it is actually available to the disabled partner).

24. "'Withdrawal' or Suicide?" *New York Times*, December 11, 1983, E7; "Mate Calls Patient 'Brainwashed'," *Santa Monica Outlook*, November 18, 1983, A3; "Struggle to Live"; "Plea by Patient for Starvation Barred by Court," *New York Times*, December 17, 1983, 8.

25. "Ruling Is Upheld in Suicide Appeal," *New York Times*, January 20, 1984, 11; Battin, "Ms Bouvia Challenges Law"; Declaration of Saul Faerstein; Declaration of Faye J. Girsh, Ed.D., and Declaration of Robert Summerour, M.D., *Bouvia v. Riverside*, 2–7; *Bouvia v. Riverside*, slip opinion, 6.

26. *Bouvia v. Superior Court*, 225 Cal. Rptr., 307, 300; Hughes and Jones, "Staff Has Tough Time with Bouvia," *Los Angeles Times*, February 3, 1984, part 1, 18; Complaint for Declaratory Relief, *Bouvia v. Riverside*, 4, 12; interview by author with Bouvia's counselor at California Department of Rehabilitation.

27. *Bouvia v. Superior Court*, 225 Cal. Rptr., 304–5.

28. *Bouvia v. Superior Court*, 225 Cal. Rptr. (J. Compton concurring), 307–8.

29. Baker, "Bouvia Attorneys File New Suit, Court Asked to Prevent Decrease of Painkillers," *Los Angeles Times*, April 22, 1986, part 2, 6; remarks of Dr. David Goldstein, U.S.C. Medical Student Bioethics Symposium, July 1986.

30. Mary Rose Barrington, "Apologia for Suicide," in Margaret Pabst Battin and David J. Mayo, eds., *Suicide: The Philosophical Issues* (New York, 1980), 97, 90.

31. Barrington, "Apologia for Suicide," 98.

32. "Pro-suicide Activists Call for Right to Assist," *Washington Times*, March 13, 1987, 6A.

33. Erwin Ringel, "Suicide Prevention and the Value of Human Life," in Battin and Mayo, *Suicide: The Philosophical Issues*, 208 n129.

34. Derek Humphry, "Mrs. Bouvia's Sad Mistakes Are Lessons," *Hemlock Quarterly* 14 (1984), 1; Plaintiff's Memorandum, 14, 21, *Bouvia v. Riverside*; "Husband Challenges Her Right to Die," *Los Angeles Herald Examiner*, November 3, 1983, A3.

35. Hastings Center, *The Hastings Center Guidelines on the Termination of Life Sustaining Treatment and the Care of the Dying* (Briarcliff Manor, New York, 1987), 28.

36. Margaret Pabst Battin, *Ethical Issues in Suicide* (Englewood Cliffs, 1982), 96, 197.

37. Battin, *Ethical Issues in Suicide*, 98.

38. Barrington, "Apologia for Suicide," 98–99 n129.

39. Barrington, "Apologia for Suicide," 90.

40. Eliot Slater, "Choosing the Time to Die," in Battin and Mayo, *Suicide: The Philosophical Issues*, 202 n129.

41. Battin, *Ethical Issues in Suicide*, 202; Lifton, *Nazi Doctors*; Finger, "Hitler's War."

42. Battin, *Ethical Issues in Suicide*, 102, 103, emphases in original.

43. David Novak, *Suicide and Morality: The Theories of Plato, Aquinas and Kant and Their Relevance for Suicidology* (New York, 1975), 66, quoted in Battin, *Ethical Issues in Suicide*, 87; Battin, *Ethical Issues in Suicide*, 87–88 (emphasis in original).

44. Battin, *Ethical Issues in Suicide*, 88.

45. Battin does note in passing, though, that "popular medical literature is filled with tales of heroic individuals who have done astonishing good from their iron lungs or their respirators or their quadriplegic wheelchairs." *Ethical Issues in Suicide*, 87. Apparently doing good for others is impossible for all but a few "heroic" disabled individuals. The odd descriptor "quadriplegic wheelchairs" also exposes the ignorance of many suicide advocates regarding matters relating to disabled people.

46. Ironically, Battin offers one of the most compelling analyses of the dangers of a "slippery slope." We can expect manipulative arguments for rational suicide to be applied to "nonterminal—as well as terminal—illness cases," such as renal failure, quadriplegia, or severe arthritis, and "to conditions where there is no *illness* as such at all: retardation, genetic deficiency, abnormal personality, and old age" (emphasis added). She suggests that so-called rational suicide might ultimately be manipulated "in a much wider variety of nonmedical situations: chronic unemployment, widowhood, poverty, social isolation, criminal conviction, and so forth," because "all these conditions have been promoted as suicide-warranting at some time in that past, and they are all also very often associated with social dependence." Battin "imagines" the paternalistic manipulation of a rational suicide by a counselor advising an old or ill person to spare both himself and his family the agony of an extended decline, even though this person would not have considered or attempted suicide on his own and would have been willing to suffer the physical distress. Could the individual "resist such pressures? Not, perhaps, in a climate in which suicide is the rational thing to do," if one is old or ill [and we might add disabled or poor or a person of colored]. "[I]n a suicide-permissive society, the choice of suicide," she predicts, "would be recognized as evidence of sound mental health." It would "be the rational—and socially favored—choice. Indeed, perhaps the choice is not so free after all." Amazingly, Battin then goes on to argue "that on moral grounds we must

accept, not reject, the notion of rational suicide" because there are circumstances, she believes, in which it would "be rational for an individual to choose death rather than to live in circumstances which for him are unacceptably or intolerably painful, physically or emotionally, or which are destructive of his most deeply held values," even though other individuals or society may have manipulated such persons into seeing their lives as "worthless" or into believing they have an obligation to end them. Battin, "Manipulated Suicide," in Battin and Mayo, *Suicide: The Philosophical Issues*, 169, 176–79.

9

The Resistance
The Disability Rights Movement and Assisted Suicide

During the past decade, I have frequently joined with disability rights colleagues in writing, speaking, testifying, and debating about the issue of physician-assisted suicide. The essay that follows attempts to weave together the general perspective and the main arguments forged by disability rights activists.

Up until 1996, most disability rights activists shied away from the controversy over physician-assisted suicide. The struggle for passage and enforcement of federal laws to protect disabled persons from discrimination and to ensure their rights to educational and employment opportunities, deinstitutionalization and independent living, equal access and reasonable accommodations seemed more urgent. Besides, many people with disabilities felt uncertain and ambivalent about this particular issue. Wasn't the disability rights movement fighting for freedom of choice, for disabled persons' right to self-determination? Hadn't disabled people, more than any other group, suffered from the overween-

This essay is drawn from my testimony regarding resolutions on assisted suicide before the American Bar Association House of Delegates Annual Meeting in San Francisco, August 6, 1997; my testimony to the California State Assembly Judiciary Committee on behalf of several disability rights organizations opposing a bill to legalize physician-assisted suicide, April 20, 1999; my formal remarks at an Educational Forum on AB 1592 "Death with Dignity Act," sponsored by the California State Independent Living Council, Sacramento, June 18, 1999; and my opening statements at "Right to Die: The Opposition," Commonwealth Club, San Francisco, August 30, 1999, and the "Death with Dignity" Forum, sponsored by the San Joaquin County Commission on Aging, Stockton, May 9, 2000.

ing power of doctors? Perhaps legalization of physician-assisted suicide would, said some, limit doctors' dominion and give disabled individuals control over at least their deaths. The contradiction in that thought—empowering doctors to bring about patients' deaths in order to limit the power of doctors regarding matters of life and death—reflected the confused and troubled thinking, not just of disabled people, but of many nondisabled folks as well. Only disabled people, though, grappled with another element of the issue that made it especially hard to face. If disability rights activists engaged with the question of assisted suicide, they would have to plumb the very depths of disability prejudice. More than tough, that confrontation would be terrifying. It felt safer to address other issues.

But then in the summer of 1996, the juggernaut known as Jack Kevorkian, and more particularly the public response to him, suddenly spurred disabled activists into action. In a dramatic turn, the disability rights movement began to mobilize in opposition to physician-assisted suicide. It now discerned a linkage between that issue and a backlash against disability rights in general. In June, activists in Oak Park, Illinois, led by a disabled attorney, Diane Coleman, announced formation of an advocacy group called Not Dead Yet. They proclaimed:

> NOT DEAD YET is declaring war on the ultimate form of discrimination: euthanasia. We've watched over the last decade as our brothers and sisters have been denied the suicide prevention that nondisabled people can take for granted, and gotten help to turn off their ventilators. We've watched as families have been allowed to withhold food and water from their disabled children. But in 1996, the courts have crossed the final line. . . . And Dr. Kevorkian was just acquitted of assisting in the deaths of two women, neither of them terminally ill. . . . We can't trust the courts and we can't trust the medical profession. We must act before it's too late.[1]

Within a few months, Not Dead Yet had enlisted activists across the United States. Over the next two years, leading figures and organizations in the U.S. disability rights movement began to speak out against physician-assisted suicide. Meanwhile, because the pro-euthanasia movement is international, disability rights campaigners in Britain, Europe, Canada, and Australia began to link with their American colleagues to fight against the well-organized and well-financed lobbying for legalization of euthanasia in most industrialized nations.

Pro-suicide advocates have tried various stratagems to counter this disability rights resistance. They have claimed that the disability rights movement is divided on the issue. In fact, while a handful of disabled activists support legalization, the overwhelming majority of disability community leaders strongly oppose it. In the United States, more than a dozen major disability rights organizations, including the National Council on Independent Living and the National Council on Disability, have taken official stands against legalization. The concerns and warnings of disabled activists regarding the consequences of legalization have met with scorn from many proponents of physician-assisted suicide, who have dismissed it as alarmist, even paranoid. That reaction is, to say the least, condescending. In addition, proponents have tried to bracket disabled activists under the right-to-life label in order to discredit them. This not only distorts the disability rights position. It portrays disabled activists as pawns of nondisabled right-to-life religious conservatives.

The news media too sometimes lump the disability rights perspective with the right-to-life outlook. More often though, they simply ignore it, just as the media have typically disregarded disability rights perspectives on most disability issues. As a result, the disability rights viewpoint has commonly been excluded from public discourse about assisted suicide. Once again, disabled voices that conflict with dominant nondisabled perceptions are effectively silenced. Disabled citizens, who are directly affected by this issue, are rendered invisible.

Yet disability rights activists have a distinctive analysis to bring to the issue of assisted suicide. They can empathize with the griefs that motivate many supporters of physician aid-in-dying, because they understand firsthand—and better than most of their fellow citizens—the undertreated pain and unnecessary suffering of far too many patients. They are also more familiar than most people with the actual workings of the U.S. health care system. That is why they insist that the debate must focus on the impact of prejudice and discrimination and of financial interests in both physician-assisted suicide and the entire health care system. These sorts of arguments distinguish the disability rights position from that of the right-to-life movement. In addition, disabled activists are not concerned with the impact of assisted suicide just on people with disabilities. They also feel responsible to point out the threats to those who are terminally ill. Once again, the disability experience provides a deeper understanding of these dangers than most people can recognize. In opposing assisted suicide, disability rights activists speak with authority.

This essay will lay out some of the basic arguments of the disability rights resistance to legalizing physician-assisted suicide.

If physician-assisted suicide is legalized, it will take place within the context of a health care system and a society pervaded with prejudice and discrimination against people with disabilities. Around the country, people with significant disabilities report that when they enter hospitals for life-sustaining treatments they are pressured by hospital staffs to sign Do Not Resuscitate forms. "Yvonne Duffy had hospital personnel constantly urging and demanding that she sign the order," while Robert Powell, a wheelchair rider, was denied admittance to a hospital when he refused to sign a DNR. The disability rights magazine *Mouth* related that a New Mexico subscriber went to a hospital emergency room during a severe asthma attack. While she struggled to breathe, a social worker carefully took the time to explain that she had a right to reject medical treatment. At last, the disabled woman demanded that the staffer summon a doctor. As she departed, the social worker insistently informed her: "It's not too late. The Right to Die is on the hospital channel 6 twenty-four hours a day. You can watch it in your room!" *Mouth* writer Joe Ehman entered a Rochester, New York, hospital for back surgery. Both before and after the operation, a squad of hospital, county, and home-health social workers pressured him to sign a Do Not Resuscitate order. Ehman shot back at them, "I'm only 30 years old! I don't want to die!" This is the hospital where Dr. Timothy Quill, a leader in promoting legalization of physician-assisted suicide, practices.[2] Disabled activists ask what "choices" these individuals were being offered. Under the pressures of cost containment, profit seeking, and prejudice, the choices were surely not free and uncoerced ones. From the disability rights perspective, nondisabled society—and especially the U.S. health care system—pays only lip service to "autonomy" and "freedom of choice" for disabled people.

Advocates note the prevalence of disability prejudice documented among medical practitioners. One study found that while more than eight out of ten emergency-care professionals surveyed thought they would have a poor quality of life if they were quadriplegic, well over eight out of ten people with quadriplegia due to spinal-cord injuries said they had an average or better-than-average quality of life. And, whereas only 18 percent of the emergency-care staffers thought they would be glad to be alive if they had a major physical disability, more than 90 percent of the quadriplegics were, in fact, glad to be alive. Disability research consistently finds that health care professionals have as negative or more negative attitudes toward living with a disability than the general public and far more negative opinions than disabled people hold. A leading psychologist researching disability calls the findings on this discrepancy of views "consistent and stunning."[3]

We should note that 14 percent of the quadriplegics in the study just cited rated their quality of life as poor. Many proponents of assisted suicide argue that disabled individuals such as these should have the right to physician assistance in order to end their unsatisfactory existence. It turns out, though, that the same proportion of the general population also grades their own quality of life poor. Yet no one but the most fundamentalist of libertarians wants to offer physician-assisted suicide to all those miserable nondisabled people.[4]

Meanwhile, pervasive disability bias affects medical practice, as the findings of research on health care professionals' views of disabled people indicate and as the examples from the disability press illustrate. Other examples abound. Disabled activists point to the *Guidelines for Health Care Providers* of the Colorado Collective for Medical Decisions. In the fall of 1996, this publication recommended that cardiopulmonary resuscitation "should be unusual if it is known that the patient had significant physical or mental impairment prior to the cardiac arrest." The guidelines did not define "significant." To activists, this recommendation seemed on the face of it prejudicial and discriminatory. I am told, although I have not verified this, that when advocates protested against this guideline as discriminatory, the collective withdrew it. Meanwhile, Joe Ehman discovered that though local home health workers in the county where he resides get certified in CPR, the county, which pays the workers' wages, prohibits them from performing it on "clients" such as him.[5]

Not Dead Yet and ADAPT (American Disabled for Attendant Programs Today) drew attention to this pervasive discrimination in their brief to the U.S. Supreme Court in the important 1997 "right to die" case, *Vacco v. Quill.* The two disability rights groups argued that a discriminatory double standard shapes delivery of U.S. health care. In violation of the Americans with Disabilities Act, that double standard, they charged, denies people with disabilities the protection of medical-practice standards, of statutes prohibiting abuse, neglect, and homicide, and of suicide-prevention laws, all of which protect nondisabled persons. Given the pervasive prejudice and discrimination against people with disabilities in the health care system, the absence of adequate health care and appropriate support services, and the application of the double standard, argued the activists to the Court, it would be impossible for lawmakers to build effective safeguards into assisted-suicide laws that would prevent the wrongful death of disabled persons, old and young.[6]

In contrast, many proponents of legalizing assisted suicide claim that disabled people would not be endangered, because the statutes would limit the practice to terminally ill individuals. Disabled activists find those reassurances unconvincing, not just because of the frequent discrimination within the health care system, but for several other reasons as well.

First, the definitions of "terminal illness" in proposed assisted-suicide laws are so broad that they implicitly include many people with disabilities. Disabled people who for decades have used—and been kept alive by—devices such as ventilators fit those definitions of "terminally ill."

More direct threats arise when terminal illness and disability are lumped together. For instance, the Hemlock Society defines mercy killing as "the killing of a terminally or incurably ill person to put him or her out of perceived misery." Likewise, in a special issue of the *Western Journal of Medicine*, Hemlock Society leader Faye Girsh implicitly equated disabled people with those who are terminally ill. An "imaginary dialogue" she created asked, Who "should have the right to ask a physician for aid in dying?" Her answer: "a person with a terminal or hopeless illness." The "living will" disseminated by the Society for the Right to Die says: "I direct that life-sustaining procedures should be withheld or withdrawn if I have an illness, disease, or injury, or experience extreme mental deterioration, such as that there is no reasonable expectation of recovering or regaining a meaningful quality of life." The word "terminal" does not even appear here. Virtually any major chronic condition might be an appropriate occasion for physician-aided death. The living will ignores the societally constructed circumstances that can deny both terminally ill people and people with disabilities a "meaningful quality of life."[7]

The same looseness and ambiguity in defining terminal illness and the same equation of disability with terminality have appeared in judges' rulings in assisted-suicide cases. Larry McAfee breathed on a ventilator due to a spinal-cord injury. Like other persons with high-level spinal-cord injuries, he was not ill, let alone terminally ill. He had a stable, chronic physical disability. Yet the Fulton County, Georgia, superior court judge who approved McAfee's petition for physician-assisted suicide described his use of a ventilator as "artificial life support" that was merely "prolonging his death." Even Atlanta's Catholic archdiocese, which anomalously endorsed McAfee's request, said that his assisted death would not be a suicide because technically he had died three years before in the motorcycle accident that disabled him. To disability rights activists in Atlanta, this prejudicially distorted the reality of McAfee's disability and his life. It evinced the bias that people with disabilities like his are virtually dead already. That in turn justified abetting his actual physical death.[8] The same prejudice surfaced in other major physician-assisted suicide court cases involving disabled individuals: Elizabeth Bouvia in California, David Rivlin in Michigan, and others. In each case, not only judges, but also assisted-suicide advocates and the news media, conflated terminal illness with disability. In each case, they ignored how the social-service and health care systems thwarted the attempts of these individuals at independent living, education, and work.

The 1989 assisted-suicide cases of David Rivlin and Larry McAfee exemplify how societal factors and public policies make the lives of some disabled people unendurable. Both were ventilator-using, spinal-cord-injured quadriplegics. And both were forced into a series of nursing homes because Michigan provided inadequate funding for independent living and Georgia refused to pay for independent living at all.[9] In states that support independent living, people with disabilities like theirs live in their own homes, raise families, go to school, and hold jobs.

David Rivlin attended Michigan's Oakland University, aiming to become a psychologist or a college teacher. He also struggled to live in his own apartment. But both goals proved impossible because of Michigan state policies. In the 1980s, Michigan granted individuals with significant physical disabilities financial aid to pay chore workers to do housekeeping and assist them with tasks such as bathing, dressing, and eating. The maximum was $666 a month. Most disabled people had to fight for that much. Many got much less. David Rivlin received less than $300 a month. That averaged out to under $10 a day or about 41 cents an hour. For that amount, no significantly disabled person could find a competent and responsible chore worker. No wonder Rivlin kept failing in his attempts at independent living. It wasn't that independent living was too costly. The State of Michigan paid the nursing home $230 a day to keep Rivlin locked up.[10]

For three years, David Rivlin clung to the hope he might escape the last of these nursing homes. In the end, he concluded he would never get out and decided he would rather be dead. So he got a court order authorizing a doctor to sedate him and disconnect his ventilator.[11]

Meanwhile, Georgia, where Larry McAfee resided, not only offered no support for independent living, no Georgia nursing home would admit a ventilator user because the state paid so little. So McAfee was shipped to a facility in Ohio. After two years, Ohio Medicaid stopped paying, so the facility sent him back to Georgia to Atlanta's Grady Memorial Hospital.

Grady placed McAfee in its intensive-care unit even though he didn't need such care. The environment of a hospital ICU subjects patients to continous emotional stress. The lights are always turned on. Medical personnel ceaselessly move about. Patients are assaulted by the constant noise of medical machines. Noise levels from the equipment and the conversation of staff continue day and night, frequently exceeding recommended standards for noise in hospital wards. Patients are caught in a disorienting atmosphere of crisis and sensory overload. As many as one-third of individuals confined to intensive care are estimated to suffer from "ICU psychosis." Although serious, this psychological disorder often goes undetected by hospital personnel. Because of the tremendous stress of ICU and the danger of this psychosis, few critically ill patients are kept in intensive care for any length of time. Patients are moved to less stressful environments as quickly as possible, because "ICU psychosis" can occur within three days after a patient has been placed in intensive care. Grady Hospital kept Larry McAfee in its ICU for eight months. (The bill mounted to over $172,000.) After three months, McAfee decided he could not take any more. He requested court authorization to have a doctor help him die.[12]

Despite their emotional battering by the social-service and health care systems, neither Rivlin nor McAfee received appropriate psychological evaluation or counseling. A court-appointed psychiatrist concluded David Rivlin was competent, yet his lawyer refused to say what, if any, qualifications the psychiatrist had in the psychology of disability, a specialized field. Some of the people who had extensive contact with Larry McAfee over the four years preceding his request for assisted suicide described emotional oscillations. At times, he showed strong interest in independent living and vocational rehabilitation. At times, he said he wanted to die. These swings reflected the tremendous stresses he struggled with, stresses due not just to his disability, but to the abusive system that held him captive. Other disabled people in similar situations exhibit the same emotional swings. Yet the judge who ruled on McAfee's request determined that he was without "emotional or psychological disabilities." McAfee got neither crisis intervention nor psychological evaluation. His lawyer did not arrange it. The judge did not order it. Instead, his lawyer sent to see him, of all people, a vocational counselor![13]

The nondisabled people around both men assumed that when a person with such a disability said he would rather be dead, he must be acting rationally. They described McAfee and Rivlin as "logical" and "lucid" in their determination to die. If someone without a disability said they wanted to commit suicide, that person would get crisis intervention therapy immediately. Let a disabled person express such despair, and he or she is assumed to be "rational." Neither David Rivlin nor Larry McAfee received crisis intervention counseling. This is exactly the sort of discriminatory double standard in health care treatment condemned by Not Dead Yet and ADAPT.[14]

None of McAfee's or Rivlin's self-designated supporters paid attention to what the two men said about their lives. Larry McAfee told *ABC's Nightline*: "If you're a citizen or resident of Georgia and you become ventilator dependent, you'd better be prepared to become an outcast unwanted by the state." His mother said he was "thrown around like a bag of rotten potatoes that nobody even wants." McAfee told *U.S. News and World Report*, "You're looked upon as a second-rate citizen." "People say, 'You're using my taxes. You don't deserve to be here. You should hurry up and leave.'" "It gets to the point," he said, "where you realize that this is your life, . . . and in my case, it's not worth pursuing." Days before David Rivlin died, a reporter who himself has a disability knew enough to ask Rivlin what he thought about society's view of disabled people. "It sucks," said Rivlin. "Transportation, attitudes, financial help, it's all bad."[15]

Disability rights activists noted the absolute failure of most nondisabled people to acknowledge the abuse and oppression by the system that causes suicidal despair in disabled people like David Rivlin and Larry McAfee. Screening all that out, they latch onto the disability as the sole reason such individuals seek death. McAfee's attorney asserted, "He's made a rational decision that he just doesn't want to exist this way," that is, as a quadriplegic. Judge Edward Johnson, ruling in favor of McAfee's request for doctor-assisted suicide, expressed admiration for his "courage." Dr. John D. Banja, assistant professor of rehabilitation medicine and lecturer in medical ethics at Emory University School of Medicine, declared to the court, "We acknowledge an individual's right to autonomy, self-determination and liberty as part of our ethical vision in this country."[16]

Atlanta disability rights leader Mark Johnson complained that throughout the McAfee case the judge, the attorneys, the media, everyone "asked the wrong questions." He could have been talking about the entire discussion regarding assisted suicide. Four Atlanta disability rights groups said they were "outraged that our state for years left Larry McAfee without enough support for independent living and now steps in willingly to help with his suicide. . . . The state creates an unbearable quality of life and then steps in and says disabled people should be assisted to die because their quality of life is so poor."[17]

But something unexpected happened. People from United Cerebral Palsy offered Larry McAfee creative possibilities to regain control of his life and to work in computer engineering, and he changed his mind about dying. In fact, he ended up testifying before the Georgia state legislature, calling upon them to fund independent living. He told them that if it had been available, he would not have despaired to the point of seeking death. Atlanta disability rights activists pressured the Georgia Department of Medical Assistance to provide him with a place in a group living arrangement. For the next eight years, Larry McAfee lived independently. In 1998, he died of a stroke.[18]

In this and comparable situations, nondisabled doctors, health care professionals, lawyers, judges, ethicists, the news media, and much of the general public typically have failed to comprehend the socially oppressive experiences that make the lives of some people with disabilities unbearable. Some assisted-suicide proponents call it paternalistic to argue that disabled individuals will be coerced into suicide. Disabled activists reply that, in fact, it is lethally patronizing to ignore the ways in which bias and discrimination make the lives of some disabled people unendurable to them and cause them to seek assisted suicide.

In the view of disabled activists, the pledge of some assisted-suicide advocates that the practice will be limited to terminally ill people is further refuted by the advocates' own colleagues. Many of the most prominent proponents have from the beginning of their movement aimed to establish physician-assisted suicide, not just for those who are terminally ill, but for persons with disabilities as well. All of Elizabeth Bouvia's attorneys were active members of the Hemlock Society. Faye Girsh, a psychologist hired by those lawyers to evaluate Bouvia's mental state, was at the time president of Hemlock's San Diego chapter and later the society's national president. In 1996, Hemlock's founder Derek Humphry told the National Council on Disability that he did not favor legalizing assisted suicide for disabled people. But in his book *Final Exit*, he admitted that once physician-assisted suicide is legalized for terminally ill persons, he hopes to see it extended to those with chronic conditions.[19]

The "slippery slope" image implies that the extension of assisted suicide to socially stigmatized persons would occur inadvertently, unconsciously, unintentionally. That image conjures up the specter of a progression from euthanasia only for terminally ill persons to the coerced deaths of those who are devalued but not dying. But disability rights activists point out that neither aspect of the metaphor accurately represents what has been happening. Pro-suicide advocates have pressed for court rulings to guarantee persons with major disabilities the "right" to physician-assisted suicide. In the McAfee and Rivlin cases, courts granted such requests under the guise of refusal of medical treatment. Disabled activists do not foresee an unintended slide down a slope. Suicides of disabled persons have already been socially and legally sanctioned. In the view of disability rights activists, there will be no slippery slope, because many right-to-die advocates have always labored to legalize assisted suicide, not just for terminally ill people, but for people with disabilities as well.

Unlike his compatriots, Jack Kevorkian never minced words about his intentions. He advocated—and practiced—assisted suicide for disabled people all along. Three-fourths of the suicides he abetted involved people with disabilities, not terminal illnesses. In March 1990, the *Detroit Free Press Magazine* reported: "Oppressed by a fatal disease, a severe handicap, a crippling deformity? . . . Show him proper, compelling medical evidence that you should die, and Dr. Jack Kevorkian will help you kill yourself, free of charge." In a February 1992 journal article, he proposed an "auction market for available organs" removed from various kinds of "subjects," including voluntarily euthanized people "hopelessly crippled by arthritis or malformations." Some of the proceeds from sales of the organs would go to family members whose financial burdens would be relieved and "their standard of living enhanced." Kevorkian not only views disabled people as having worthless and burdensome lives, he sees them as a drain on society. He told a Michigan Court in August

1990: "The voluntary self-elimination of individual and mortally diseased and crippled lives taken collectively can only enhance the preservation of public health and welfare."[20]

This statement and Kevorkian's actions regarding people with disabilities alarmed many disability rights activists. They felt disturbed too, though not really surprised, that advocates of physician-assisted suicide failed to condemn Kevorkian's—to speak plainly—neo-Nazi bigotry against disabled people. Instead, the pro-euthanasia advocates confined themselves to lamenting that his actions were unregulated, but praised him for having forced to public awareness the need for legalized physician aid-in-dying.

Disability rights activists expressed outrage too that the news media failed to report Kevorkian's viciously prejudiced views of disabled people. The media instead typically portrayed him as some sort of eccentric folk hero. Some virtually championed him. Mike Wallace and *60 Minutes* gave him a supportive forum regarding the death of a man with ALS (amyotrophic lateral sclerosis). It seemed significant to disability rights activists that on two earlier occasions, *60 Minutes*, with Wallace as its correspondent, had made the case for Elizabeth Bouvia's assisted suicide. None of these stories about Bouvia or Kevorkian included the dissenting disability rights perspective. Another disturbing media moment occurred when *Time* magazine, to commemorate its seventy-fifth anniversary, held a huge celebration of "leaders." One of its honorees was Jack Kevorkian. Just five days before *Time*'s party, Kevorkian had abetted the suicide of a young quadriplegic man. Many activists saw *Time*'s feting of a serial killer whose agenda targeted disabled people, along with *60 Minutes'* unbalanced reporting, as indicating the depth and extent of disability bigotry.[21]

Disability bias combined with gender bias in Kevorkian's suicide-abetting campaign. Seven out of ten of his "patients" were women. The vast majority of them were not terminally ill. They had disabilities. Autopsies discovered that several of them had "no evidence of disease whatsoever." This same disturbing pattern appears in other "mercy killings." Two out of three such killers are men; two out of three of those killed are women. The men are typically the husbands of the women they kill. The wives are commonly sick or disabled, but only about one in three of those women is terminally ill. And the husbands' "mercy" is far from gentle. Most often, they blow their wives' brains out with a gun. Or they suffocate them or poison them. Why would most "mercy killers" be men? The Hemlock Society claims that it is because terminally ill people and their "caregivers" don't get enough support. But the leading expert on these sorts of homicides, psychologist Silvia Sara Canetto, points out that while most of the killers are men, most caregivers are women. Perhaps, Professor Canetto suggests, these murders may stem from the inability of some men "to accept a reversal in caring responsibilities." She also sees connections between such killings and the devaluation of women's lives in society at large. Most pertinent here, women, especially women with disabilities, receive poorer medical care than men. Some women may internalize this institutionalized prejudice as a lower sense of self-worth, says Professor Canetto; they may then ask for assisted suicide when they become sick or disabled. But, she cautions, such a request may mask a plea for support: "Do you care enough to want me alive and to be willing to share in my suffering?" Professor Canetto concludes that "one should be wary of those who present mercy-killing as a gift to women. These are fatal gifts, embedded in a long tradition of legitimizing women's sacrifice."[22]

"Sacrifice" of their lives is presented as a way disabled people could do something useful for society. At one point, Jack Kevorkian announced that he planned to "donate" the organs of the "patients" he had killed. Some of the public reactions to his organ-harvesting scheme were as troubling as the project itself. One transplant surgeon dismissed the idea as "totally unrealistic." Another expert said it was "simply not feasible," though he praised Kevorkian's "generosity." Neither expressed moral outrage at this additional expression of his contempt for sick people and people with disabilities.[23]

Meanwhile in California, Sandra Jensen, a woman with Down's syndrome, was rejected as a heart-lung transplant recipient. The efforts of disability rights activists got that discriminatory decision reversed. Ms. Jensen received a transplant and, contrary to biased preoperative expectations, did quite well in the recuperative phase. Still, the initial responses to her need for a transplant and to Kevorkian's harvesting plan suggested that people with disabilities were thought of by some influential people as organ donors, but not organ recipients.[24]

Jack Kevorkian automatically and arrogantly assumed that disabled people seeking suicide want to die because of their disabilities. He ignored societally caused factors. Wally Spolar, a man with multiple sclerosis from El Paso, Texas, sought help to die because, said Kevorkian's attorney Geoffrey Fieger, "he feared ending up in one of those rat-infested nursing homes to be warehoused by 'Nurse Ratched.'" So Kevorkian helped Spolar kill himself. Meanwhile, Texas disability rights activists demanded that the state fund independent living rather than force disabled people into nursing homes. "Unless Texas puts its money where its mouth is, gets its priorities right," declared ADAPT of Texas, "many more will follow suit." Wally Spolar "could see his choices: warehousing or death."[25]

To the ADAPT activists, Kevorkian viewed Spolar through the prism of ignorance and prejudice. He disregarded the social factors that make the lives of some disabled people unendurable: public policies that force them into nursing homes, improper medical treatment, inadequate pain management, denial of appropriate psychological supports, discrimination in obtaining health insurance, resulting financial distress, the attitude that they burden their families and society, and the deep prejudice that their lives are worthless.

Kevorkian, like all pro-suicide advocates, claims to support individual autonomy. But in fact, he would give doctors the power to decide that some people, including people with disabilities, would be better off dead. In May 1993, *Time* magazine asked him how he decided "whom to help? Does the patient have to suffer from a life-threatening illness?" "No, of course not," replied Kevorkian, ". . . but your life quality has to be nil." "And who decides that?" asked *Time*. "That's up to physicians," said Kevorkian, "and nobody can gainsay what doctors say."[26]

All too many people with disabilities have had all too many doctors dismiss their "quality of life" as "nil" and recommend withholding medical treatment that would sustain their lives. Those doctors assumed that they would be better off dead and that their families would be better off with them dead. Disability rights activists worry that while right-to-die advocates are suspicious of doctors who seek to sustain life, they naively trust doctors who deliberately bring about death.

The catchphrase "quality of life" is frequently invoked to justify physician-assisted suicide. When proponents of assisted suicide set quality of life as a justifiable reason for facilitating people's deaths, they almost always invoke the loss of "dignity" while simultaneously raising the specter of "dependency." Advocates of Oregon's Measure 16, the state's assisted-suicide law, originally claimed that doctor-induced death would be a "last resort" when nothing else could be done to alleviate "unrelenting and intolerable suffering." In fact, the vast majority of Oregonians who have sought suicide under that law feared, not pain, but losing autonomy or control of bodily functions. They feared becoming disabled. Instead of serving as a last resort, the legally sanctioned reasons for suicide were widened, just as disability rights activists predicted. The simple fact of terminality is not the reason individuals seek assisted suicide. They choose to die early not because they are going to die sooner or later. They want to escape the presumed humiliation of "dependency."[27]

The advocates fan that fear of "dependency." Janet Good, a sometime collaborator with Jack Kevorkian in abetting the suicides of several individuals with disabilities, told the *Washington Post:* "Pain is not the main reason we want to die. It's the indignity. It's the inability to get out of bed, or get onto the toilet, let alone drive a car and go shopping, without another's help. I can speak for literally hundreds of people whose bedside I've sat at over the years. . . . They've had enough when they can't go to the bathroom by themselves. Most of them say, 'I can't stand my mother; my husband, wiping my butt.' That's why everybody in the movement talks about death with dignity. People have their pride. They want to be in control."[28]

Stephen Drake, a leader of Not Dead Yet who himself has a disability, responded to Good's statement:

> Many people with disabilities need such assistance in the bathroom, assistance which they are in charge of and which they do not regard as undignified. It's a shame that Ms. Good doesn't convey a more respectful attitude toward her "clients." Instead she reinforces and lethally acts out the devaluing attitudes of our society that tell sick or disabled people they lack dignity because they need assistance with basic activities of daily living, and would be better off dead. Have we really gotten to the point in this country that we will sanction and abet the suicides of people because they can't wipe their own behinds? People who have internalized society's contempt as self-hatred? That Janet Good thinks this justifies facilitating suicides shows what little progress we have made in rooting out disability prejudice.[29]

To disability rights activists like Drake, Good's view of dignity and dependency shows once again that the supposed safeguards built into statutes such as Oregon's Measure 16 are paper barriers that will easily be cut down. This law and other proposed policies pledge to limit physician-assisted suicide to persons diagnosed as terminally ill with six months or less to live. First of all, such predictions of death are notoriously inaccurate. Thus, they are useless and dangerously misleading in determining who would be eligible for physician-assisted death. More to the present point, if needing help is undignified, and death is better than dependency, there is no reason to deny assisted suicide to people who will have to put up with dependency for six or sixteen *years*, rather than just six *months*. If dignity and dependency rather than terminality are the real criteria of eligibility, then the six-month rule is entirely arbitrary and unjust and will be struck down.

Deployment of notions like "dignity" and "dependency" and "quality of life" fail to note that these are not objective descriptions of illness or disability. Instead, they are highly value-laden concepts that in and of themselves shape perceptions. They are rooted in American values that uphold complete physical self-sufficiency and absolute personal autonomy as cultural ideals. They express a myth, the myth that real Americans are rugged individualists who quite literally stand on their own two feet. The ideal, the authentic, American is not in any way dependent on others. Or at least, so the myth teaches us to pretend. To become sick or disabled in America is to lose one's social validity. It is to acquire a relentlessly and radically negative identity. It is to become the inversion of what a real American is supposed to be.

The disability rights movement has fought this culture's dominant values and myths about personal autonomy because those myths and values have inevitably generated discrimination against people with disabilities. Disability rights activists have demanded recognition that quality of life is constructed by public policies and socioeconomic conditions. They fought for the Individuals with Disabilities Education Act, the Americans with Disabilities Act, and access and accommodations, and the right to full health care. They are fighting to protect all of those rights from the current fierce attack. And they have fought for independent-living and government programs to liberate people with disabilities from nursing homes. Many people with disabilities have said they would rather be dead than imprisoned in such places. The disability rights movement has struggled to eliminate the pressures that have forced some disabled people to choose between the nursing home and the grave.

The few disabled leaders who favor legalization of assisted suicide base their stance on what they claim is the central goal of the disability rights movement: personal autonomy. Part of the problem is that those advocates implicitly accept the definition of personal autonomy dominant in American culture. In contrast, the disability rights movement in general has understood self-determination in a significantly different way from the majority culture.

In addition, the disability rights movement has always aimed at more than empowering individuals to make their own choices. It has addressed a much wider range of issues. Disability rights activists have sharply criticized reigning notions of individual autonomy for helping to mask the structural arrangements of power and privilege, advantage and opportunity that marginalize people with disabilities. They have taken a critical view of the allocation of economic resources and the distribution of social and political power. They have also espoused an alternative view of the nature of community and the relationships of individuals to one another within communities. They have been affirming alternative values concerning sexuality and gender, learning and work, and what constitutes personhood. This distinctive perspective has important implications, not just for people with disabilities, but for modern societies in general. Disability-based analysis can contribute to the critically needed reconstruction of contemporary social, economic, and political systems. In a sense, the threat of the physician-assisted suicide campaign is also an opportunity to develop both a more rigorous ideology of disability and disability rights, and a more thorough critique of dominant nondisabled values and arrangements from a disability perspective.[30]

Out of this wider set of concerns and this broader critical outlook, disability rights activists have insisted that the current debate about physician-assisted suicide must focus on more than cultural values about personal autonomy and "quality of life." It must also examine the role in this issue of economic interests and the structural maldistribution of economic, social, and political power. The United States has yet to guarantee all Americans a basic right to health care. Medical decisions are increasingly made, not by doctors, let alone by patients, but by profit-minded managed-care corporations. Abuse under this system is not just inevitable, but already occurring, and it is causing some people to die.

Yet no plan for physician-assisted suicide even begins to grapple meaningfully with these economic realities. Oregon's Measure 16 and proposals in other states modeled on it require doctors receiving requests for assisted death to inform patients about alternative options, such as "comfort care, hospice care, and pain control." But none of these policies guarantee desperate patients access to any of those other options.[31]

AB 1592, a bill introduced in 1997 in the California legislature to legalize assisted suicide, would, in addition, have prohibited insurers from coercing patients into choosing that option. This naive provision failed to recognize that direct coercion by health care insurers is unnecessary. Managed-care bureaucrats are already overruling doctors' decisions about appropriate and necessary, sometimes life-sustaining treatments in order to cut costs and boost profits. About the time AB 1592 was introduced, Dr. Linda Peeno disclosed the realities of her job as a medical coverage reviewer for Humana, one of the nation's largest managed-care corporations. "In the spring of 1987, as a physician, I caused the death of a man," she confessed. From her office in Louisville, Kentucky, Dr. Peeno denied a heart transplant to a patient in California. She knew her decision was a death sentence for the man, but she explained that corporate pressure on reviewers to deny such claims was overwhelming. The company rewarded her with advancement. "Everyone was thrilled when I denied that coverage," she reported. "If I had approved it, I would have been gone the next day." Dr. Peeno told her story to the California State Assembly's Health Committee as she testified in support of legislation to regulate managed care. The managed-care companies opposed the bill. A few months later, a federal class-action lawsuit accused Humana of misleading health plan members by failing to inform them of the financial incentives it offered doctors and case reviewers like Dr. Peeno to keep costs down by limiting or denying care.[32]

Despite such corporate practices, the Sacramento lobbyist for Death with Dignity, Inc., could make the extraordinary claim that "there are no economic arguments which would cause a managed care system or a physician to push physician-assisted dying for a patient. There are no financial incentives or advantages for this."[33] Such an assertion is, at best, dangerously naive.

Speaking of financial advantages, Death with Dignity, Inc., could afford to hire a paid professional lobbyist because, like the physician-assisted suicide movement in general, it is well financed. The disability rights movement cannot afford paid lobbyists. Disabled activists insist that if we want to understand the forces behind the push to legalize physician-aided death we must "follow the money."

In that regard, disabled activists point out that not only do measures to legalize physician-assisted suicide fail to guarantee patients access to medical care options they might choose instead of death, but also the pro-suicide campaign actively promotes the economic interests of managed-care corporations. Those companies have made plain their financial stake in legalization of physician-assisted suicide. After Measure 16 became law, most health maintenance organizations in Oregon added assisted suicide to the list of "benefits" they would cover. Caring for dying patients can run into tens of thousands of dollars of expenses that cut into corporate profits, while the lethal medication to kill the same patients costs a mere forty-five bucks. No wonder an Oregon HMO with the ironic name of the Ethix Corporation announced that it "welcomed broad coverage for assisted suicide in a medical economic system already burdened." It turned out that the leading proponent of Measure 16, Barbara Coombs-Lee, was a vice president at Ethix. This rather important bit of occupational data, which some observers might regard as a conflict of interest, did not get much attention during her campaign for the initiative.[34]

Sometimes supporters of assisted suicide admit that the managed-care system is unjust. The *San Jose Mercury News*'s endorsement of AB 1592 employed astonishing and disturbing logic: "If California's managed health care system had the confidence of the public—if people believed their doctors and insurance companies would stand by them after disease had stolen their ability to fight for control over their own life and death—there would not be a need for AB 1592. . . . But we are a long way from the time when Californians will have no fear of painful, impersonal death."[35] In other words, because corporate managed care treats people so badly, we should authorize that system to abet despairing patients in committing suicide.

If profits drive corporate managed care, the thrust to hold down public spending propels managed care in government-funded health insurance for poor people. The situation created in Oregon is ominous for those who depend on Medicaid. In 1994, the same year Measure 16 became law, Oregon's Medicaid program instituted health care rationing for the poor. It ranked 745 health services according to their efficacy, importance, and public demand. The Oregon Medical Assistance Program would henceforth pay for only the top 578 treatments. In 1998, OMAP's managers added doctor-assisted suicide to the "treatments" covered under the list's "comfort care" category. Meanwhile, they decided to limit the number of doses of a particularly strong and effective pain medication. Protests forced the bureaucrats to back down, but they did successfully put barriers in the way of funding a "state-of-the-art anti-depressant medication." The OMAP managers also cut over 150 services needed by terminally ill, disabled, and elderly Medicaid recipients, while the state pared in-home support services funding by 5 percent. A newspaper profile revealed that Barbara Coombs Lee was "closely involved in passage" of Oregon's health plan. Oregon's governor John Kitzhaber, a former emergency room physician and the chief architect of this health care rationing system, admitted—or perhaps he was boasting—that "only three states spend less per person on health care for the poor." The British magazine *The Economist* praised Kitzhaber "for rationing health care in the face of limited resources and observed that Oregon no longer pays for such treatments as 'efforts to fight the final stages of AIDS.'" Politicians' and bureaucrats' implementation of these cost-cutting measures while they willingly fund assisted suicide amounted to a declaration of class warfare against the poor, many of whom are sick or disabled.[36]

Class as well as disability bias has shaped judicial rulings too. The U.S. Ninth Circuit Court of Appeals offers a prime example of why disability rights activists distrust the judiciary. In a decision that sought to legalize physician-assisted suicide, that court made money a reason to die but failed to ensure access to treatment. It declared: "in a society in which the costs of protracted health care can be so exorbitant, we are reluctant to say that it is improper for competent, terminally ill adults to take the economic welfare of their families and loved ones into consideration." Yet the court went on to say that it had no authority to make any rulings about access to health care. It left that to the legislature. It is telling that while many judicial decisions have affirmed patients' "liberty interest" in refusing or terminating medical treatment, and a few recent rulings have found a "liberty interest" in physician-assisted suicide, no court has ever even "considered the possibility that a patient might have a coexisting liberty interest in demanding or receiving specific medical care or medically mediated procedures." More pertinent, no U.S. court would ever find that an American citizen has a general right to health care.[37]

Not only did the Ninth Circuit Court declare its incapacity to establish such a right. It sneered at concerns that legalization might expose "the poor and minorities to exploitation." It dismissed such warnings as "disingenuous," "fallacious," and "meretricious." The court wrote, "The argument that disadvantaged persons will receive more medical services than the remainder of the population in one, and only one, area—assisted suicide—is ludicrous on its face."[38]

No wonder Not Dead Yet declared, "we can't trust the courts." To disability rights activists, only affluent, privileged white people who enjoy the advantages of the current economic system could so arrogantly scorn the concerns of many people in minority communities, as well as people with disabilities who are often poor. Only people with such advantages could convince themselves that physician-assisted suicide could operate without abuse. People with disabilities cannot afford to indulge in such naivete. To disability rights activists, rulings like the Ninth Circuit Court's decision simply try to mask the injustices, indeed the savagery, of the current health care and economic systems. Such verdicts rationalize social coercion as personal autonomy. As one activist put it, "In a profit-oriented system pervaded by prejudice and ignorance about disability, so-called patient choice to die will not long remain any choice at all."[39]

Health care "choices" are never made in a vacuum. Given the absence of real options, death by assisted suicide becomes not an act of personal autonomy, but an act of desperation. It is fictional freedom, it is phony autonomy. The rhetoric of "choice" is deployed to hide the realities of coercion. The propaganda of personal freedom conceals a eugenic agenda. As always, eugenics is ultimately a program to defend economic interests.

Given the current transformation in the health care system under managed care, no law legalizing physician-assisted suicide, no matter how carefully crafted, could operate fairly. Inevitably the combination of a "right to die" but no right to treatment will have a deadly impact on socially and economically disadvantaged groups who are heavier users of the health care system and already find themselves discriminated against within that system. Seniors, people with chronic or progressive conditions or disabilities, poor people, members of racial minorities, and anyone who is, in fact, terminally ill will be put at serious risk. A Canadian disability rights leader warned that "the growing momentum" for assisted suicide, "coupled with the global retreat from social welfare creates an intensely fearsome environment for people like us. . . . Never has the social message been clearer. You are worthless. You are a burden. We would be better off without you. Anything we give you you should be grateful for and if we give you nothing it is because that is what you deserve."[40]

In response to that threat, a California coalition of advocates for poor people, people with disabilities, racial minorities, and seniors, along with health care professionals and religious groups, joined forces in April 1999 to defeat AB 1592, a bill to legalize physician-assisted suicide in the state. Startling the assembly leadership of both parties with the vehemence of its opposition, that alliance "killed the bill." It jolted people who regard themselves as liberal or progressive by condemning AB 1592 and similar proposals as dangerously reactionary.

To counter the campaign for physician-assisted suicide and to redirect public attention to what disability rights activists regard as the real issues, advocates have set forth an agenda of their own. They espouse the following principles:

- Any committee, conference, or public body convened to discuss the euthanasia issue or to draft or apply rules governing the refusal of medical treatment must include representatives of the disability rights movement. Symposia to debate aid in dying often do not include disabled discussants, unless they are supporters of assisted suicide. In the Bouvia and McAfee cases, the courts welcomed and even solicited the views of nondisabled persons but ignored the amicus briefs filed by disability rights groups. The disability rights movement has a distinctive perspective to contribute to this public debate. Given that the lives of people with disabilities are at stake, inclusion of that viewpoint is a matter, not just of balance, but of justice.
- Assistive devices and supportive services for people with significant disabilities must not be regarded as "artificial life supports" that merely prolong their dying. They are appropriate means of assistance in daily living.
- The equation of disability with terminal illness reflects, not a person's medical condition, but his or her devalued social status.
- Bids for assisted suicide are not refusals of medical treatment. Nor are they simply a response to a person's physical disability. Social factors—segregation, the denial of self-determination, cultural devaluation—are always present and typically primary in generating such despair. Suicidal gestures are a response to social deprivation and the internalization of societal prejudice. Until people with major disabilities are guaranteed their rights to self-determination, independent living, equal access to society, and appropriate psychological counseling, medical professionals must never support or assist the suicide of a disabled person. To do so in the present soci-

etal circumstances of devaluation, discrimination, and segregation is simply the ultimate act of oppression.

- Persons who are terminally ill or disabled who request assisted suicide must receive psychological evaluation and crisis intervention counseling, just like anyone else. They must also be evaluated by professionals knowledgeable about the psychology of disability and the oppressive social experience of people with disabilities.

- Saving people's lives, rehabilitating them, and teaching them the medical and physical management of their now-disabled bodies is futile if they are denied the right and the means to control those lives. Health care professionals must support the disability rights movement's efforts to secure adequate, nationwide government funding for self-directed independent living. People with either terminal illnesses or chronic disabilities have a right to adequately funded personal-assistance services that will support them in living in their own homes. They should not find themselves forced into nursing homes or institutions.

Society must indeed guarantee terminally ill persons the right to die with dignity. That right includes: competent pain management, adequate hospice care, appropriate psychological support services, and sufficient health insurance coverage so that none need fear that the costs will break their families financially. Death with dignity also means the right to die in one's own home with proper supportive assistance. But death with dignity does not mean having a doctor speed up one's dying with a lethal medication in order to guarantee HMOs bigger profits.

Disability rights activists declare that it would be unconscionable for a society that has failed to guarantee its citizens these rights—as well as a general right to health care—even to consider establishing a so-called right to physician-assisted suicide.

Notes

Acknowledgments: Linda Clever, Diane Coleman, Steve Drake, Carol Gill, Marilyn Golden, Mark Johnson, Kristi Kirschner, Rita Marker, Eleanor Smith, Wesley Smith, and Larry Voss all encouraged, stimulated, or prodded me to develop my thinking on this subject. I thank them.

1. "Kevorkian Action Planned," Justice-For-All Moderator <jfa@TNET.com>, 11 June 1996.

2. "Joint Statement from Evan Kemp and Justin Dart," November 15, 1996; Carl Weiser, "Protesting Assisted Suicide Disabled People Shout, 'We're Not

Dead Yet!'" *Louisville Courier-Journal*, January 9, 1997, 4A; Joe Ehman, "The Politics of D.N.R. (Do Not Resuscitate)," *Mouth Magazine* 6:6 (March–April 1996), 14–16.
3. K. A. Gerhart, J. Kozoil-McLain, S. R. Lowenstein, and G. G. Whiteneck, "Quality of Life Following Spinal Cord Injury: Knowledge and Attitudes of Emergency Care Providers," *Annals of Emergency Medicine* 23 (1994), 807–12. The research on health care professionals' attitudes toward life with various disabilities and its implications for legalization of assisted suicide are reviewed by Carol J. Gill, "Health Professionals, Disability, and Assisted Suicide: An Examination of Relevant Empirical Evidence and Reply to Batavia," *Psychology, Public Policy, and Law* 6:2 (March 2000), 526–45. Gill summarizes:

> If the attitudes of health professionals regarding life with a disability significantly influence their patients' view of disability, and if physicians and other professionals would play central roles in legalized assisted suicide, the disability attitudes of health professionals warrant examination. In general, research indicates that people with disabilities encounter a great deal of devaluation from the general public despite societal support of disability access improvements and anti-discrimination laws (Vernaci, 1991). Furthermore, studies consistently demonstrate that disability attitudes of health professionals are as negative and sometimes more negative than public attitudes (Gething, 1992; Ralston, Zazove, & Gorenflo, 1996; Roush, 1986). More specifically, health professionals significantly underestimate the quality of life of persons with disabilities compared to the actual assessments of people with disabilities themselves. In fact, the gap between health professionals and people with disabilities in evaluating life with disability is consistent and stunning. In a survey study of attitudes of 153 emergency care providers, only 18 percent of physicians, nurses and technicians imagined they would be glad to be alive with a severe spinal cord injury. In contrast, 92 percent of a comparison group of 128 persons with high-level spinal cord injuries said they were glad to be alive (Gerhart, Koziol-McLain, Lowenstein, & Whiteneck, 1994). Furthermore, only 17 percent of the professionals anticipated an average or better quality of life should they acquire this disability compared with 86 percent of the actual spinal cord injury comparison group. The investigators express concern that these inaccurate and pessimistic professional views of life with disability are implicitly conveyed to patients and their families while they are in the midst of decision-making about new disabilities. In another survey of emergency personnel (Hauswald & Tanberg, 1993), 82 percent indicated that they preferred death to severe disability. Bach and Tilton (1994) found that hospital staff significantly underestimated life satisfaction of quadriplegic individuals using ventilators. The tendency of health professionals to overestimate depressed mood in persons with spinal cord injuries has been well documented (Bodenhamer, et al., 1983; Cushman & Dijkers, 1990; Ernst, 1987). Other studies have indicated that compared with individuals with disabilities themselves, health professionals significantly underestimate

the well-being and life satisfaction of ventilator-assisted polio survivors (Bach & Campagnolo, 1992); primary care physicians underestimate the global quality of life of their elderly patients with chronic conditions (Uhlmann & Pearlman, 1991); and physicians substantially overestimate the willingness of laryngectomy patients to die rather than lose their ability to use their voice (Otto, Dobie, Lawrence & Sakai, 1997). Physicians also tend to overestimate the negative effect on families of having a child with spina bifida (Blaymore, Liebling, Morales, & Carlucci, 1996) and to underestimate the future capabilities of children with developmental disabilities (Wolraich, Siperstein, & O'Keefe, 1987).

Sources cited by Gill: C. A. Bach and R. W. McDaniel, "Quality of Life in Quadriplegic Adults: A Focus Group Study," *Rehabilitation Nursing* 18:6 (1993), 364–67; J. R. Bach and D. I. Campagnolo, "Psychosocial Adjustment of Post-Polio Ventilator Assisted Individuals," *Archives of Physical Medicine and Rehabilitation* 73:10 (1992), 934–39; J. R. Bach and M. C. Tilton, "Life Satisfaction and Well-being Measures in Ventilator Assisted Individuals with Traumatic Tetraplegia," *Archives of Physical Medicine and Rehabilitation* 75 (1994), 626–32; Blaymore Bier, J. A. Liebling, Y. Morales, and M. Carlucci, "Parents' and Pediatricians' Views of Individuals with Meningomyelocele," *Clinical Pediatrics* 35: 3 (1996), 113–17; E. Bodenhamer, J. Achterberg-Lawlis, G. Keverkian, A. Belanus, and J. Cofer, "Staff and Patient Perceptions of the Psychosocial Concerns of Spinal Cord–Injured Persons," *American Journal of Physical Medicine and Rehabilitation* 62 (1983), 182–93; L. A. Cushman and M. P. Dijkers, "Depressed Mood in Spinal Cord Injured Patients: Staff Perceptions and Patient Realities," *Archives of Physical Medicine and Rehabilitation* 71 (1990), 191–96; F. A. Ernst, "Contrasting Perceptions of Distress by Research Personnel and Their Spinal Cord Injured Subjects," *American Journal of Physical Medicine and Rehabilitation* 66 (1987), 12–15; L. Gething, "Judgments by Health Professionals of Personal Characteristics of People with a Visible Physical Disability," *Social Science and Medicine* 34 (1992), 809–15; M. Hauswald and D. Tanberg, "Out-of-hospital Resuscitation Preferences of Emergency Health Care Workers," *American Journal of Emergency Medicine* 11:3 (1993), 221–24; R. A. Otto, R. A. Dobie, V. Lawrence, and C. Sakai, "Impact of a Laryngectomy on Quality of Life: Perspective of the Patient versus that of the Health Care Provider," *Annals of Otology, Rhinology, and Laryngology* 106:8 (1997), 693–99; E. Ralston, P. Zazove, and D. W. Gorenflo, "Physicians' Attitudes and Beliefs about Deaf Patients," *Journal of the American Board of Family Practice* 9:3 (1996), 167–73; S. E. Roush, "Health Professions as Contributors to Attitudes Towards Persons with Disabilities: A Special Communication," *Physical Therapy* 66:10 (1986), 1551–54; R. F. Uhlmann and R. A. Pearlman, "Perceived Quality of Life and Preferences for Life-sustaining Treatment in Older Adults," *Archives of Internal Medicine* 151:3 (1991), 495–97; R. L. Vernaci, "Disabilities Scary for Many: Survey," *Nashville Banner*, October 11, 1991, 5; M. L. Wolraich, G. N. Siperstein, and P. O'Keefe, "Pediatricians' Perceptions of Mentally Retarded Individuals," *Pediatrics* 80:5 (1987), 643–49.

4. Gerhart et al., "Quality of Life Following Spinal Cord Injury."

5. "Joint Statement from Evan Kemp and Justin Dart," October 1, 1996; Ehman, "Politics of D.N.R.," 14.

6. Amici curiae brief of Not Dead Yet and American Disabled for Attended Programs Today in Support of Petitioners, Dennis C. Vacco, et al., vs. Timothy E. Quill, et al., Respondents, U.S. Supreme Court, October 1995, http://www.notdeadyet.org/brief.html.

7. F. J. Girsh, "Physician Aid in Dying—What Physicians Say, What Patients Say, What Politicians Say," *Western Journal of Medicine* 157 (August 1992), 188–89; Society for the Right to Die, *The Living Will* (New York, 1967).

8. Duane Riner, "A Matter of Life and Death, Judge Rules Man Can Disconnect Ventilator," *Atlanta Constitution*, September 7, 1989, A17.

9. James A. McClear, "A 'Driving Wish' to Die," *Detroit News*, May 19, 1989, Life/1A; Jim Neubacher, "Whose Life Is It, Anyway?" *Detroit Free Press*, May 29, 1989; Margot Dougherty and Sandra Rubin Tessler, "Controversy: "Tiring of Life Without Freedom, Quadriplegic David Rivlin Chooses to Die among Friends," *People*, 32 (August 7, 1989), 56–58; Joseph P. Shapiro, "Larry McAfee, Invisible Man," *U.S. News and World Report*, February 19, 1990, 59–60.

10. McClear, "Driving Wish"; Dougherty and Tessler, "Tiring of Life Without Freedom," 58; Mary Johnson, "Drab Curtains," *Disability Rag* 10 (September–October 1989), 24.

11. "Accident Victim: Life More Than Surviving," *Daily Reporter* (Coldwater, Michigan), May 20, 1989; "Court OKs Death Wish," *USA Today*, July 7, 1989, 2A; McClear, "Driving Wish"; Neubacher, "Whose Life Is It, Anyway?"; Dougherty and Tessler, "Rivlin," 58.

12. Carol Easton and Florence MacKenzie, "Sensory-Perceptual Alterations: Delirium and the Intensive Care Unit," *Heart and Lung, the Journal of Critical Care,* 17:3 (May 1988), 229–35, article reviewing literature on intensive care psychosis; Duane Riner, "Quadriplegic Petitions Court to Let Him Die," *Atlanta Constitution*, August 15, 1989, A1, A18; Duane Riner, "Quadriplegic Tells Judge: I Wake Fearing Each Day," *Atlanta Constitution*, August 17, 1989, C1, C2; Shapiro, "Larry McAfee, Invisible Man," 60; Hal Straus, "Victim of Accident Is Stuck at Grady—But He's Not Sick," *Atlanta Constitution*, April 9, 1989.

13. McClear, "Driving Wish"; United Press International, "Man Disabled 18 Years Seeks Doctor to Cut Off Life Support," *Indianapolis Star,* July 7, 1989, A11; Dianne B. Piastro, "He Needed Help to Live," *Long Beach Press-Telegram,* August 1, 1989, C2; United Press International, "Quadriplegic Tells Why He Wants to Die," *San Francisco Chronicle,* August 17, 1989, A2; Riner, "Fearing Each Day," *Atlanta Constitution,* August 17, 1989, C2; Duane Riner, "A Painful Case: May Quadriplegic Die?" *Atlanta Constitution,* September 5, 1989, A1; attorney Randall Davis interviewed on *Today* (NBC), September 13, 1989.

14. "Accident Victim: Life More Than Surviving," *Daily Reporter* (Coldwater, Michigan), May 20, 1989; McClear, "Driving Wish," *Detroit News,* Life/6A; "Rivlin," *People,* 56; UPI, "Quadriplegic Tells Why He Wants to Die"; Riner, "Fearing Each Day"; Riner, "A Painful Case."

15. *ABC News Nightline*, December 28, 1989; Shapiro, "Larry McAfee, Invisible Man," 60; Rivlin interview, Cable News Network, July 21, 1989.

16. UPI, "Quadriplegic Tells Why He Wants to Die"; Peter Applebome, "Judge Rules Quadriplegic Can Be Allowed to End Life," *New York Times* (National Edition), September 7, 1989, A12; Riner, "A Painful Case," A1, A11.

17. Paul K. Longmore, "The Shameful Mistreatment of Larry McAfee," *Atlanta Journal-Constitution*, September 10, 1989; "Suicide?" Press Release of four Atlanta disability rights groups, September 5, 1989.

18. Duane Riner and Ben Smith III, "Quadriplegic Decides He'll Pursue Life," *Atlanta Journal-Constitution*, January 18, 1990, A1; Associated Press, "Quadriplegic Who Sought Death Now Seeks Job," *St. Paul Pioneer Press Dispatch*, January 18, 1990, 3A.

19. Paul K. Longmore, "Elizabeth Bouvia, Assisted Suicide, and Social Prejudice," chap. 8 in this volume; Derek Humphrey, "Mrs. Bouvia's Sad Mistakes Are Lessons," *Hemlock Quarterly* 14 (1984), 1; Derek Humphry, *Final Exit: The Practicalities of Self-Deliverance and Assisted Suicide for the Dying* (Eugene, 1991), 58–62.

20. Lori A. Roscoe, Julie E. Malphurs, L. J. Dragovic, and Donna Cohen, "Dr. Jack Kevorkian and Cases of Euthanasia in Oakland County, Michigan, 1990–1998," *New England Journal of Medicine* 343:23 (December 7, 2000); Raja Mishra, "A Study of Deaths Raises Questions on Kevorkian Image," *Boston Globe*, December 7, 2000, http://www.boston.com/dailyglobe2/342/nation/A_study_of_deaths_raises_questions_on_ Kevorkian_image+.shtml; Patricia Anstett, "Kevorkian Cases Linked, Study Says Most Who Sought Help with Suicide Were Vulnerable," *Detroit Free Press*, December 7, 2000, http://www.freep.com/news/locoak/nkevo7_20001207.htm; Wes Allison, "USF Researchers Say Most of Dr. Kevorkian's Patients Had No Terminal Illness," *St. Petersburg Times*, December 8, 2000, http://www.sptimes.com/News/120800/TampaBay/Study_Kevorkian_pati.shtml; "In Royal Oak: The Death Machine," *Detroit Free Press Magazine*, March 18, 1990, 24; Jack Kevorkian, "A Controlled Auction Market Is a Practical Solution to the Shortage of Transplantable Organs," *Medicine and Law* 11:1–2 (1992), 51, 53; Jack Kevorkian, written statement to Oakland County, Michigan, Superior Court, August 17, 1990.

21. *60 Minutes*, story on Kevorkian's killing of Thomas Youk, CBS News, aired November 22, 1998; *60 Minutes*, story on Elizabeth Bouvia, CBS News, producer Paul Lowenwarter, aired March 23, 1986; *60 Minutes*, follow-up story on Elizabeth Bouvia, CBS News, producers Deborah DeLucha Sheh and Paul Loewenwarter, 1996; Jim Yardley, "Celebrities Galore at Time Magazine Gala for 75th Anniversary," *New York Times*, March 4, 1998.

22. Silvia Sara Canetto and Janet D. Hollenshead, "Gender and Physician-Assisted Suicide: Analysis of the Kevorkian Cases, 1990–1997," *Omega: The Journal of Death and Dying* 40:1 (1999–2000), 165–208; Lori A. Roscoe, Julie E. Malphurs, L. J. Dragovic, and Donna Cohen, "A Comparison of Characteristics of Kevorkian Euthanasia Cases and Physician-Assisted Suicides in Oregon," *Gerontologist* 41:4 (August 2001), 439–46; Lynne Marie Kohm and Britney N. Brigner, "Women and Assisted Suicide: Exposing the Gender Vulnerability to Acquiescent Death," *Cardozo Womens' Law Journal* 4 (1998), 241–320; Silvia Sara Canetto and Janet D. Hollenshead, "Older Women and Mercy Killing," *Omega: The Journal of Death and Dying* 42:1 (2001), 83–99; Silvia Sara Canetto and Janet D. Hollenshead, "Men's Mercy Killing of Women: Mercy for Whom? Choice for Whom?" *Omega: The Journal of*

Death and Dying 45 (2002), 275–280; "Women Most Frequently Targets of Mercy Killing; Men Most Frequently Commit the Killing,"(visited July 13, 2002), http:// www.newswise.com/articles/2001/9/MERCY.CSU.html.

23. Jane Daugherty, Brian Harmon, and Doug Durfee, "Experts Denounce Kevorkian's Organ Donor Proposal, Legal and Medical Authorities Call Plan Unethical, Unfeasible," *Detroit News*, October 24, 1997.

24. "Down Syndrome Woman Denied Organ Transplant," *San Francisco Chronicle*, August 12, 1995, A19.

25. Associated Press, "Kevorkian Takes Part in Another Suicide," Nando.net, October 10, 1996; "Right To Life, Liberty and the Pursuit Of Happiness or Right to Die, What Will Texas Choose for Texans with Disabilities?" ADAPT of Texas press release, October 18, 1996, disabilitynewsletter@juno.com, October 19, 1996.

26. "Kevorkian Speaks His Mind," *Time*, May 31, 1993, 39.

27. Arthur E. Chin, Katrina Hedberg, Grant K. Higginson, and David W. Fleming, "Legalized Physician-Assisted Suicide in Oregon—The First Year's Experience," *New England Journal of Medicine* 340:7 (February 18, 1999); A. D. Sullivan, Katrina Hedberg, and David W. Fleming, "Legalized Physician-Assisted Suicide in Oregon—The Second Year," *New England Journal of Medicine* 342:8 (February 24, 2000), 598–604; Katrina Hedberg, D. Hopkins, and K. Southwick, "Legalized Physician-Assisted Suicide in Oregon, 2001," *New England Journal of Medicine* 346:6 (February 7, 2002), 450–52; A. D. Sullivan, Katrina Hedberg, and D. Hopkins, "Legalized Physician-assisted Suicide in Oregon, 1998–2000," *New England Journal of Medicine* 344:8 (February 22, 2001), 605–7; Katherine Foley and Herbert Hendin, "The Oregon Report. Don't Ask, Don't Tell," *Hastings Center Report* 29:3 (May–June 1999), 37–42; "Physician-assisted Suicide: When Pain Trails Other Concerns," editorial, *AMA News*, March 23, 2001, http://www.ama-assn.org/sci-pubs/amnews/ amn_01/edsa0319.htm; "Opinion: Death by the Numbers: Physician-assisted Suicide; Look Closely at the Statistics from Oregon and Elsewhere That Are Driving the Physician-assisted Suicide Debate," http://www.ama-assn.org/sci-pubs/amnews/ amn_02/edsa0318.htm, *American Medical News* (a publication of the AMA), 3/18/02.

28. Richard Leiby, "Whose Death Is It Anyway? The Kevorkian Debate. It's a Matter of Faith, in the End," *Washington Post*, August 11, 1996, F1.

29. *The Real Hemlock Society* (visited February 8, 1998), www.normemma.com/ arhemlock.htm.

30. For examples of alternative disability analysis, see James Charlton, *Nothing about Us Without Us* (Berkeley, 1998); Laura Hershey, "Economic Literacy and Disability Rights," *Disability Studies Quarterly* 16:4 (Fall 1996), 15–18; Paul K. Longmore, "Conspicuous Contribution and American Cultural Dilemmas: Telethon Rituals of Cleansing and Renewal," in David Mitchell and Sharon Snyder, eds., *Discourses of Disability: The Body and Physical Difference in the Humanities* (Ann Arbor, 1997), 134–58; Marta Russell, *Beyond Ramps: Disability at the End of the Social Contract* (Monroe, Maine, 1998).

31. For criticism of "Proposed Assisted Suicide 'Safeguards'" see http://www. notdeadyet.org/docs/ndysafeguards.html.

32. William Carlsen, "Doctor to Confess Role in Man's Death," *San Francisco Chronicle*, April 15, 1997, A13; Milt Freudenheim, "Humana Sued in Federal Court over Incentives for Doctors," *New York Times*, October 5, 1999.

33. Statement of Donne Brownsey at an educational forum on AB 1592, "Death with Dignity Act," sponsored by the California State Independent Living Council, Sacramento, June 18, 1999. For a critical analysis of this issue, see Susan M. Wolf, "Physician-Assisted Suicide in the Context of Managed Care," *Duquesne University Law Review* 35 (Fall 1996), 455–79.

34. "HMOs Stand to Gain Big," from OaksGroup@aol.com, to Kill_the_Bill@ onelist.com, subject: [Kill_the_Bill] Barbara Coombs Lee, May 5, 1999; http:// lifeadvocate.com/11_97/feature4.htm; Gail Kinsey Hill, "Lee: A Crusader for Assisted Suicide," *Oregonian*, August 24, 1997.

35. Editorial, "When Death Is Your Choice," *San Jose Mercury News*, May 10, 1999, http://www.mercurycenter.com/premium/opinion/edit/HOSPICE.htm.

36. Peter Steinfels, "Beliefs: Oregon Medicaid's Doctor-Assisted Suicide," *New York Times*, March 7, 1998; Erin Hoover, "Coverage of Assisted Suicide Looks Certain," November 24, 1998, *Oregonian*, http://www.oregonlive.com/todaysnews/ 9811/st112405.html; Patrick O'Neill, "Kitzhaber Proposes New Programs, No New Taxes; The Oregon Health Plan Would Face Some Cuts, Tougher Screening under the Governor's Proposal," *Oregonian*, December 2 1998; Associated Press, "Oregon Health Plan Will Cover Assisted Suicide Costs," December 2, 1998; Physicians for Compassionate Care, "Assisted Suicide Report Plagued by Shortcomings," press release, February 23, 2000; Nat Hentoff, "Free Ticket to Eternity," *Washington Post*; February 6, 1999, A21; "Questions Asked about Assisted Suicide Chief Petitioner Answers Questions on Measure 16," http://nl12.newsbank.com/nl-search/we/ Archives?p_action=doc&p_docid=0EB0888D68E1573C&p_docnum=6.

37. *Compassion in Dying v. State of Washington*, No. 94–35534, U.S. Court of Appeals for the Ninth Circuit, 79 F.3d 790; 1996 U.S. App. LEXIS 3944, Online. LEXIS-NEXIS® Academic Universe (6 July 2001), p. 120; Ann Dudley Goldblatt, "Knocking on Heaven's Door: Medical Jurisprudence and Aid in Dying," in Ronald P. Hamel and Edwin R. DuBose, eds. *Must We Suffer Our Way to Death? Cultural and Theological Perspectives on Death by Choice* (Dallas, 1996), 71. In making her quoted observation about judicial findings, Goldblatt's point was that there is not a legal basis for patients to compel doctors to provide assistance in dying as a treatment.

38. *Compassion in Dying v. State of Washington*, p. 115.

39. Michael Volkman quoted in Harvey Lipman, "Disabled Group Urges Supreme Court to Reject Assisted Suicide," *Albany Times Union*, January 8, 1997, B2.

40. Sandra Carpenter, Senior Manager, Ontario Ministry of Citizenship, Culture and Recreation, Citizenship Policy Branch, Disability Issues Unit, Toronto, Canada, personal communication to author, October 1996.

10

Medical Decision Making
and People with Disabilities

A Clash of Cultures

As has become obvious throughout the preceding essays, the discrepancy between "insider" and "outsider" perspectives regarding
the nature and meaning of the experience of *disability* appears in
every sphere of society. But nowhere is it more palpable than in
the disparity between disabled and nondisabled views of medical
decision making. Once again, disability rights activists have a distinctive disabled perspective to contribute to the current debate
about changing health care policies and ethics.

In discussions of medical decision making as it applies to people with disabilities, a major obstacle stands in the way. The perceptions and values
of disabled people (particularly disability rights advocates and disabled
scholars) on the one side and of many nondisabled people (particularly
health care professionals, ethicists, and health policy analysts) on the
other side, regarding virtually the whole range of current health and
medical-ethical issues (treatment decision making, health care access
and health care rationing, medical cost containment, and assisted sui-

The original version of this essay was written for "Medicine's New Recipes," a bioethics conference sponsored by the Pacific Center for Health Policy and Ethics, University of Southern
California Law Center, at the request of Vicki Michel, who, with Alex Capron, has distinguished herself by a readiness to include a disability rights perspective in the current debate.
From Paul K. Longmore, "Medical Decision Making and People with Disabilities," *Journal
of Law, Medicine, and Ethics* 23:1 (Spring 1995), 82–87. © 1995. Reprinted in slightly different
form with permission of the American Society of Law, Medicine, & Ethics. May not be re-
produced without express written consent.

cide), seem frequently to conflict with one another. This divergence in part grows out of the sense, common among people with disabilities, that their interactions with "the helping professions," medical and social-service professionals, are adversarial. But those differences of opinion also stem more basically from a clash of fundamental values.

This paper addresses, in historical perspective, the ways in which the status of persons with disabilities as a stigmatized minority group affects medical decision making. It also examines the efforts of disability rights activists to prevent discrimination against persons with disabilities in current medical culture. Finally, it raises questions about how the rights of people with disabilities will fare as new care standards are developed and implemented.

In recent years, a majority of Americans with disabilities have come to view themselves as members of a stigmatized minority group.[1] That minority group consciousness is being expressed by mounting political activism. The adversarial relationships and conflict of values between medical professionals and persons with disabilities can only be understood within the context of this minority status and consciousness.

At the heart of this minority consciousness is a rejection of the reigning medical model of disability. That paradigm has dominated not only medical treatment decision making regarding persons with disabilities, but also, more broadly, modern cultural definitions of disability, social perceptions of people with disabilities, and the social options and roles permitted to disabled persons. The medical model defines *disability* as the physical and psychological experience of biological defect deriving from any one of a series of illnesses or injuries located within the bodies of "afflicted" individuals. Medical practitioners have seen cure, or at least correction of functioning, as the only possible way to bring about the social integration of people with disabilities.

The emergent minority group consciousness defines *disability* primarily as a socially constructed condition. The difficulties of persons with disabilities in social and vocational functioning are seen not as the exclusive and inevitable consequence of bodily impairments, but as the product of the interaction between individuals with such impairments and the arrangements of the social and architectural environments. In particular, according to this analysis, historic and pervasive cultural devaluation of physically different persons has produced socioeconomic discrimination against them. It follows that people with a variety of disabilities, despite considerable differences in etiology, have historically confronted a common set of stigmatizing cultural values and social hazards.[2]

Disability minority group consciousness and mounting activism among people with disabilities have arisen in opposition to what is now widely condemned within their community as the historical legacy of oppression. In the United States during the late nineteenth and early twentieth centuries, professionals in medicine, social services, and education increasingly attributed to the "defective classes," which included virtually anyone with a disability, a lack of moral and emotional self-control, blaming them for the poverty, vice, crime, and dislocations of the new industrial order. People with mental retardation, epilepsy, or cerebral palsy were often permanently institutionalized as dangers to society. Others with physical disabilities were at times segregated by such ordinances as Chicago's "ugly law." Reacting to a growing Deaf subculture, an "oralist" movement began in the 1880s to oppose sign language and to insist that deaf people learn speech and speech reading. Led by Alexander Graham Bell, the oralists took over deaf education and sought to disperse the Deaf community. Eugenicists lobbied for sterilization of people with various disabilities. By 1931, more than half the states had adopted sterilization laws. Proponents of euthanasia advocated putting to death people with certain kinds of disabilities, an idea implemented in Nazi Germany under the T-4 Euthanasia program.[3]

Meanwhile, modern welfare policy defined *disability* as complete incapacity for productive labor and, in effect, incompetency to manage one's life. It thereby brought many people with disabilities under permanent medical and social-service supervision, while relegating them to economic dependency. This public policy created a large stigmatized and segregated category of persons and held it in a permanent state of clientage. In terms of social values, this categorization came to define the limits of legitimate need, on the one hand, and of social normality, on the other. It also served the ideological and economic interests of various professional groups in the modern welfare state.[4]

The disability rights movement rejected these reigning perspectives and practices. It secured passage of federal laws barring discrimination and ensuring the rights of access and reasonable accommodations, educational opportunities and employment, deinstitutionalization and independent living, medical and support services, employment and family life. That movement has met resistance on every front.

As part of that opposition to the civil-rights campaign of Americans with disabilities, adversaries have resurrected the arguments of the early-twentieth-century eugenics and euthanasia movements: people with disabilities are unproductive, their lives have low quality and little meaning, they burden their families, they drain scarce social and economic resources.[5] Disability rights activists in Colorado discerned consistency in the policy positions of Richard Lamm, one-time governor and sometime U.S. Senate candidate. Writing in the *Denver Post*, disabled columnist Laura Hershey noted: "Equal education and integrated accessible transportation have been central issues in disabled people's historic struggle for equality. . . . Lamm is a longtime opponent of lift-equipped buses and special education for severely disabled children, both of which he says are 'not cost-effective.' Lamm talks about 'hard choices.' Hard on whom? And whose choice? Once again, a politician is telling us that our basic needs . . . are too expensive, and unimportant. In times of economic hardship, tight resources and general confusion, sometimes the easiest thing to do is to find somebody to blame."[6] Disability rights activists like Hershey see a linkage between Lamm's views on education and accessibility and his positions on medical cost containment and the right, indeed the duty, to die.

Nondisabled people may question the connections disabled activists detect. What connection does the Chicago "ugly law" or Lamm's opposition to accessible public transit have with medical decision making or health care policy? Disabled activists and social scientists start from the premise that all individual and institutional behavior toward people with disabilities, including health care decisions, is shaped by historically deep-seated cultural presuppositions about disability and about what sort of persons Americans ought to be. When medical decisions regarding individuals with disabilities are made and when health care policies that will impact persons with disabilities individually and as a class are formulated, disability rights advocates and disability studies scholars argue, the historically intense and still largely unacknowledged devaluation of such persons inevitably comes into play. In everything from freak shows to telethons, movies to medical ethics, people with disabilities have been depicted as the antithesis of what Americans ought to be. They have been and are the ultimate Other, assert proponents of the minority model. As a result, that ongoing historical reality continues to shape social perceptions as well as health policy and health care choices.[7]

For instance, Jack Kevorkian could visit David Rivlin in a Michigan nursing home and see only a man who had "to be turned and fed and everything done for him. [A] highly intelligent man, who had decided that his life now had no meaning and no need to go on, and he wanted a doctor to come forward to help him, and, of course, with the situation today, no one dared." "After that case, I knew we had to have a device to help people like Mr. Rivlin, and that's when I started making it." Disability rights activists saw instead a man thwarted in his attempts at independent living, education, career, and romance by public policies that spent $230 a *day* to keep him in a nursing home, but less than $300 a *month* for him to live in his own apartment. Those policies would have denied him any support had he married, as he wished to do at one point. Activists note that while the United States spends approximately $53 billion annually on long-term care, only 18 percent of that amount goes to in-home services.[8]

Discussion of treatment choices and of limiting the treatment afforded persons with disabilities often revolves around views of the "quality of life." Here, particularly, the opinions of disabled and nondisabled people sharply diverge, but the values that shape those views typically remain unexamined. The conventional wisdom of nondisabled people seems to be that costly heroic medical interventions frequently keep alive infants and older persons with disabilities who should be allowed or caused to die, while the conventional wisdom and common experience in the disability rights community is that adequate and appropriate treatment is frequently denied because of devaluation and discrimination.[9]

Researchers with disabilities describe a conflict of values, perspectives, and interests between persons with disabilities and their own families, and at other times between, on the one hand, disabled persons and their families, and, on the other, health care providers. Some nondisabled researchers studying parental and physician attitudes toward newborns with disabilities have reached similar conclusions. For instance, they find a connection between social class and stigmatization. Infants with Down's syndrome, "the most stigmatized of the retarded, physically and socially, represent an assault on middle-class strivings and aspirations and culturally determined goals." They are "seen as a serious impediment to social mobility. . . . Families with less status concern seem to be far less traumatized." Other research has found health professionals resisting or refusing treatment of infants with disabilities because of devaluing attitudes. Doctors may reject newborns with disabilities because physicians feel they have failed. Such feelings of failure are not simply personal psychological reactions; they originate from the social unacceptability of the characteristics of infants with disabilities.[10]

Nondisabled physicians, parents, and other nondisabled persons often seem to assume that persons with disabilities see their own lives as inherently diminished due to their disabilities. But Beatrice Wright, a leading authority on the social psychology of disability, notes that social psychologists have repeatedly documented "the ease with which devalued groups are regarded as unfortunate, despite the fact that the members of those groups do not view themselves as unfortunate." For example, "persons with physical disabilities at a rehabilitation center . . . rated themselves as individuals at least average in terms of how fortunate they were, whereas, as a labeled group, they were rated below average by others." "The difference," explains Wright, "can be understood in terms of the kind of information being processed. Whereas the label attached to a group defines the salient aspect to be observed and little else, . . . when one rates oneself a host of personal and situational aspects enter the field for consideration." In others words, "outsiders," nondisabled people, latch onto a single trait (for example, paraplegia or arthritic pain), while "insiders," people with disabilities, take into account the full range of their experience. Their evaluation of their own lives is not restricted by a stigmatizing label. It is not just that insiders have grown used to their disabilities and have learned to deal with them. They have incorporated the disabilities into their identities, into their very selves. And they see their experiences as yielding much that is positive in their personal growth.[11]

According to Wright, the research findings are consistent. They hold, not just among people with disabilities, but also among individuals with potentially fatal diseases. One investigation "demonstrated that hospital patients felt less depressed, anxious, and hostile than their medical therapists judged them to feel." Another study "showed that the closer the subject is to the position of the patient, the more likely positive effects of a life-threatening illness, cancer, will be perceived." "To my knowledge," concludes Wright, "all research on insider versus outsider perspectives shows not only that the meaning of the experience differs, but also that the insider is generally more inclined than the outsider to take into account positives in the situation. Insiders place the significance of the handicap or trouble in a life context so that the span of realities connected with it are wide. Only some aspects are negative, others are clearly positive (e.g. coping, identity), and it is this broad context that restrains negative spread. To outsiders the other person's handicap or problem tends more or less to stand alone."[12]

The divergence, indeed conflict, between insider and outsider perspectives, between disabled and nondisabled people, leads to radically different ethical and policy choices. Thus, Helga Kuhse and Peter Singer can assert that the readiness of many pediatricians to cause newborns with disabilities to die supports their argument for infanticide. They would apply that practice not only to infants with very severe disabilities, but even to youngsters whose only disability may be riding a wheelchair. In contrast, a disabled civil-rights lawyer looks at the same physician choices and sees discrimination.[13]

Such divergences emphasize the importance of incorporating disabled views into the current debate about health care decisions, policies, and spending. Yet the inclusion of a disability rights perspective in that discourse is rare. Disability rights groups have complained for years that projects such as Health Vote and the debate over the Oregon Medicaid health care rationing plan have excluded their perspective. In March 1994, members of the activist disability rights group ADAPT went so far as to disrupt a meeting of Michigan's commission on euthanasia by chanting "Extermination Without Representation."[14]

Disability rights perspectives have usually been excluded from public discourse. When they have been included, nondisabled persons have often discounted them as alarmist. As a result, some activists and social scientists with disabilities are skeptical that adding one or two individuals to bodies such as hospital ethics review panels would adequately represent the rights and interests of people with disabilities. For instance, the disabled political scientist Harlan Hahn has suggested that

> composition of [a medical ethics review] committee is likely to repeat the mistakes of similar bodies formed under P.L. 94-142 [the Individuals with Disabilities Education Act] which frequently have failed to protect the rights of disabled children because of the ability of professionals to intimidate parents and advocates for the child. . . . This approach . . . seems to assume that there will be no divergence of interests between disabled and nondisabled. As a minority influenced by a social legacy that encompasses a suspicion of professional authority as well as genocide and infanticide, disabled people are not likely to remain content with a policy that denies them an opportunity to play a major role in decisions that affect the fate of other members of their group.[15]

It is then perhaps understandable when disabled activists are similarly skeptical that treatment and medical guidelines could safeguard people with disabilities. Disability rights advocates might reasonably contend that as long as the historical and continuing reality of institutionalized prejudice persists, not just unresolved but largely unacknowledged, no ethical dicta or practice guidelines could begin to protect people with disabilities or to assure them equal access to appropriate health care. Practice guidelines could easily—virtually unconsciously—be ignored.

Does this leave us at an impasse? Can we bridge the apparent gulf between disabled and nondisabled perspectives? At this juncture, only one course of action seems not only useful but essential: the perspectives and values of the disability rights community, as well as attention to the historical and contemporary oppression of people with disabilities, each needs to be incorporated into the ongoing debate about medical practice, ethics, and policy.

Notes

1. Louis Harris and Associates, *ICD Survey of Disabled Americans* (New York, 1986), 112, 114.

2. For general statements of the medical and minority group models and their contemporary and historical applications, see: Victor Finkelstein, *Attitudes and Disabled People: Issues for Discussion* (New York, 1980); John Gliedman and William Roth, *The Unexpected Minority: Handicapped Children in America* (New York, 1982), 1–51; Paul K. Longmore, "The Life of Randolph Bourne and the Need for a History of Disabled People," *Reviews in American History* 13:4 (1985), 81–87; Paul K. Longmore, "Uncovering the Hidden History of Disabled People," *Reviews in American History* 15:3 (1987), 355–64; and William Roth, "Handicap as a Social Construct," *Society* 20:3 (1983), 56–61.

3. Hugh Gallagher, *FDR's Splendid Deception* (New York, 1985); Harlan Lane, *When the Mind Hears: A History of the Deaf* (New York, 1985); Longmore, "Uncovering the Hidden History of Disabled People"; Carol Paden and Tom Humphreys, *Deaf in America: Voices from a Culture* (Cambridge, Mass., 1988); William R. F. Phillips and Janet Rosenberg, eds., *Changing Patterns of Law: The Courts and the Handicapped* (New York, 1980); Peter L. Tyor and Leland V. Bell, *Caring for the Retarded in America: A History* (Westport, 1985); John Vickrey Van Cleve, ed., *Deaf History Unveiled: Interpretations from the New Scholarship* (Washington, D.C., 1993); John Vickrey Van Cleve and Barry Crouch, *A Place of Their Own: Creating the Deaf Community in America* (Washington, D.C., 1989); Wolf Wolfensberger, *The Origin and Nature of Our Institutional Models* (Syracuse, 1975); Marcia Pearce Burgdorf and Robert Burgdorf, Jr., "A History of Unequal Treatment: The Qualifications of Handicapped Persons as a 'Suspect Class' under the Equal Protection Clause," *Santa Clara Law Review* 15:4 (1975), 863–64.

4. On the history of public disability welfare and social-insurance policy, see: Edward Berkowitz and Kim McQuaid, *Creating the Welfare State: The Political Economy of Twentieth-Century Reform* (Lawrence, Kan., 1980); Edward Berkowitz, *Disabled Policy: America's Programs for the Handicapped* (New York, 1987); Harlan Hahn, "Rehabilitation and Public Policy," *American Behavioral Scientist* 28:3 (1985), 293–318; and Deborah Stone, *The Disabled State* (Philadelphia, 1986).

5. See for example: Helga Kuhse and Peter Singer, *Should the Baby Live? The Problem of Handicapped Infants* (New York, 1985); Peter Singer, *Practical Ethics* (New York, 1979).

6. Laura Hershey, "Once Again, a Politician Calls our Basic Needs Too Costly, and Unimportant," *Denver Post*, May 28, 1992, 7B.

7. Douglas Biklen and Lee Bailey, eds., *Rudely Stamp'd: Imaginal Disability and Prejudice* (Washington, D.C., 1981); Robert Bogdan, *Freak Show: Presenting Human Oddities for Amusement and Profit* (Chicago, 1988); Harlan Hahn, testimony, U.S. Civil Rights Commission, *Protection of Handicapped Newborns, Hearing Held in Washington, D.C., June 12–14, 1985* (Washington, D.C., 1985), 116–20; Paul K. Longmore, "Screening Stereotypes: Images of Disabled People in Television and Motion Pictures," *Social Policy* 16:1 (1985), 31–37; Paul K. Longmore, "Elizabeth Bouvia, Assisted Suicide, and Social Prejudice," *Issues in Law and Medicine* 3:2 (1987), 141–70.

8. Jack Kevorkian interviewed on *Sally Jessie Raphael*, KCAL (Los Angeles), June 14, 1990; Paul K. Longmore, "The Strange Death of David Rivlin," *Western Journal of Medicine* 154 (1991), 615–16; *Polio Survivors Newsletter*, December 1992–January 1993, 1.

9. Mary Johnson, "Killing Babies: Left and Right," *Disability Rag* 6 (1985), 22–23; Timothy M. Cook, "Disability Law: Medical Treatment—Who Decides?" *Mainstream* 11:5 (1987), 19; Sonya Ross, "Rulings for Suicide Disturb Disabled," *Oregonian*, September 13, 1989; Carol J. Gill, "Suicide Intervention for People with Disabilities: A Lesson in Inequality," *Issues in Law and Medicine* 8:1 (1992), 37–53; Carol Gill, "'Right to Die Threatens Our Right to Live Safe and Free," *Mainstream* 16:11 (1992), 32–36.

10. Carol J. Gill, "The Family/Professional Alliance in Rehabilitation Viewed from a Minority Perspective," *American Behavioral Scientist* 28:3 (1985), 424–28; Carol J. Gill, "Disability and the Family," *Mainstream* 18:13 (1994), 30–35; Hahn testimony, U.S. Civil Rights Commission, *Protection of Handicapped Newborns*; Fletcher, "Attitudes Towards Defective Newborns," unpublished manuscript, 25–27.

11. Beatrice Wright, "Attitudes and the Fundamental Negative Bias: Conditions and Corrections," in Harold E. Yuker, ed., *Attitudes Towards Persons with Disabilities* (New York, 1988), 8–9.

12. Wright, "Attitudes and the Fundamental Negative Bias," 9–10.

13. Kuhse and Singer, *Should the Baby Live?* 35–36; Cook, "Disability Law,"19.

14. "Leaving Disabled People Out Prompts Boycott Call," *Disability Rag* 6:7 (1985), 11; Frances Strong, letter, *Disability Rag* 7:2 (1986), 36; "Panel on Assisted Suicide Split as Rest of Society," *San Francisco Examiner*, March 6, 1994, A6.

15. Harlan Hahn, "Public Policy and Disabled Infants: A Sociopolitical Perspective," *Issues in Law and Medicine* 3:1 (1987).

FOUR

PROTESTS
AND FORECASTS

11

The Second Phase
From Disability Rights to Disability Culture

Every so often participants in social-change movements need to
pause, look back over their past efforts, and look forward to try to
forecast where they are headed. We need on occasion to review
and sum up in order to continue to move ahead with clear purpose. I tried to offer that sort of appraisal in this 1995 speech.
The speech/essay that follows had several goals. It attempted to
summarize the agenda and analysis of the disability rights movement. In particular, it reviewed disability rights ideology, both as
it has critiqued dominant social thought and practice and as it
has framed and promoted alternative approaches. In addition, it
sought to reflect on a deeper and culturally more radical extension of that ideology by exploring the emergence of a disability-
based critique of reigning values and the development of an alternative constellation of disability-based values and norms. Finally,
it considered the role of disability studies in relation to disability
rights advocacy and disability culture formation.

The movement of disabled Americans has entered its second phase. The
first phase has been a quest for civil rights, for equal access and equal
opportunity, for inclusion. The second phase is a quest for collective
identity. Even as the unfinished work of the first phase continues, the
task in the second phase is to explore or to create a disability culture.

Originally published in slightly different form in *Disability Rag* 16 (September–October 1995),
3–11, and online in *The Ragged Edge;* based on a keynote address to "This/Ability: An Interdisciplinary Conference on Disability and the Arts," at the University of Michigan, May 19,
1995.

This historic juncture offers a moment for reflection and assessment. It is an opportunity to consider the aims and achievements of the disability movement over the past generation and in the last few years.

In August 1985, the *Disability Rag* reported an incident that captured the essence of the disability movement's first phase:

> "It comes to a point where you can't take it any more," said Nadine Jacobson, sounding for all the world like Rosa Parks. She and her husband Steven were arrested July 7th for refusing to move from seats in the emergency exit row of a United Airlines flight on which they were to leave Louisville after the NFB [National Federation of the Blind] convention here. "You lose some of your self-respect every time you move," she told *Louisville Times* reporter Beth Wilson. United has a policy of not letting blind people sit in emergency exit rows, because it believes they might slow an evacuation in an emergency, though there seems to be no airline policy against serving sighted passengers in emergency exit rows as many drinks as they want for fear they might become too intoxicated to open an emergency door properly in the event of a disaster. NFB members say it's discriminatory treatment, plain and simple. The airline says it is not. The Jacobsons pleaded "not guilty" to the charge of disorderly conduct.

Six months later, the *Rag* related that the Jacobsons had been acquitted of the charge. A half year after that, in the fall of 1986, it announced that Congress had passed the Air Carrier Access Act, which amended the Federal Aviation Act to prohibit discrimination against persons with disabilities in airline travel. Yet over the next three years, the *Rag* reported instances of discrimination against blind and wheelchair-riding travelers, FAA regulations that restricted the rights of disabled airline passengers, including a rule prohibiting them from sitting in exit rows, and the opposition of the National Federation of the Blind, the Eastern Paralyzed Veterans Association, and ADAPT to these practices and policies.

Despite the problems with its implementation, the Air Carrier Access Act was one of some fifty federal statutes in a quarter century of legislation that reflected a major shift in public-policy making regarding Americans with disabilities. That process began in 1968 with the Architectural Barriers Act and culminated in 1990 with the ADA. In between came such legislative high points as Section 504 and P. L. 94-142.[1] This body of laws departed significantly from previous policies because it sought not just to provide more "help" to persons regarded as disadvantaged by disability, but rather expressed and implemented a fundamental redefinition of "disability" as a social more than a medical problem.

The new-model policies coincided with, and to a degree reflected, the emergence of disability rights activism. Airline accessibility was only one of the issues spurring that activism. Deaf and disabled activists moved on everything from the presidency of Gallaudet University to the pervasive impact of telethons. But whatever the particular issue at hand, activists were redefining "disability" from the inside.

This activism was the political expression of an emerging consciousness among a younger generation of Americans with disabilities. A 1986 Louis Harris survey of adults with disabilities documented that generational shift in perspective. While only a minority of disabled adults over the age of forty-five regarded people with disabilities as a minority group like blacks or Hispanics, 54 percent of those aged eighteen to forty-four agreed with that perspective. In addition, substantial majorities in every age bracket believed that people with disabilities needed legal protection from discrimination, but the largest percentage of respondents holding that view were in the youngest age group, eighteen to thirty. And yet only one-third were aware of Section 504. It appeared that the great mass of disabled people had not yet become politically active. Their views reflected a proto-political consciousness, the emerging minority group consciousness of a new generation.

That younger generation has spurned institutionalized definitions of "disability" and of people with disabilities. At its core, the new consciousness has repudiated the reigning medical model that defines "disability" as physiological pathologies located within individuals. That definition necessarily prescribes particular solutions: treatments or therapies to cure those individuals or to correct their vocational or social functioning. Cure or correction has been viewed as the only possible means by which people with disabilities could achieve social acceptance and social assimilation.

Those who are not cured or corrected have been defined as marginalized by disability. They have been relegated to invalidism. This has meant not just physical dependency or institutionalization but, most fundamentally, social invalidation.

While the medical model claims to be scientific, objective, and humane, within its practice has lurked considerable anxiety toward the people it professes to aid. In one respect, the medical model has been the institutionalized expression of societal dis-ease about people who look different or function differently. It regards them as incompetent to manage their own lives, as needing professional, perhaps lifelong, supervision. It sometimes sees them as a threat to society.

The new disability perspective has presented a searching critique of the medical model. It has argued that by locating the problem in the bodies of individuals with disabilities, the medical model cannot account for, let alone combat, the bias and discrimination evident in such actions as the mistreatment and arrest of Nadine and Steven Jacobson. Indeed, disability rights advocates have argued that implementation of the medical model in health care, social services, education, private charity, and public policies has institutionalized prejudice and discrimination. Far from being beneficial, or even neutral, the medical model has been at the core of the problem.

In place of the medical model, activists have substituted a minority group model of disability. "Disability," they have asserted, is primarily a socially constructed role. For the vast majority of people with disabilities, prejudice is a far greater problem than any impairment; discrimination is a bigger obstacle for them to "overcome" than any disability. The core of the problem, in the activists' view, has been historically deep-seated, socially pervasive, and powerfully institutionalized oppression of disabled people.

To combat this oppression, the disability movement not only called for legal protection against discrimination, it fashioned a new idea in American civil-rights theory: the concept of equal access. Traditional rehabilitation policy defined access features and accommodations such as architectural modifications, adaptive devices (wheelchairs, optical readers), and services (sign-language interpreters) as special benefits to those who are fundamentally dependent. Disability rights ideology redefined them as merely different modes of functioning, and not inherently inferior.

Traditional civil-rights theory permitted differential treatment of minorities only as a temporary expedient to enable them to achieve parity. Disability rights ideology claimed equal access and reasonable accommodations as legitimately permanent differential treatment because they are necessary to enable disabled persons to achieve and maintain equal access.

"Access" could have been limited to physical modifications in the personal living and work environments of disabled individuals. Instead, disability activists have pressed forward a broad concept of equal access that has sought to guarantee full participation in society. To ensure equal opportunity, they have declared, equal access and reasonable accommodations must be guaranteed in law as civil rights.

To nondisabled opponents, disabled activists have not sought equal opportunities, they have demanded special treatment. Disabled people could not, the critics have complained, on the one hand, claim equal opportunity and equal social standing, and, on the other, demand "special" privileges such as accommodations and public financial aid (e.g., health insurance). Disabled people could not have it both ways. According to majority notions, equality has meant identical arrangements and treatment. It is not possible in American society to be equal and different, to be equal and disabled.

On this basic issue of the nature of equality and the means of accomplishing it, disabled activists and their nondisabled opponents have had radically different perceptions. And that difference was not new in the 1970s and 1980s. It has a long history.

To take just one example, in 1949 a spokesperson for the National Federation of the Blind testifying before a Congressional committee argued simultaneously for Aid to the Blind (ATB), a social-service program of financial assistance, and for civil-rights protections. The disability of blindness was a physical condition that incurred significant expenses and limitations, he argued, and therefore required societal aid. But it was also a social condition that involved discriminatory exclusion. He quoted the famous legal scholar and blind activist Jacobus ten Broek's "Bill of Rights for the Blind" to the effect that the real handicap of blindness, "far surpassing its physical limitations," was "exclusion from the main channels of social and economic activity."

Throughout the history of disabled activism, advocates like this NFB representative simultaneously called for "social aid" and civil rights. Unlike their nondisabled opponents, they saw no contradiction in this position. It was possible in America, they implicitly proclaimed, to be equal and to require aid and accommodations, to be equal and different. Indeed, for Americans with disabilities, any other approach to equality seemed impossible.

The disability movement's critique of the medical model has also argued that the complete medicalization of people with disabilities has advanced the agenda of professional interest groups. People with disabilities have served as a source of profit, power, and status.

An estimated 1.7 million mentally, emotionally, or physically disabled Americans have been defined as "incurable" and socially incompetent and have been relegated to medical warehouses. Another 10 to 11 million disabled adults, 70 percent of working-age adults with disabilities in the United States, are unemployed and welfare dependent, while uncounted others languish below the poverty line.

According to the disability movement's analysis, the immediate causes of this marginalization have been public policies. Health care finance policies force disabled people into institutions and nursing homes rather than funding independent living. Income maintenance and public-health insurance policies include "disincentives" that penalize disabled individuals for trying to work productively. Disabled adults have also been relegated to dependency because of continuing widespread inaccessibility and pervasive job market discrimination.

But according to this analysis, the ultimate cause of their marginalization is that people with disabilities are highly profitable. For that reason, they have been kept segregated in what is virtually a separate economy of disability. That economy is dominated by nondisabled interests: vendors of overpriced products and services; practitioners who drill disabled people in imitating the "able-bodied" and deaf people in mimicking the hearing; a nursing-home industry that reaps enormous revenues from incarcerating people with disabilities.

Thus, concludes this analysis, millions of deaf and disabled people are held as permanent clients and patients. They are confined within a segregated economic and social system and to a socioeconomic condition of childlike dependency. Denied self-determination, they are schooled in social incompetency, and then their confinement to a socially invalidated role is justified by that incompetency. According to this critique, disabled issues are fundamentally issues of money and power.

The disability rights movement marked a revolt against this paternalistic domination and a demand for disabled and Deaf self-determination. That revolt and that demand have been at the center of the controversy over telethons. Who should have the power to define the identities of people with disabilities and to determine what it is they really need? Or, parallel to this dispute, how could the hearing majority on the Gallaudet University Board of Trustees reject two qualified Deaf educators to select yet another hearing president? "Who has decided what the qualifications [for president] should be?" asked Gallaudet student government president Greg Hlibok. "Do white people speak for black people?" Hence the students' demand for a Deaf majority on the board of trustees.

But the attack on the medical model has gone beyond merely questioning the motives of nondisabled interest groups. At a still deeper level, that critique has explained the relentless medicalization of people with disabilities as an attempt to resolve broader U.S. cultural dilemmas. In a moment of intense social anxiety, the medical model of disability has helped reassure nondisabled people of their own wholeness as human beings, their own authenticity as Americans. It has done so by making "disability," and thus people with disabilities, the negation of full and valid American humanity.

In order for people with disabilities to be respected as worthy Americans, to be considered as whole persons or even approximations of persons, they have been instructed that they must perpetually labor to "overcome" their disabilities. They must display continuous cheerful striving toward some semblance of normality. The evidence of their moral and emotional health, of their quasi-validity as persons and citizens, has been their exhibition of the desire to become like nondisabled people.

This is, of course, by definition, the very thing people with disabilities cannot become. Thus, they have been required to pursue a "normality" that must forever elude them. They have been enticed into a futile quest by having dangled before them the ever-elusive carrot of social acceptance.

Recognition that "overcoming" is rooted in nondisabled interests and values marked the culmination of the ideological development of the disability movement's first phase. And that analytical achievement prepared the way for a transition into the second phase.

The first phase sought to move disabled people from the margins of society into the mainstream by demanding that discrimination be outlawed and that access and accommodations be mandated. The first phase argued for social inclusion. The second phase has asserted the necessity for self-definition. While the first phase rejected the medical model of disability, the second has repudiated the nondisabled majority norms that partly gave rise to the medical model.

That repudiation of dominant values has been most obvious in rejections of the medically proclaimed need to be cured in order to be validated. At the time of the Gallaudet student revolt, Eileen Paul, co-founder of an organization called Deaf Pride, proclaimed, "This is a revolt against a system based on the assumption that Deaf people have to become like hearing people and have to fit into the dominant hearing society."

As they spurned devaluing nondisabled definitions, Deaf people and disabled people began to celebrate themselves. Coining self-affirming slogans such as "Disabled and Proud," "Deaf Pride," and "Disability Cool," they seized control of the definition of their identities. This has been not so much a series of personal choices as a collective process of reinterpreting themselves and their issues. It is a political and cultural task.

Beyond proclamations of pride, Deaf and disabled people have been uncovering or formulating sets of alternative values derived from within the Deaf and disabled experiences. Again, these have been collective rather than personal efforts. They involve not so much the statement of personal philosophies of life as the assertion of group perspectives and values. This is a process of Deaf cultural elaboration and of disabled culture building.

For example, some people with physical disabilities have been affirming the validity of values drawn from their own experience. Those values are markedly different from, and even opposed to, nondisabled majority values. They declare that they prize not self-sufficiency but self-determination, not independence but interdependence, not functional separateness but personal connection, not physical autonomy but human community. This values formation takes disability as the starting point. It uses the disability experience as the source of values and norms.

The affirmation of disabled values also leads to a broad-ranging critique of nondisabled values. American culture is in the throes of an alarming and dangerous moral and social crisis, a crisis of values. The disability movement can advance a much-needed perspective on this situation. It can offer a critique of the hyperindividualistic majority norms institutionalized in the medical model and at the heart of the contemporary American crisis. That analysis needs to be made, not just because majority values are impossible for people with disabilities to match up to, but, as important, because they have proved destructive for everyone, disabled and nondisabled alike. They prevent real human connection and corrode authentic human community.

Another manifestation of the disability movement's analysis and critique has been the attempts over the past dozen years to develop "disability studies" within research universities. Every social movement needs sustained critical analysis of the social problems it is addressing. Such movements develop their own cadres of intellectuals and scholars who arise from the community and often connect it with academic institutions. Disability studies has been conceived as a bridge between the academy and the disability community.

But what should disability studies look like? Professor Simi Linton, a disabled scholar-activist, and her colleagues at Hunter College in New York have proposed a useful working definition of disability studies:

> Disability Studies reframes the study of disability by focusing on it as a social phenomenon, social construct, metaphor and culture, utilizing a minority group model. It examines ideas related to disability in all forms of cultural representation throughout history, and examines the policies and practices of all societies to understand the social, rather than the physical and psychological, determinants of the experience of disability. Disability Studies both emanates from and supports the Disability Rights Movement, which advocates for civil rights and self-determination. The focus shifts the emphasis away from a prevention/treatment/remediation paradigm, to a social/cultural/political paradigm. This shift does not signify a denial of the presence of impairments, nor a rejection of the utility of intervention and treatment. Instead, Disability Studies has been developed to disentangle impairments from the myth, ideology and stigma that influence social interaction and social policy. The scholarship challenges the idea that the economic and social status and the assigned roles of people with disabilities are inevitable outcomes of their condition.

This definition captures the fundamental features of disability studies as it has grown out of the disability rights movement.

If disability studies is to serve the disability community and movement effectively, it needs to define an agenda. That project should include the following goals:

- Disability studies should serve as an access ramp between the disability community and research universities. It must forge a fruitful connection between the disability community/movement and such institutions.
- The traffic of ideas and persons on that ramp should flow in both directions. It must be a two-way street. The disability perspective, the insights, experience, and expertise of people with disabilities, must inform research, producing new questions, generating new understandings.
- At the same time, academic researchers can help bring new rigor to the disability rights movement's analysis and activism. Collabora-

tion between scholars and advocates can produce a deeper critique of disability policy and of the social arrangements that affect people with disabilities and can generate a more fully elaborated ideology of "disability" and disability rights.

- Complementing these endeavors, disability studies should also forge a link with disabled artists and writers. This collaboration can support the current flowering of disability arts. It will also promote disability-based cultural studies that can uncover disabled values, explain the social/cultural construction of "disability" by the majority culture, and critique dominant nondisabled values.

- To implement this agenda, disability studies must obtain support for faculty and graduate students. That support must come in two forms: funding to pay for research and teaching, and affirmative action to recruit faculty and students with disabilities to develop disability studies. We need to build a phalanx of disabled disability-studies scholars and intellectuals.

- To succeed and to remain true to its purpose, disability studies needs the active support and involvement of the disability community. Disability studies can then help advance both phases of the disability movement.

Those two phases are not separate and successive chronological periods. They are complementary aspects of the disability movement. The concept of equal access represents a politics of issues. It is the effort of Americans with disabilities to build an infrastructure of freedom and self-determination. The proclamation of disability and Deaf pride and the elaboration of disability and Deaf cultures express a politics of identity. They are an affirmation, a celebration, of who we are, not despite disability or deafness, but precisely because of the disability and Deaf experiences.

These two phases of the disability movement are reciprocal. Each is essential to the other. Together they declare who we are and where we intend to go.

Note

1. The Education for All Handicapped Children Act, subsequently renamed the Individuals with Disabilities Education Act.

Princeton and Peter Singer

If the disparity of perspectives and the clash of values between disabled and nondisabled people is frequently as deep as many of the preceding essays argue, it is imperative that we work to make space for disabled perspectives in public and academic discourses. Yet disabled viewpoints and disability studies analyses continue to be excluded from many of our public arenas and most of our colleges and universities. To be sure, there are hopeful signs. A small but growing number of schools offer disability studies courses; a few have even mounted degree programs. In addition, the National Endowment for the Humanities has called attention to the intellectual significance of this emerging field by funding disability studies projects. Still, by and large, our major universities continue to support research and teaching about disability that approach it only from the perspective of medical pathology. They make no room for a minority group analysis. That narrow framing and the ways in which it excludes other modes of thought might have been examined during the furor over the appointment of Peter Singer to an endowed professorship at Princeton University. Instead, the controversy revolved around issues of the quality and sanctity of life and issues of free speech and academic freedom. Unfortunately virtually everyone involved overlooked a third major question: in the end, which voices and views are privileged in the academy and which are shut out?

A shorter version of this essay was originally published in *New Mobility*, October 1999.

Disability rights activists have criticized the philosopher Peter Singer for his prejudicial views against people with disabilities and have condemned Princeton University for hiring him. But the protest has failed to raise a number of important questions.

Who on the Princeton faculty researches, writes, and teaches about the experience of disability from a minority group perspective? There are undoubtably many faculty at Princeton who address disability issues, as there are at all our major universities. Scholars in many fields teach and write about disability, but the overwhelming majority approach that study from a medical model. How many teachers at Princeton and other American universities lead their students in examining these issues from a minority model?

And how many of the faculty who teach about disability are people *with* disabilities? How many of them understand the experience of disability from the inside?

Our leading universities have women faculty who teach and write about the experience and social status of women. Many of them do so from a feminist perspective that seeks to counter the historic subordination of women to men. Those schools also have faculty of color who teach and write about the experience and social status of racial and ethnic minorities. They do so from the perspectives of those historically segregated groups. Many of these faculty are distinguished scholars who produce respected and influential work.

All of this is as it should be. This diversity reflects the concerted attempt in American higher education during recent decades to redress past exclusions and imbalances. But most of our universities overlook a current exclusion and imbalance.

How many faculty members with disabilities do Princeton and other schools have? How many faculty teach about the experience and social status of people with disabilities? And what effort is Princeton, what efforts are our other universities, undertaking to recruit faculty members who publicly identify as disabled persons? How many universities are seeking out scholars who do intellectual work that advances social justice for disabled people?

The answer is that only a handful of major universities is making any effort to hire faculty with disabilities. Only a few are searching for scholars who research and teach about disability from a minority-model perspective. Disability studies is apparently not even on the radar of Princeton or most of our universities.

Indeed, one would not expect Princeton to recruit faculty with disabilities or to develop disability studies given its dismal record of support for students with disabilities. In November of 2000, a *Daily Princetonian* columnist noted that while the university has committed itself to promoting diversity, it omits people with disabilities from that agenda. The campus is pervasively inaccessible. It has large programs to support women students, minority students, and gay, lesbian, bisexual, and transgendered students, but not disabled students. All of this violates both Section 504 and the Americans with Disabilities Act. We are left to consider this disturbing fact: "one of the richest universities in the country" could find funds to endow a chair for a man who advocates killing disabled people, but it can't come up with the money to accommodate disabled students.

No wonder only thirty-six Princeton undergraduates—a minuscule 0.8 percent of the campus population in fall 2000—reported having disabilities. The student columnist sensibly urged that the Princeton community consider why there are so few disabled students, "given that disabilities affect one in five Americans." "Are people with disabilities less intelligent? Less motivated?" he asked. "Hardly. More likely the lack of physical accessibility or administrative support—as well as an unfriendly atmosphere—immediately deter these students from even considering Princeton." Princeton students with disabilities confirmed that assumption.

The columnist went on to say that "skeptics may wonder why the university should invest in the effort and expense to attract more students with disabilities." His answer: beyond legal and moral obligations, "we want a diverse community." Students with disabilities could "contribute to the diversity on campus, to the spectrum of human life. They stand as living models of perseverance, motivation and grace. And when students leave this place to enter the real world they will no longer feel uncomfortable approaching a co-worker who seems a little different."[1]

The student columnist was on the right track in recognizing that the presence of people with disabilities would enhance Princeton's diversity. Unfortunately he expected their contribution to come only at the level of personal character, of inspirational modeling.

These narrow expectations are not really his fault. They inevitably result from the absence of, not just fellow students with disabilities, but, more important, faculty with disabilities and disability studies curricula.

If Princeton lags behind many other schools in ensuring equal access and reasonable accommodations, its deficiencies in hiring disabled faculty, developing disability studies courses, and incorporating minority group analysis of disability into the university's intellectual discourse remain characteristic of most of American higher education.

Active interaction with disabled teachers, as well as intellectual and moral engagement with disability studies, would open to students like this thoughtful young man unexpected new understanding of the experience and meaning of "disability." Integration of disability studies concepts and materials in the general curriculum would demonstrate the significance of the field for every academic discipline, for all intellectual inquiry. Disability studies deepens our comprehension of the broad range of questions education has always posed: What makes a person human? What is justice? What is community? What is equality? Disability studies touches upon many themes, from American notions of individualism and equality, to social and legal definitions of what constitutes a minority group, to values and beliefs regarding gender and sexuality, to unspoken ideas about autonomy, fitness, and citizenship, appearance, progress, and the "health" of society. Exploration of these issues from a disability studies perspective thus has philosophical as well as political implications.

The valuable potential contributions to learning that would result from disability studies curricula and disabled faculty, but their continuing scarcity in higher education, prompt some additional questions. Why do Princeton and almost all of our major universities privilege the intellectual perspectives on disability of scholars who view it as medical pathology and social deficiency, but typically make no place for scholars who take a minority model approach? Why has Princeton given an endowed professorship to a philosopher who advocates executing disabled babies, but—as far as I can discover—has failed to hire in any faculty position at any rank in any discipline even a single instructor who offers a minority group analysis of the social segregation and marginalization of people with disabilities?

The absence of the latter perspective is especially significant because, while many established academicians would condemn a philosopher who advocated killing girl babies or black or brown babies, they do not balk at the claim that parents should have a right to kill disabled babies. They implicitly regard disabled people's lives as worth less than those of nondisabled people, perhaps even worthless altogether. As they see it, disability is different from race and gender, so Singer's views fit within the parameters of acceptable moral and intellectual discourse.

Defenders of his appointment charge Singer's critics with infringing on his academic freedom and freedom of speech. But they fail to ask why the minority group perspective on disability issues is virtually excluded from intellectual discourse at Princeton and almost every other major university in the United States. They fail to question why the experience and voice of disabled people are absent from the faculties of those schools. They fail to realize that these exclusions distort intellectual discourse. They are oblivious that this constitutes a form of intellectual censorship and invalidation.

My point is not to call for Singer's ouster. Rather, I simply want to ask why his perspective is accorded, not just academic standing, but a highly privileged place, an endowed chair, while the perspectives of people with disabilities are granted no place at all.

When will Princeton—when will all our universities—begin to foster balance and diversity by adding the voices of disabled scholars and by enabling students to study "disability" from a minority group perspective?

Since the completion of this essay, Princeton has launched a compliance effort to make that university physically and programmatically accessible and accommodating and, it appears, to begin to incorporate people with disabilities into its promotion of diversity. This is a commendable step in the right direction.

Note

1. Nathan Arrington, "Inaccessible Is Unacceptable: When It Comes to Comfortably Accommodating Disabled Students, Princeton Has a Long Way to Go," *Daily Princetonian*, Tuesday, November 21, 2000, http://www.dailyprincetonian.com/Content/2000/11/21/edits/338.shtml; Emma Soichet, "Handicapped Accessible?" *Daily Princetonian*, Monday, November 13, 2000, http://www.dailyprincetonian.com/Content/2000/11/13/page3/.

Why I Burned My Book

One afternoon in 1992, I sat in a large wood-paneled seminar room in Stanford University's History Corner. One of the doctoral students gave an interesting talk on mid-twentieth-century U.S. welfare policies, following which the group of faculty and graduate students discussed the history of American welfare. As I listened, it struck me that no one seemed to have much sense of what it was really like to "be on welfare." I wondered if I were the only person there who had actually had that experience. It has often occurred to me that the same lack of direct experience has hobbled the study of disability in general and disability policy in particular, though few scholars in these fields seem aware of that limitation.

My own interest in disability policy and its history grew partly out of the impact of public policies on me personally. The ways in which policy construed "disability" severely constricted my life and work. That direct encounter with the implementation of disability policies not only spurred me to investigate their origins and historical development; it provided me with a perspective other scholars commonly lack.

At the same time, I found that in order to have any hope of building a career as a professional historian and college teacher, indeed, in order to do any kind of work at all, I was inexorably drawn into disability rights advocacy regarding those same policies. Personal inclination made me a historian. Personal encounter with public policies made me an activist.

Based on a keynote address at "On the Move '89," Sixth Annual Conference for People with Disabilities, YWCA, Riverside, California, May 20, 1989.

In October 1988, I organized a demonstration in Los Angeles to protest so-called work disincentives in federal disability-related welfare policies. The account that follows expands on a speech I made a few months later in which I recounted both that protest and the experience that led up to it.

This essay draws together the themes woven throughout this collection: the discrepancy between "insider" and "outsider" perspectives; the disparities of power between people with and without disabilities; the conflict of agendas between disability rights activists and nondisabled policy makers and professionals; the interplay between disability rights advocacy and disability studies analysis; the continuing struggle of disabled people to gain a voice and to shape our destinies. This story seems a fitting way to conclude this book.

I want to tell you why I burned my book. A deed as shocking as burning a book demands an explanation. It seems particularly mystifying and, therefore, all the more disturbing when the perpetrator has avowedly devoted his life to books. In order to account for that act, I will have to tell you a good deal about myself. I must say, though, that I feel uncomfortable having to disclose so much about my personal life. I would prefer to keep it private. I would rather write biography than autobiography. But it seems to me that some of us are going to have to talk frankly about what it is really like for us as disabled people if we ever hope to break down the barriers of prejudice and discrimination that "cripple" our lives.

I—and most disabled Americans—have been exhorted that if we work hard and "overcome" our disabilities, we can achieve our dreams. We have heard that pledge repeatedly from counselors and educators and "experts," and from our government too. We have seen it incarnated by disabled heroes on television, those plucky "overcomers" who supposedly inspire us with their refusal to let their disabilities limit them. We are instructed that if we too adopt an indomitable spirit and a cheerful attitude, we can transcend our disabilities and fulfill our dreams.

It is a lie. The truth is that the major obstacles we must overcome are pervasive social prejudice, systematic segregation, and institutionalized discrimination. Government social-service policies, in particular, have forced millions of us to the margins of society. Those policies have made the American Dream inaccessible to many disabled citizens.

In saying these things, I risk getting myself labeled as a maladjusted disabled person, a succumber to self-pity, a whining bitter cripple who blames nondisabled people for his own failure to cope with his condition. That charge—or the fear that we might provoke it—has intimidated many of us into silence. As I said, some of us are going to have to risk telling the truth.

The truth is I am a model "rehabilitant." I am, from one perspective, a disabled overachiever, a "supercrip." That shouldn't surprise anyone. I had polio. The rehabilitation system drilled people who had polio in overcoming and then held us up as legendary exemplars of healthy adjustment to disability. American culture has lionized us for our alleged refusal to accept limitations.

So what did I do? I earned my B.A., M.A., and Ph.D. in American history, intending to become a college teacher. And when I published my first book, one reviewer remarked that it drew on "a truly astounding amount of research." Of course it did. Would a postpolio supercrip do anything less? How characteristically disabled of me to undertake so grandiose a project.

Still, I don't want to reduce my work to "overcoming." At the core of my efforts, I pursued a rather simple personal dream: I wanted to write about American history and to teach it to college students.

A succession of dedicated teachers helped me move toward those goals by demonstrating their belief in my talents: Tim O'Keefe at the University of Santa Clara; Norman Cohen, Cliff Kroeber, and Bob Winter at Occidental College; and especially Robert Dawidoff, my dissertation adviser at the Claremont Graduate School. Leonard Levy of Claremont and Bob Middlekauff of the Huntington Library later helped me get my first publications. Martin Ridge of the Huntington sought to support my research. The endorsement of my scholarship and teaching by these mentors, their confidence that I could have a professional future, were especially important because their support buoyed me up against waves of bias from other quarters. Even while they urged me on, other teachers sapped some of my energy with wounding words of prejudice and occasional overt acts of discrimination.

One undergraduate professor told me that because of my disability no college would ever hire me as a teacher. I guess he thought he was helping me face the hard facts. His opinion that I should pursue a more realistic objective reminded me of something I read around that time in *The Autobiography of Malcolm X*. Early in the book, Malcolm reports the impact on him of a conversation with one of his teachers. The teacher told the talented and eager teenager that his dream of attending college and law school was unrealistic. Like Malcolm, I felt that my teacher was not only discounting my abilities, but counseling me to give in to discrimination.

A couple of years later as I was completing my master's degree, the chair of the history department told me he thought I would do well in doctoral studies, because, he said, "You're not bitter like most cripples." But he also informed me matter-of-factly that because of my disability no college would ever hire me as a teacher.

I went ahead and applied to several Ph.D. programs in history anyway. One school rejected me because of my disability. Fortunately, in 1971 the Claremont Graduate School accepted me. At the end of my first year there, I applied for a fellowship, but the departmental committee turned me down. I asked for a meeting with them. I wanted them to tell me to my face why they had refused my fellowship application. They explained that because of my disability no college would ever hire me as a teacher. In other words, they didn't want to squander the department's money on me. They suggested I consider archival work. I pointed out that archival work is more physical than teaching. Besides, I said, I want to teach, and I'm going to teach whether you help me or not. They said they felt sure I would succeed, because "we really admire your courage."

The committee's decision to deny me a fellowship because of my disability was an act of discrimination, but it was not an illegal act. In 1972, there was no Americans with Disabilities Act. There was no Section 504. No law prohibited disability-based discrimination. Had it not been for Robert Dawidoff's personal commitment to me and my work, bias might well have defeated my efforts to get my Ph.D. and become a college teacher. At some point, I likely would have given up.

A personal benefactor had paid my first year's tuition. For the second year and for several years thereafter, I had no funding to pay for my doctoral studies. I was living on Supplemental Security Income, a federal income maintenance program for poor people with disabilities.[1] SSI at first provided me with $135 a month. Over five years, the allotment was raised to $185 a month. Somehow—looking back, I cannot imagine how—I scrimped and scraped together enough to pay the tuition for a single course each year. Because I could not afford the cost of attending classes full-time, I had to petition the Claremont Graduate School to waive its residency requirement, the academic regulation requiring doctoral students to complete all course work within a specified time. I snailed along, enrolling in just one course a year for several years.

If individual acts of discrimination on the part of some of my teachers hurt or hindered me, over the long run the discrimination institutionalized in government policies and programs was far more debilitating. At the time of my acceptance to graduate school, I applied to the California Department of Rehabilitation for financial aid. A rehabilitation counselor in the Pasadena office told me that DR did not fund doctoral study. But, he said, they could train me to become a computer programmer. I told him no, thanks. Now, there's nothing wrong with computer programming. It's honorable work. It's just not what I wanted to do. I wanted to teach college.

For several years through the mid-1970s, I hunted for money to pay for my graduate education. I applied for student fellowships. I got none. I asked about financial aid from disability-related charities like the Easter Seal Society. They said they didn't provide that kind of help. I even managed, after a considerable campaign, to become a contestant on the TV game show *Tic Tac Dough*. I lost.

Finally one day, not knowing where else to turn for advice or assistance, I happened to call the Rehabilitation Counseling Department at Cal State University, Los Angeles. A secretary put me through to one of the professors. I explained my situation. He told me I had been—how shall I put it?—*misinformed* by the counselor at the state Department of Rehabilitation. Nothing in the law or public policy or DR's own regulations, explained the professor, prevented it from financially supporting my Ph.D. studies in history. DR could help me in whatever way I needed. I just had to persist with them tenaciously, he said. I had to refuse to take no for an answer.

Armed with this information and advice, I went back to the Department of Rehabilitation. This time the people in the Pasadena office agreed to enroll me as a client. DR would begin funding my graduate education. But—here was the catch—it would pay no more than the cost of tuition at one of California's public universities. At the Claremont Graduate School, a private institution, tuition stood at three times the rate of tuition at the state's public institutions, such as UCLA. In practical terms, DR's cap on tuition payments meant that I could now take two courses a year, instead of just one.

Perhaps I could have gotten DR to pay more if I had asserted myself with the agency as the Cal State professor had warned me I would have to do. But at that point, I was still rather naive about the system, still intimidated by it. I hadn't yet realized just how tenacious and aggressive one had to be to make the bureaucracy move.

After several more years during which I labored along in my doctoral studies, the Department of Rehabilitation notified me that it intended to close my case. I had taken too long to complete my degree, explained my rehab counselor. I've taken so long, I replied, because you people won't pay the full tuition. You could have gone to a public university that charges lower tuition, she said. I'm a student in a highly regarded graduate program in history, I told her. Don't I have a right to go to the best school I can get into? You could have stopped with a master's degree, she said; that's enough for an entry-level position. It's not enough to teach college, I answered. I need a Ph.D. to become a college teacher. At last, the counselor confessed that her superiors put pressure on her and other counselors to close out cases in order to improve the agency's overall statistics.

I already knew about DR's practice of terminating cases to make itself look more effective in rehabilitating clients to successful employment. Everyone knew about it. It's one of the ways the voc rehab bureaucracy keeps itself in business. Still, the rehab counselor shouldn't have openly admitted the practice to a client, at least not to this particular client. I quoted her words in a letter to my state assembly member.

My assembly member intervened with top-level administrators in Sacramento. DR reversed itself. They would continue me as a client. They also switched me to a new counselor, a man who himself had a disability. He offered me support DR had never before provided, most important, money to pay for transcription of my dictated research notes. At last I had the means to make significant progress on my dissertation and doctorate.

A few months after the new counselor started working with me, I got a call from his supervisor. He wanted to know if I was satisfied with the counselor. I said I most definitely was. The supervisor said he was glad to hear that, because he had recommended promotion of the counselor to senior rank against the opinion of his (the supervisor's) superiors. I asked why the superiors had opposed promoting my counselor. Because of his disability, said the supervisor. They didn't think he could do the job.

If the struggle to find ways to pay for my graduate studies slowed my progress, an even greater financial dilemma threatened to stop me altogether. My disability incurs enormous expenses. I have no use of my arms, limited use of my right hand, and, because of a severe spinal curvature I use a ventilator a great deal of the time. As a result, I employ aides in my home to do the housekeeping and to assist me with tasks like showering, shaving, dressing, and eating. As of October 1988, at the time I burned my book, the wages paid to my personal assistants, plus the rental of my ventilators, exceeded $20,000 a year. (By the turn of the century, those costs topped $45,000 a year.) Disability-related living and work expenses have posed the fundamental problem of my adult life. The plain fact is, I am unlikely ever to earn enough in an academic career to cover such costs.

My situation is not unusual. Enormous numbers of Americans with major disabilities grapple with high disability-related expenses. They too could work, at least part-time, but could never earn enough to pay for the services and devices they need.

Necessity has forced many of us to maintain eligibility for federal Supplemental Security Income (SSI) or Social Security Disability Insurance (SSDI) or both. Both programs provide monthly cash benefits. But that is not what makes them vital to us. Indeed, virtually any of us could earn the $350 to $700 monthly allotments we typically receive.

Far more important, SSI and SSDI eligibility make us eligible for other, more essential assistance. For instance, throughout my adult life I have paid my personal assistants through California's In-Home Support Services program. Medi-Cal (the California version of Medicaid) has paid for my ventilators. Without this financial aid, I would have had to spend my adult life in some sort of nursing home. At far greater cost to taxpayers, I might add. In most states, people with disabilities like mine have found themselves in a far more horrendous situation: they get little or no aid for independent living. They are shackled to their families or imprisoned in nursing homes. They are denied access to life and to work. Independent living has enabled me to work productively.

The catch is that for most of my adult life, in order to maintain eligibility for this government aid, I had to refrain from work. Using a combination of medical and economic criteria, federal disability policy defined—and still defines—"disability" as the total inability to engage in "substantial gainful activity." In the 1970s and 1980s, policy makers reckoned as "substantial gainful activity" gross earnings exceeding $300 a month. (Eventually they raised the SGA level to over $700 for nonblind disabled persons.) Anyone who earned above that meager amount was, to their way of thinking, no longer disabled, despite any ongoing medical condition or functional limitations they might have. If you worked and earned more than that, the government would cut off all financial aid to you.

All through the 1970s and much of the 1980s, the all-or-nothing $300-a-month earnings threshold blocked me from getting teaching experience. If I had taken even part-time work as a college instructor—which is the way doctoral students usually seek to make themselves more competitive in the higher-education job market—I would have jeopardized the financial aid that paid for my in-home assistance and my ventilator, the aid that enabled me to live independently and, in fact, to work. As a result, my résumé remained almost blank. What college, I wondered, would hire someone with what amounted to zero formal teaching experience and virtually no record of any kind of work at all? And if I did somehow manage to land a faculty position, how would I, on a college teacher's salary, replace the $20,000 a year in assistance that had made it possible for me to get to that point?

Year after year in graduate school, I fretted about how I could make myself marketable as a college teacher and how I would get by financially if I ever did get a job. Semester after semester, I considered quitting the Ph.D. program. Why beat my head against a stone wall? What was the point? In virtually every semester of graduate school, there came a moment when I had to sit down and decide once again that I would hang in there for one more term.

If the policy definition of disability as complete incapacitation for productive work ever made sense, it certainly made none by the late twentieth century. Advances in technology made it possible for even significantly disabled people to work. I completed my doctoral dissertation using a Dictaphone and a word processor.

The historical roots of these public policies that deliberately and systematically deny disabled Americans the right to work require some explanation. In her elegantly persuasive study *The Disabled State*, Deborah Stone, a political scientist, demonstrated that policy makers created the "disability category" in poor relief and social welfare in order to distinguish unambiguously between two economies, one putatively based on "need," the other allegedly grounded in "work." They sought to keep workers in the labor market by restricting admission to the "need-based" system. Invention of the disability category, Stone argues, attempted to achieve these objectives by defining "disability" as utter incapacity to perform productive labor.[2]

The designers of disability-related early-modern poor relief and modern social-service programs believed that many nondisabled or only partially disabled workers would make false claims in order to win exemption from work. Given that expectation, the policy makers identified prevention of fraud as the central problem in welfare administration. They attempted to detect imposture, Stone shows, by adopting a "clinical concept" of disability. They assumed that this medical model would supply a scientific means of quantifying "disability," thereby objectively measuring and verifying it. Application of medical definitions would supposedly catch fraud, thereby ensuring that only those with legitimate claims to societal aid would get it.

The trouble was—and is—that disability-related poor relief and social welfare have always operated on a foundation of false postulates about the nature of disability. The policies rest on the assumption that physical or mental impairments by themselves produce "disabilities," limitations in social and vocational functioning. These premises undoubtably have had great appeal because they offer certain advantages for public-policy making and program administration. They give assurance that determination of eligibility for aid can be a fairly clear-cut process. Doctors and other professionals can reduce both impairment and disability to a set of numbers, numbers that will show who objectively qualifies to receive benefits. This assumedly will not only prevent fraud; it will also make program administration more efficient, while helping to keep a lid on public spending.

In reality, this ideological framework for disability welfare policies seriously misconstrues the causes and character of disability. Disability is not an entity that a clinical examination can correlate with the numbers on a schedule of impairments. It is not located in pathological individual bodies. It is not simply caused by impairments or by physiological features that depart from the typical. Instead, disability is produced through the dynamic interplay of a complicated constellation of factors that includes, not only stigmatized physical and mental limitations and physiological differences, but also physical and architectural environments, social arrangements and cultural values, and the impact of public policies themselves. In addition, all of the factors that make "disability" and shape the human experience of disability have, like all historical phenomena, changed over time. Disability, then, is not a fixed *thing*. It is an elastic and dynamic social category. It is not an objective condition. It is a set of socially produced, highly mutable, historically evolving social identities and roles. Throughout the modern history of disability welfare and rehabilitation programs, some policy makers, program administrators, and medical and rehabilitation professionals have acknowledged these realities about the true complex nature of disability. Nonetheless, policies and programs have continued to operate on the traditional simplistic definitions of disability, its causes and character.

Both politicians and disability policy bureaucrats continue to operate from these premises. And they still see fraud as the major concern. For example, in 1981 the newly installed Reagan administration asserted that more than one out of four Social Security Disability Insurance recipients failed to match the program's eligibility requirements. That is, they did not fit the SSDI definition of disability; they were not really disabled. This view was not unique to conservative Republicans. The preceding, liberal Democratic Carter administration had expressed the same opinion. The difference was that the Reaganites launched a massive effort to "purify" the SSDI rolls of the alleged horde of illegitimate claimants. Tens of thousands of disabled people found themselves kicked off SSDI, thereby losing medical insurance and other essential assistance. As it turned out, the vast majority did meet the program's definition of disability. Most eventually had their benefits restored. But, it is disturbing to note, a significant number who would have won reinstatement did not appeal. Many disabled citizens who are eligible for assistance struggle by on whatever meager resources they can muster rather than traversing the energy-sapping, dehumanizing bureaucratic labyrinth. Even more disturbing, at least a dozen purged SSDI recipients died before they received notification that the bureaucracy had booted them off the program erroneously. The allegation of widespread fraud was never proved. It was a phony issue.[3]

Most scandalous of all, the Social Security Administration resisted federal court rulings regarding its eligibility reviews. SSA did yield when the courts overturned its decisions in individual cases, but it dug in its heels when federal judges enjoined it to make basic changes in how it conducted those reviews. The courts directed the agency to ensure recipients' due process rights and to employ less mechanistic definitions of disability. For several years, SSA refused to obey these rulings. It euphemistically called its defiance of the courts "nonacquiescence." If you or I refused to "acquiesce" to the decision of a federal court, we would find ourselves looking out through the bars of a cell. Top-level federal bureaucrats are different from you and me. To disability rights activists, SSA's stance evidenced that the problems in the federal social-insurance/social-welfare system stem not only from a policy ideology that distorts the realities of disability, but also from the tenacious exertions of an entrenched bureaucratic institution to safeguard its prerogatives and powers, no matter what the cost in the lives of ordinary people with disabilities.[4]

In addition to designing mechanisms for detecting fraud, policy makers historically have sought to forestall fakery by making both the process of determining eligibility and the experience of receiving benefits—so to speak—arduous. They fashioned what amounted to ceremonies of social degradation for persons seeking or getting assistance. Disabled people who have suffered through this gauntlet know what I am talking about. The politicians and bureaucrats who designed these deliberate indignities figured that only the most destitute, only the "truly needy," would put up with such ignominious treatment.

This institutionalized system of social humiliation has a long history. An integral feature of the English Poor Law system, it went under the euphemistic name of the principle of "less" or "least eligibility" (in modern parlance, desirability or preferability). Though the archaic descriptor is no longer used, the demeaning practice has been continued. The great blind scholars Jacobus ten Broek and Floyd Matson described it in their classic mid-twentieth-century studies of U.S. welfare and disabled people. They depicted an institution that from start to finish deliberately robs disabled people of their dignity. "Through an interminable succession of investigations beginning with the application interview and culminating, but not ending in the issuance or withholding of the cash grant," they wrote, "the disabled client finds himself confronted with a presumption not of innocence and eligibility but of guilt and probable fraud. . . . Nor is this surveillance a one-time only procedure briefly annoying but soon over and done with; it is continuous and recurrent, ceasing only with the client's death or his transfiguration into a state of self-sufficiency. For the disabled recipient of aid, Big Brother is always watching." To ten Broek and Matson, the hoary principle of "less eligibility today no longer signifies the pauper's badge, workhouse gruel, bodily punishment, and loss of franchise in general, but it does involve certain major deprivations: the loss of the right to privacy with continuing review of resources, expenditures, and living circumstances; the pressure on relatives to contribute and the resulting strain on family life; and a lower material standard of living than others enjoy."[5] In my own experience and the experience of many disabled people I have talked with, little has changed since the 1950s and early 1960s when ten Broek and Matson wrote their brilliant and scathing analyses. Their gendered language is now outdated; their critique still applies.

In ten Broek and Matson's view, the modern welfare system not only demeans people with disabilities; it thoroughly disempowers them. "Whatever modest degree of self-control and responsibility, the disabled person may have possessed before entering this web of bureaucracy and paternalism," they noted, "is soon wrested from him by the process of means-test aid. It is the agency of welfare, not the recipient, who decides what life goals are to be followed, what ambitions may be entertained, what services are appropriate, what wants are to be recognized, what needs may be budgeted, and what funds allocated to each. In short, the recipient is told what he wants as well as how much he is wanting. . . . If the recipient does not comply and conform, he may be removed from the roles and have his budget reduced. The alternatives are obedience or starvation."[6]

Seeking the origins and causes of this system of suspicious scrutinizing, ten Broek and Matson traced the underlying ideology back through "Victorian pieties" about "the moral depravity and natural inferiority of the poor." They found its earliest roots in Elizabethan Poor Law images of poor people and disabled people as "victims of their own vices." Some of their observations still resonate decades later in an era when politicians across the spectrum boast that they have "ended welfare as we know it." For example, the two disabled scholars pointed out that the "concept of the characterological causation of poverty and dependency has not only a venerable history but a contemporary reality. In the eyes of that law there are not broad social problems of poverty or injustice to be solved but only individual wrongs to be righted, personal sins of commission to be expiated and corrected. And the proper corrective, in most cases, is some form of punishment."[7]

Many policy scholars have noted that the badge of moral depravity historically was affixed on the able-bodied poor. Only a few have recognized with ten Broek and Matson that poor-relief and welfare policies have always inflicted a parallel moral stigma on people with disabilities. In fact, many policy scholars regard induction into the disability welfare category as a "privileged" status that "exempts" people with disabilities from work rather than excluding them from productive contribution to society. This was not ten Broek and Matson's view. It is not the view of disability rights advocates. In their opinion, while public policies have ostensibly separated the "unworthy" from the "worthy" poor, those policies have also effectively erased that distinction by marking people in both categories as unworthy. All are morally flawed, all socially discredited. All are punished.

If the punitive element in welfare administration stems from ancient notions of moral defectiveness, ten Broek and Matson traced the sources of the system's paternalistic component to an ideology of poverty and disability that drew its rationale from modern medicine, psychology, and social work. All "welfare clients," they noted, "including the blind and the disabled, have been categorically judged incompetent to manage their lives and affairs." A fundamental though unspoken assumption of welfare administration regards the client as "irrational, irresponsible, abnormal, and incompetent."[8]

It should come as no surprise that this supposition of client abnormality and incompetency shapes the operation of welfare programs, for it appears implicitly, if not explicitly, in many explanations of the causes of poverty, just as it pervades disability, rehabilitation, and special-education research and training. Ten Broek and Matson focused on the consequences of this attitude for people with disabilities under the welfare system. In fact, that notion has stood as a core formative principle of most modern disability programs, whether in custodial institutions or community-based support services, medical and vocational rehabilitation or special education, public assistance or private charity. Virtually all late-twentieth-century disability programs of whatever type established mechanisms for clients to appeal adverse decisions, while many programs ostensibly guaranteed them a voice in the drafting of individualized education or rehabilitation plans. But in actual practice, programs have usually operated on the assumption that people with every sort of disability are incapable and irresponsible regarding management of their own lives. In tandem, this presumed personal and social incompetency, along with the putative moral defectiveness of disabled people, make necessary, make inevitable, their placement under professional supervision. Indeed, so pervasive are the deficiencies of disabled people, so omni-incompetent are we, that an array of professionals with many kinds of expertise must superintend our lives. These arrangements force many people with disabilities to remain as permanent clients of, not just one, but many programs and agencies. Professionals and bureaucrats continue to wield the greater power.

As ten Broek and Matson concluded, the "chief effect" of these features that historically have characterized disability-related social-service policies and programs has been "to perpetuate dependency and discourage initiative." "Continuous surveillance, loss of independence, and inadequate allowances all combine to produce conditions which run sharply counter to the principles of personal rehabilitation." These tendencies make the recipient "a ward under agency guardianship, in flat contradiction of the declared goal of helping 'individuals meet their essential needs and recover and maintain their personal capacities for self-direction.'" Noting that rehabilitation involves, not just physical, but social and psychological, elements, ten Broek and Matson declared, "Integrity of personality cannot be built upon a foundation of humiliation." "A system of aid . . . which continually impresses upon the recipient a sense of his helplessness and dependency, which withdraws from him the daily experience of management of his own affairs, and which enfolds him in an atmosphere of custodialism and guardianship—weakens the fiber of self-reliance, deters self-improvement, and threatens the very independence that is indispensable to salvation." Their observations about recipients of Aid to the Blind capture the experience of all disabled recipients: "The blind aid recipient is soon made aware, and continually kept conscious, of the inferior position into which he has been thrust. He comes to feel that he is the victim of unique discrimination; that other groups in society—organized labor, farmers, industrialists—make no such sacrifice in personal liberty when they receive a helping hand from the government. And with this deepening realization, his resentment is compounded, his frustration and insecurity are intensified, his alienation from self and society is completed. He feels himself robbed of self-respect and the right to resume a useful role in society." The recipient is schooled in "passive adjustment . . . to an immutable social reality." Which is to say, the welfare system compels people with disabilities to acquiesce in their own inferiority and marginalization.[9]

Not only do the deprivation of dignity and independence defeat the goal of rehabilitation, in ten Broek and Matson's view the financial provisions of the aid programs stymie that objective in material ways. First of all, "the smallness of the grant continually hinders and prevents rehabilitation." The amount of financial assistance provided to disabled recipients barely staves off destitution, if it does so at all. And "destitution," they declared, "is a poor foundation from which to accomplish the difficult task of self-reconstruction—economic, social, and psychological. Yet destitution is made a condition of eligibility for public assistance." Here they put their finger on one of the Catch-22's that have always been central to disability welfare policies.[10]

But the enforcement of poverty on disabled recipients does not end with these provisions. "Rehabilitation is struck still another blow by the means-test requirement that a recipient utilize all his property and income to meet his current needs." Policy planners would later call this rule "the resource limit." In the 1980s, an SSI recipient who was single could accumulate no more than $1800 in "resources." A couple, both receiving SSI, could accrue just $2000. Recipients who somehow had resources in excess of those limits had to "spend down" in any given month to get their resources below the threshold before the month ended. In other words, policy prohibited—and continues to prohibit—any savings, any planning for the future, any effort toward development or accomplishment. As ten Broek and Matson argued: "Reasonable accumulations of personal property, if not required to be applied to the meeting of immediate needs, might be used as stepping stones to independence of the relief rolls. Retention of reasonable amounts of income, *especially earned income*, also performs a vital function in the rehabilitative process, both for its incentive value, and as a means of moving from public aid to self-support."[11]

Disability rights activists a generation after ten Broek and Matson have argued that even if savings do not ultimately lead to "independence of the relief rolls," disabled recipients should be allowed to save what they can. The combination of earnings and savings surely would encourage, perhaps not economic independence, but at least economic productivity—and with it payment of some taxes. It certainly would enhance their quality of life, while putting a stop to the ludicrous requirement that they "spend down," which often means spend wastefully.

There has been one way recipients in recent decades might permissibly gather some savings. The Social Security Administration calls it a Plan to Achieve Self-Support (PASS). The plans are time-limited schemes for accumulating specified amounts toward purchase of particular items SSA has approved as appropriate means toward vocational rehabilitation. Here again the bureaucracy determines what disabled individuals really need and what activities they may legitimately undertake.

In addition, those who have applied for a PASS have often found it hard to get local SSA offices to approve their requests. Given the institution's ideology of poverty, disability, and welfare, the whole idea of recipients saving any money at all rather than spending every penny on current needs violates the bedrock principle that only the utterly destitute, totally incapacitated, and therefore truly worthy should receive aid. In practice, SSA has operated the PASS as a minor concession to rehabilitation.

Given the system's premises, given its ideology of both poverty and disability, the conflict between welfare and rehabilitation criticized by ten Broek and Matson was inevitable. Policy makers set out to discourage all but the "truly needy" from applying for aid in order to maintain a sharp separation between the "work-based" and "need-based" economies. As a result, they made it not only hard and humiliating to go from work to welfare, but also virtually impossible to move in the other direction, from welfare to work. In order to limit access *into* the so-called need-based economy, they deliberately limited exit *out of* that system as well. Thus, the effort to restrict able-bodied workers' access to social-service benefits simultaneously constituted people with disabilities as a stigmatized category, a segregated caste relegated to a permanent state of clientage. That disabled caste was deployed to define the boundaries of legitimate need. In the end, it came also to define the features of social normality by incarnating their inversion.

The mechanisms used to restrict disabled people's access to the labor market and society came in the late twentieth-century to be called, in one of the system's modern euphemisms, "work disincentives." Those so-called disincentives are, in fact, penalties, punishments designed to keep disabled people out of work, out of society, and out of life. Likewise, if we try to marry or raise a family, the government penalizes many of us through—here's yet another euphemism—"marriage disincentives." Throughout the recent decades, politicians have talked incessantly about "family values." Yet the policies they perpetuate have relentlessly undermined the families of disabled Americans. Marriage and work penalties hit disabled women even harder than disabled men. Marriage sometimes mitigates women's poverty, but the disability policy disincentives exacerbate the impoverishment and isolation of women with disabilities by helping to keep their employment and poverty rates high and their marriage rates low. Meanwhile, disabled students who get government welfare benefits and accept scholarships face education disincentives. So, whether we seek to learn, to work, or to love, the state punishes millions of us. It cuts off assistance with the high disability-related expenses many of us face, costs we probably could never earn enough to cover. These policies reinforce the degraded social status that has helped make the disability category in social welfare unattractive. Robbing us of our dignity has also helped intensify the stigma and segregation many of us endure.

During much of the twentieth century, these sorts of practices—the arduous and degrading process of obtaining assistance, the stigmatization of those granted it, and the work and marriage restrictions placed on recipients—interacted with intense social prejudice. Just as ten Broek and Matson described, people with many kinds of disabilities found themselves not only defined as incapable of work, but viewed as incompetent to manage their lives—and even sometimes as a threat to society. More and more were placed under the supervision of professionals. Some were permanently incarcerated in institutions. The systematic denial of the chance to work, joined with restrictions on education, marriage, and most forms of social intercourse, has entailed what John Gliedman and William Roth call "perhaps the most radical act of social declassification possible."[12] For a great many people with disabilities, it amounted to social death.

Meanwhile, invention and maintenance of the disabled caste advanced the ideological and economic interests of an array of professional groups in the modern welfare state. "Disability" became a multibillion dollar industry. Many states still keep adults with physical or developmental disabilities imprisoned in nursing homes and other public and private facilities that exploit them for profit. Even those of us at large in society pull in high profits for vendors of a great many services and products. A few years ago, I designed a device for my use in the bathroom. Knowing it would prove handy for people with similar disabilities, I sought ways to make it available. It would cost only a few dollars to manufacture, but a vendor eagerly told me we could sell it for at least fifty dollars a unit. The government would pay for it, he said. Hence comes the overpricing of everything from hearing aids to wheelchairs. This greedy arrangement between the private and public sectors, between vendors and the government, keeps many people with disabilities in a permanent state of clientage. We have to stay clients in order to get the devices and services we require.

The long history of poor-relief and social-service policies that have
marginalized and sought to disempower people with disabilities might
lead us to believe that they have suffered helplessly and passively as victims of enormously powerful institutions. But the historical evidence
uncovered thus far suggests active resistance on the part of at least some
disabled people. Two brief examples will illustrate that opposition.

Abram Courtney's pamphlet *Anecdotes of the Blind*, published in 1835,
tried to convince the public of the capabilities of blind people and to promote their education. He recounted his adjustment to complete blindness in his teens and twenties and reported his encounters with other
blind people, describing their activities and occupations. He made particular mention of two blind men who had married. Desiring to work
productively and to support himself, Courtney became an itinerant peddler. He hired a boy to assist him as he traveled through upstate New
York, Ohio, and Pennsylvania selling his wares. Customers initially
bought his goods because of the novelty of a blind peddler and out of
pity. But on his subsequent trips, he frequently encountered the view,
often expressed with hostility, that he should go to the almshouse. In
other words, he was told he should withdraw from society. Along with
his attempt to educate the sighted public, Courtney expressed indignation at the prejudice he met with on his travels in Jacksonian America.
Paraphrasing Shakespeare's Shylock, he wrote: "If you prick a blind man,
does he not bleed? If you tickle him, does he not laugh? If you treat him
with contumely, does he not feel mortification and bitterness of heart?
Shall he not also have an honest pride?"

Exactly a century later in the Depression-era America of 1935, a
group of disabled young adults banded together as the League of the
Physically Handicapped. They demonstrated against job discrimination
in federal work relief programs. They sent a delegation from New York
City down to Washington, D.C., to the Works Progress Administration
headquarters to protest job bias in WPA projects. They were not only
taking political action to compel changes in institutional practices. They
were redefining "disability" as a social, economic, and even political condition, rather than simply a medical or physical phenomenon. And like
Abram Courtney, they were attempting to fashion a new social identity.

As with other minorities, we tend to see disabled people as passive victims of fate or history. Abram Courtney and the League of the Physically Handicapped indicate that in important ways, individually and col-

lectively, people with disabilities have been actors in our own history. As with other minorities, we have sought to carve out maneuvering room for ourselves within the constraints of social ideologies and arrangements. We have attempted to modify social beliefs in order to expand our social power. In particular, we have sought ways to use our talents and to contribute to society through productive work.

I have spent much of my life seeking ways to elude social stigma and outwit discrimination. I have wanted to escape the roles of dependent cripple or inspirational overcomer. I, like the members of the League of the Physically Handicapped, have tried to work productively and to fashion for myself an alternative social identity. Like Abram Courtney, I have claimed as my right "an honest pride." Yet for my entire adult life, many government policies have been deliberately designed to prevent me, not just from pursuing my profession, but from attaining the socially respected place in society that goes with honest work. Millions of other Americans with disabilities find their attempts at productivity and pride blocked by these same segregationist work penalties and the social prejudice those policies express.

In the late 1970s, in the tradition of ten Broek and Matson, and, without knowing it, as successors to Courtney and the League, disability rights activists started calling for removal of work disincentives from Supplemental Security Income and Social Security Disability Insurance. In 1980, Congress authorized the Social Security Administration to create a national demonstration program called Section 1619 that would allow SSI recipients to go to work and retain medical insurance and other assistance. Year after year, SSA failed to publicize this program. The Reagan administration took no stand on the issue. Instead, it allowed SSA's top officials to obstruct reform. In 1983, the General Accounting Office recommended that Congress require SSA to conduct such experiments. In 1986, disability rights advocates once again lobbied for permanent reform, and once again the Social Security Administration fiddled with its statistics to predict that enabling us to work and pay taxes would cost taxpayers billions. A Social Security spokesperson even had the audacity to tell the *Los Angeles Times* that government policy contained no work disincentives.

The Social Security Administration of course claimed that allowing us to work while we received assistance with our disability-related living and medical expenses would cost the government billions of dollars. A national pilot project launched in 1980 proved just the opposite. The government and society got millions back from disabled people who had at last become workers and taxpayers. Despite this, for seven years the Reagan administration ignored the issue, while the Social Security Administration blocked permanent institutionalization of the SSI reforms. Finally in 1986, Congress overrode SSA's resistance. It ordered permanent elimination of most work disincentives from SSI. The new rules in Section 1619 would permit recipients to earn up to a threshold amount equivalent to the cash value of all the assistance they received plus the amount of their "impairment-related work expenses."

For twenty years, I had wondered and worried how I would ever fulfill my dream of teaching and writing American history. I had finally finished my Ph.D. in 1984 but still could not take even a part-time teaching position without jeopardizing the financial aid that paid for my ventilators and in-home assistance. With the arrival of Section 1619, the work penalties that had blocked me were at long last gone. Or so I thought.

In March of 1988, I learned that although Section 1619 would permit me to earn a living as a college teacher, the reformed rules would not allow research fellowships or publishing royalties. The Social Security Administration would continue to regard such income as "unearned," like royalties from oil well stocks.

The Huntington Library, a world-renowned research institution in San Marino, California, fifteen minutes from where I lived, had just offered me a fellowship to continue my work on George Washington's role in post-revolutionary America. I would have to turn that fellowship down. More problematic, in October the University of California Press would publish my book, *The Invention of George Washington*. I needed that first book to make myself attractive in the college-teaching job market. UC Press expected the book to sell pretty well. That was the problem. Even if it yielded only modest royalties, that money would not fit the Section 1619 definition of "earned" income. So I could lose some or all of the assistance I depended on to work and live and, literally, to breathe.

Don't ask me how the policy makers decided that earnings from a book it took me ten years to write would be "unearned." They live in an Alice-Through-the-Looking-Glass realm, where significantly disabled people who work are not really disabled after all.

I wrote President Reagan and other top federal officials to describe my situation. Scholarly careers, I explained, are rarely lucrative. I could earn a full-time salary as a college teacher, obtain grants occasionally, publish scholarly books, and still not have enough income to pay for my disability-related living and work expenses. If I cannot apply for and accept research fellowships or publish books, I said, I cannot advance in my profession. If I lose the government aid that pays for my in-home assistance and ventilators, I cannot live independently *or* work.

President Reagan vigorously advocated getting the government off Americans' backs. He could have initiated changes in SSI policy, as I requested him to do. He did not. Instead, he forwarded my letters to the commissioner of Social Security, Dorcas Hardy.

At first, Commissioner Hardy referred me to the Glendale, California, Social Security office. This was simply, as the members of the League of the Physically Handicapped would have put it, "the runaround." She knew that the claims representatives in the local office could only inform me of the regulations about which I had already complained to the president.

Then in June 1988, Commissioner Hardy offered a suggestion. "If you can establish an employer-employee relationship" with the University of California Press regarding publication of your book or with the Huntington Library regarding research there, she wrote, "your income may be treated as earnings under Section 1619." (Note the noncommittal "may." No guarantees, no venturing out on a limb by the bureaucratically cautious commissioner.) Despite my skepticism about this proposed solution, I checked it out with Dr. Martin Ridge, director of research at the Huntington Library. He told me that the Huntington could not legally pay me fellowship money in the form of a salary. Neither could I establish an employer-employee relationship with my publisher. They had bought a literary property of my creation. They had not hired me.

Commissioner Hardy's advice was not just unworkable. It sidestepped the central issue. The suggestion that a scholar who happens to have a disability should seek to establish an employer-employee relationship with a grantor or publisher struck me as discriminatory. Scholars without disabilities do not seek or obtain such arrangements. Why should I be required to do so just because I'm disabled? Why should I not work under the same arrangements as others in my profession?

Commissioner Hardy had another idea. "If the Internal Revenue Service determines that you are self-employed in a trade or business," she said, "your income may be treated as earnings under Section 1619. Otherwise, your income must be classified as unearned." (That noncommittal "may" again, followed by an emphatic "must." Bureaucrats make sure to protect not just their backsides, but also their administrative prerogatives.) Well, I studied the Internal Revenue Service publications concerning fellowships and royalties. I discovered that the IRS makes no distinction between self-employment and salaried employment. It classifies research fellowships and publishing royalties as taxable *earned* income. I would have to pay income taxes on any book royalties. It seemed to me only fair for the Social Security Administration to acknowledge that I earned such income and to treat it as earnings under Section 1619.

Finally on August 26, 1988, Commissioner Hardy notified me that SSA would regard any income I obtained from research fellowships and book royalties as "unearned" and that this would adversely affect my eligibility for SSI.

When I read the commissioner's peremptory warning that SSA would punish me if I received any royalties from my book, something in me reached a breaking point. Years of finding myself trapped and thwarted by this system, years of feeling demeaned and degraded by it, came to a head. I said to myself, "I've had enough." I decided in that moment that when my book came out in October I would burn it in protest.

I spent the next two months carefully planning the book burning. I mailed a series of flyers to activists in the Southern California disability community to keep them up-to-date on the preparations. I phoned dozens of people urging them to participate in the protest. I contacted television and print news reporters. I spent hours on the phone trying to educate a *Los Angeles Times* writer about the intricacies of government disability policies.

I also figured that if I really were going to burn my book, I had better do it right. First off, I didn't want to set *myself* on fire. At the same time, I wanted to make the burning of the book visually dramatic. So one afternoon I went over to my friend Vince Pinto's house. I brought with me several books I had been planning to throw away. I picked those particular books because they had glossy paper dust jackets like the jacket my book would have. Vince and I and his aide spent an hour at Vince's backyard barbecue practicing how I would burn my book.

We quickly hit upon a method. We wadded up some newspaper, stuck it under the barbecue grill, and soaked it with lighter fluid. We also saturated the books with lighter fluid and stood each one in turn on top of the grill. Next, Vince's aide handed me a long fireplace match he had already lit. I turned a half-turn to my right and ignited the newspaper kindling. The flames started up under the books, then consumed them.

We all agreed that I was ready.

My planned protest got enthusiastic support from the Southern California disability community. Leaders of the California Council of the Blind, the Greater Los Angeles Council on Deafness, several independent-living centers, local chapters of the California Association of the Physically Handicapped, Able Advocates of Santa Barbara, and ADAPT of Southern California endorsed the demonstration.

On October 18, some forty people gathered in front of the federal building on Los Angeles Street in downtown L.A. There were adults with disabilities who were trying to work, or wanted to and could work, but were thwarted by work penalties. There were college students with disabilities who wondered if they would be prevented from following the careers they dreamed of pursuing when they graduated. There were parents of disabled children who wanted those youngsters to have a useful and fulfilling future. There were teachers and counselors who labored to help people with disabilities get an education or job training. They were paid with government funds to do this, but government policies baffled their efforts. We all came together to demand an end to work and marriage penalties.

Vince and his aide transported Vince's barbecue in his wheelchair-lift-equipped van. We set it up on the sidewalk in front of the main entrance to the federal building. Parker Center, the headquarters of the Los Angeles Police Department, stands right across the street. Several LAPD cops, along with security personnel from the federal building, warily stood watch during the protest and book burning.

I had hired a Deaf commercial-art student from Pasadena City College to make brightly colored placards bearing slogans television viewers would be able to read easily. One placard declared: "We Want to Work! Why Won't the Government Let Us?" Another demand I borrowed from the League of the Physically Handicapped: "Jobs. Not Tin Cups."

A row of placard holders stood to one side, as another group of demonstrators paraded in an elongated circle. Two of them led the protesters in disability rights chants. Wheelchair riders carried placards on their laps.

After awhile I stepped up to the wooden lectern I had borrowed and read a statement explaining the reasons for our demonstration. Then I moved over to Vince's barbecue. A friend handed me a lighted match. I turned and ignited the newspaper wads under the grill. A copy of my book stood on top of the grill. The front cover of the book jacket had a striking design: a photographic reproduction of Antoine Houdon's famous white marble bust of Washington against a red and blue background with the words *"The Invention of George Washington"* and "Paul K. Longmore" above and below. The image was bold, noble, majestic. At first the flames licked the bottom of the book. Then they engulfed my name and George Washington's head and the book's title.

I somberly watched the fire consume my book. I had planned the protest. I had rehearsed how to burn the book. I had even thought about what sort of expression I should have on my face. But I could never have prepared for the emotional effect on me of the act itself. I was burning my own book, a book I had spent ten years of my life laboring over, a book that had earned me my Ph.D. in history, a book I felt proud of and, in fact, loved. It was a moment of agony.

Everyone in the crowd looked on quietly, soberly. Several wept. As with my own reaction, their emotional response surprised me. I asked my friend Carol Gill, a disabled psychologist who participated in the protest, why she thought so many people had reacted so strongly. She said she believed that those friends and colleagues were partly expressing their love for me. At the same time, she said, the entire protest and especially the burning of the book gave tangible form to the pain they felt about their own lives. They too felt thwarted by a government that stymies their efforts to work and make a life. They too felt dehumanized by a society that devalues them.

The demonstration ended. The protesters dispersed. An LAPD officer approached the three or four of us who were cleaning up. He asked my name. He wrote it down. I asked if there was a problem. He said he just wanted the information for the record.

That evening, news broadcasts on KNBC-TV (the NBC affiliate in Los Angeles) and KHJ-TV (an independent station) aired stories about the book burning. The next morning, the front page of the *Los Angeles Times* Metro section ran a long story on the protest. The article included a large photo of me watching my book burn.[13]

Subsequent events gave hope that the book burning might have the political impact we sought. In November, a high-ranking Social Security Administration official privately admitted to a disability rights advocate that the book burning had given the agency "a black eye" and that the work disincentives were "stupid." That same month, the *New York Times* published an opinion piece of mine on the work penalties issue.[14]

In December, National Public Radio broadcast a story about a quadri-plegic man in Montana who received $15,000 a year in Medicaid. That financial aid enabled him to live independently. Then he won election to the state legislature. Because of the modest salary he would receive from that part-time job, the Social Security Administration told him it would cut off his assistance even though he would not be earning enough to live on.

In January 1989, the new Congress convened in Washington. It took up the Social Security Work Incentives Act, a bill first introduced in the previous session. The proposed legislation aimed to eliminate the ma-jor work penalties in Social Security Disability Insurance. Congressmen Robert Matsui (Democrat, California) and Steve Bartlett (Republican, Texas) carried the bill in the House; Senators Robert Dole (Republican, Kansas) and Donald J. Riegle, Jr. (Democrat, Michigan), brought it be-fore the Senate. When disability rights advocates alerted Congressmen Matsui and Bartlett about the book burning and our demands, they de-cided to add to their bill an amendment that would address the SSI work penalties we had protested. The new provision would classify publish-ing royalties, speaking honoraria, and research grants and fellowships as "earned" income for purposes of reckoning the income threshold under Section 1619.

In February 1989, I learned that the Social Security Administration was vigorously opposing the entire bill. Once again SSA twisted statis-tics to claim that reform would cost $5 billion over five years. Concerned about the budget deficit, Congress began pulling back. The bill's provi-sions were seriously weakened. In negotiations with congressional staff-ers, SSA agreed to recognize publication royalties as "earned" income for SSI recipients, but the bureaucrats dug in their heels about research scholarships, grants, and fellowships. They adamantly insisted on con-tinuing to regard that sort of income as "unearned." The few changes SSA would agree to got folded into the Omnibus Budget Reconciliation Act. That legislation allowed honoraria and publishing royalties. Today, almost a decade and a half later, the rule barring grants and fellowships remains in place. Over the years, a number of disabled undergraduate college and graduate students have had to turn down scholarships or face losing the personal-assistance services and medical coverage they required.

Meanwhile, the struggle to root out work penalties has continued. In late 1999, Congress passed and President Clinton signed a new Ticket to Work and Work Incentives Improvement Act. It won support and praise across the political spectrum as the most important disability-related federal legislation since the Americans with Disabilities Act of 1990. Politicians, both Left and Right, and some disability rights activists exuberantly forecast that WIIA (later TWIIA) would remove SSI/SSDI work "disincentives" and enable millions of disabled Americans to go to work. In fact, contrary to the hyperbolic claims, TWIIA is only an incremental move toward the removal of work penalties. The act's greatest value lies, not in the specifics of its modest provisions, but in initiating a key ideological shift in disability policy: it permits the first small steps toward delinkage of medical insurance coverage from impoverishment. In other words, in states that choose to participate some disabled people could qualify for Medicaid and other publicly funded support services without having to remain destitute. They could go to work while retaining eligibility for that vital assistance. This represents an important conceptual breakthrough in disability-related social-service policy making. But for the present and for many years to come, perhaps for decades, that conceptual advance will result in only limited practical changes because of the act's circumscribed provisions.

TWIIA does not institute permanent, comprehensive nationwide reform to eliminate work disincentives from SSI and SSDI. Rather, it authorizes, but does not require, individual states to establish time-limited "demonstration" projects, which is to say, experimental programs, to offer Medicaid to specified pilot groups of workers with disabilities. TWIIA also permits states to cap both the total expenditures for these projects and the numbers of participants enrolled in them. In addition, it allows states to liberalize or do away with the income and resource limits in currently existing benefits programs, but it does not direct them to do so.

The effectiveness of these experiments in promoting productive employment will depend on the package of features they offer in their Medicaid buy-in programs. If states fail to provide adequate access to health insurance and support services, many disabled people will continue to find it impossible to go to work. An instance of that sort of dereliction has apparently already occurred in Minnesota. That state has reportedly adopted a flawed Medicaid buy-in, return-to-work policy.

Not only will defectively designed state-option demonstration programs continue to block disabled people from seeking productive work; they will also expose the long-term campaign for reform of disability policies to a significant political risk. Opponents of change want to keep in place the traditional system that dichotomizes "work" and "need." They will seize on the small numbers of disabled persons who seek employment under faulty TWIIA pilot projects as evidence of the failure of work incentives. They have already attacked work incentives provisions such as the Plan to Achieve Self Support and Section 1619. Low employment rates due to deficient Medicaid buy-in programs will hand them ammunition to shoot down comprehensive national reforms.

A more immediate political obstacle already confronts disability rights advocates. TWIIA's neo-federalist approach necessitates cumbersome state-by-state lobbying for adoption of demonstration projects. The few states with well-organized and highly politicized disability organizations, such as California, have already mobilized to get their legislatures to adopt appropriately designed programs. But in most states, disability rights advocacy is less experienced, extensive, and effective politically. In those places, one can reasonably predict that the demonstration projects will vary widely in quality and efficacy. And, of course, some states will opt not to try TWIIA experiments at all. In many states, disabled citizens will find that they do not enjoy the equal protection of the laws.

Whatever the merits of particular state experiments, all of the TWIIA demonstration projects will expire within a few years. At that point, it will take an act of Congress to extend them. Some disability rights advocates hope and expect that the projects will generate a database that will persuade Congress to enact comprehensive national reforms. But they admit that the accumulation of that data may take a decade. That is, assuming that the state projects work as effectively as the highly optimistic forecasts predict. One would not be unduly pessimistic to expect the opponents of change to stall full-scale reform for as long as fifteen to twenty years. In other words, the multitude of disabled people who want to work and could work may be forced to languish in the "need-based" SSI/SSDI system for another generation.

As for me, well, my book, *The Invention of George Washington*, never earned the kind of royalties I had both hoped and feared it would draw. So, fortunately or unfortunately, it never put me in danger of losing the assistance I needed. On the other hand, it did help me finally get a tenure-track teaching position. Several schools turned down my applications for full-time openings in Early American history and even for part-time lectureships. A faculty member at one of those schools told me frankly that some of his colleagues doubted if I could do the job, given my disability. At times I wondered if every search committee would bear out the warnings of my old professors that no school would ever hire me. But at last, the history department at San Francisco State University offered me a position, indeed, welcomed me as a colleague. At long last, in my mid-forties, I began my teaching career. Working sedulously, I tried to make up for lost time. I now hold the rank of full professor.

I do not tell you this to brag about my achievements or to boast about my tenacity and perseverance or to exhort other disabled people to try harder. That is the sort of individualistic claptrap usually fed to us. It keeps us believing that if our lives are limited, it is because of our disabilities or our lack of pluck. I recount my professional progress to make the point that I was liberated from the thrall of crippling public policies by successful disability rights lobbying. No matter how hard I worked, I could never have succeeded without the removal of work penalties. What tore them out of my way was the *political* tenacity and perseverance of our disability community. I got this far because of the achievements of the disability rights movement.

So here I am, having achieved in my profession much of what I had dreamt of as a young man. It took far longer than I expected or wanted. It came much later than it should have. The government denied me years of productive work, years I will never get back. Still, I am here.

But now I face a new worrisome dilemma. Both federal and state disability benefits programs regard retirement pensions as "unearned income." If and when I retire from my job and begin receiving the pension I am currently paying into, I will incur a substantial "share of cost" —that is, payment out of my own pocket—before I can receive any government financial assistance to pay for my ventilators or my personal-assistance services. The "share of cost" will likely be so high that I will not qualify for any government aid at all. But my pension will not cover both my ordinary living expenses and the tens of thousands of dollars I will face annually in disability-related expenses.

As in the past, I am not the only disabled person confronting this problem. Thanks to SSI Section 1619, growing numbers of Americans with significant disabilities are seeking and holding jobs and pursuing careers. Some have had to take early retirement because middle age and hard work have exacerbated their functional difficulties. To their shock and dismay, they have discovered that by retiring and beginning to receive pensions, they become ineligible for the government assistance that has enabled them to live independently and work. They don't know how they're going to survive. They are alerting the rest of us to the danger we too will soon face.

For decades, the government warned us that if we got jobs it would take away the assistance that made it possible for us to live independently and to work. Now the government is warning us that if we retire from our jobs it will take away that assistance. In other words, the old premises about people with disabilities remain in place. The old penalties that try to deter disabled people from productive work still threaten us. We still must fight policies that exclude or punish us.

The core of what I said in my statement just before I burned my book in October 1988 unfortunately remains true today:

"We, like other Americans, should have the right to work productively. Work and marriage penalties . . . , far more than our disabilities, thwart our efforts and our lives. We demand an end to these discriminatory government policies."

"We are here today, not just for ourselves, but on behalf of millions of Americans with disabilities. My book represents, not just my work, but the work that we all want to do and could do. The burning of a copy of my book symbolizes what the government does to us and our talents and our efforts. It repeatedly turns our dreams to ashes. We find that outrageous, and we will no longer quietly endure that outrage."

"We, like all Americans, have talents to use, work to do, our contributions to make to our communities and country. We want the chance to work and marry without jeopardizing our lives. We want access to opportunity. We want access to work. We want access to the American Dream."

Notes

Acknowledgments: I am grateful to Doug Martin, a longtime activist on these issues and a longtime friend, for correcting my errors and clarifying my explanations about disability policies and politics in this essay.

1. In the academic year 1971–72, I received financial assistance through a federal program called Aid to the Totally Disabled. Late in 1972, Congress created the Supplemental Security Income program by combining ATD with two other programs, Aid to the Blind and Old Age Assistance.

2. Deborah Stone, *The Disabled State* (Philadelphia, 1986).

3. Edward Berkowitz, *Disabled Policy: America's Programs for the Handicapped* (New York, 1987), 122–44; Kenneth A. Rasmussen, "An Overview of the History of Disability Policy: An Historian's and Insider's Perspective," paper presented at the Society for Disability Studies, Fourth Annual Meeting, Oakland, California, June 26, 1991, 28–31.

4. Rasmussen, "Overview of the History of Disability Policy," 31–32.

5. Jacobus ten Broek and Floyd W. Matson, "The Disabled and the Law of Welfare," *California Law Review* 54 (1966), 811–12, reprinted in William R. F. Philips and Janet Rosenberg, eds., *Changing Patterns of Law: The Courts and the Handicapped* (New York, 1980), 830. See also Jacobus ten Broek and Floyd Matson, *Hope Deferred: Public Welfare and the Blind* (Berkeley, 1959), 131–35.

6. ten Broek and Matson, "The Disabled and the Law of Welfare," 830–31.

7. ten Broek and Matson, "The Disabled and the Law of Welfare," 831–33; ten Broek and Matson, *Hope Deferred*, 149–50.

8. ten Broek and Matson, "The Disabled and the Law of Welfare," 831–32.

9. ten Broek and Matson, *Hope Deferred*, 136–8, quoting *Social Security Bulletin* 8:3 (March 1945), 17; ten Broek and Matson, "The Disabled and the Law of Welfare," 831–33.

10. ten Broek and Matson, *Hope Deferred*, 139.

11. ten Broek and Matson, *Hope Deferred*, 139–40, italics added.

12. John Gliedman and William Roth, *The Unexpected Minority: Handicapped Children in America* (New York, 1982), 24.

13. "Disabled Historian Burns Book," *Los Angeles Times*, October 19, 1988.

14. Paul K. Longmore, "Crippling the Disabled," *New York Times*, November 26, 1988.

Index

accessibility, advocacy/concepts, 19, 21, 22–23, 29, 154–55, 190, 206, 215, 216, 217, 221; architectural, 28; as civil right, 112, 143–44, 154, 206, 215, 216, 217, 218–19, 221; enforcement of laws on, 21, 23, 26, 28, 29, 30; equal access concept and, 49–50, 130, 154, 218–19, 228; resistance to, 23, 24–25, 27–30, 31n. 1; 58, 155, 207; segregation and, 20, 21, 25, 108; social construction of disability and, 49–50, 57, 205

accessibility, obstacles/objectives: airline, 23, 28, 31n.2, 216, 217; airport, 23–24; architectural, 24–26, 27, 28, 29, 108, 143–44, 170n.11, 227; business, 24–25, 27–28, 29; education and, 26–27, 105, 108, 227, 228; employment and, 23; Greyhound and, 23, 31n.1; hospital, 105, 108; hotel, 25, 29; housing, 25–26, 28, 103; information, 25; intercity buses, 23, 31 n 1; paratransit and, 22–23, 155; parking lot, 24, 29; public transportation, 21–23, 28, 29, 58, 112, 154–55, 170n.11, 207; railroads, 58; rental cars, 24; signage and, 25; telecommunications, 25

accessibility, policies/laws: Air Carrier Access Act, 23, 28, 216; Architectural Barriers Act of 1968, 170n. 11, 216; Architectural and Transportation Barriers Compliance Board, 170n. 11; business, 24–25, 27–28, 29; education and, 26–27, 105, 108, 227, 228; employment and, 23; enforcement of, 21, 23, 26, 28, 29, 30; Fair Housing Amendment Act of 1988, 25–26; Federal Aviation Act, 216; guide

dog laws and, 154; white cane laws and, 154. *See also* activism; civil rights; minority group model/social construction; policies, public

activism, agenda of, 4, 19, 154, 215, 224; disability rights perspective excluded/included, 163, 167, 176–77, 186, 196, 210, 211; education and, 125, 154, 155, 206, 247; history of, 9–10, 19, 50–51, 53–54, 56, 57, 60, 61–115, 145–46, 154–55, 206, 215–17, 219, 247–48; identity politics and, 57, 62, 69–70, 77, 79, 81, 82–84, 86, 110–11, 114, 221–22, 224, 247–48; inclusive versus disability-specific, 86–87, 109–10, 114–15; politicization of disability in, 31, 54, 57, 62, 64, 69–70, 71, 81, 83–84, 86, 87, 108–11, 112–15, 132–33, 145–46, 154, 215–21, 247; Rehabilitation Acts of 1972 and 1973, 103–5; Section 504, 50, 104–11, 154; resistance to, 154–55, 158, 176, 190, 206–7, 219, 248–49, 250–51, 253–54; self-determination and, 7–8, 9, 112, 114, 220, 224, 231, 247–48; U.S. social-reform movements and, 54, 64, 66, 69, 70–71, 80, 81–82, 84–85, 102, 107, 108, 109, 110, 112

activism, groups/organizations involved in: Able Advocates of Santa Barbara, 252; American Coalition of Citizens with Disabilities (ACCD), 106, 109; American Disabled for Attendant Programs Today, formerly American Disabled for Accessible Public Transit (ADAPT), 179–80, 183, 188, 210, 216, 252;

261